Yellow Perils

Yellow Perils

China Narratives in the Contemporary World

EDITED BY

Franck Billé and Sören Urbansky

University of Hawai'i Press
Honolulu

23   22   21   20   19   18   6   5   4   3   2   1

Library of Congress Cataloging-in-Publication Data

Names: Billé, Franck, editor. | Urbansky, Sören, editor.

Title: Yellow perils : China narratives in the contemporary world / edited by Franck Billé and Sören Urbansky.

Description: Honolulu : University of Hawai'i Press, [2018] | Includes bibliographical references and index.

Identifiers: LCCN 2018004207 | ISBN 9780824875794 (cloth : alk. paper)

Subjects: LCSH: China—Foreign public opinion—Case studies. | Chinese—Foreign countries—Social conditions—Case studies. | Racism—Case studies. | Model minority stereotype—Case studies.

Classification: LCC DS740.4 .Y447 2018 | DDC 303.48/251—dc23

LC record available at https://lccn.loc.gov/2018004207

Cover art: "China loves Africa #37" by Kenyan artist Michael Soi.

University of Hawai'i Press books are printed on acid-free paper and meet the guidelines for permanence and durability of the Council on Library Resources.

Contents

Acknowledgments

P ART OF THE RESEARCH featured in this book was made possible through an Economic and Social Research Council (ESRC) grant, which funded the project "Where the Rising Powers Meet" (ES/ J012335/1) that ran at the University of Cambridge between 2012 and 2015.

The authors also gratefully acknowledge the additional financial support from the German Research Foundation's Graduate School for East and Southeast European Studies (LMU Munich/University of Regensburg), which funded and hosted a workshop in Munich in July 2015.

In addition, the institutional support of the LMU Munich, the University of Cambridge, the Mongolia and Inner Asia Studies Unit (Cambridge), and the University of California, Berkeley, was invaluable and provided wonderfully collegial and supportive environments.

Heartfelt thanks go as well to our colleagues, who generously offered comments and suggestions on early drafts of chapters presented at conferences in Cambridge, Chicago, Munich, and Makuhari. Particular thanks go to Amy Matthewson and Flair Donglai Shi, whose own work on the Yellow Peril led to many stimulating conversations.

This book in its final form would not have been possible without the input and guidance of our wonderful editor Pamela Kelley and her editorial associate Debbie Tang. It was a pleasure to work with both of them, and with copy editor Jennifer McIntyre, who made sure our prose always remained legible!

Finally, we would like to thank Michael Soi for the cover image, Jose Santos for the overall cover design, and Anja Dreves for compiling the index.

CHAPTER 1

~

Introduction

FRANCK BILLÉ

IN NOVEMBER 2011, after several months of intense discussion, Icelandic interior minister Ögmundur Jónasson formally rejected a bid by Chinese billionaire Huang Nubo to purchase 115 square miles of wild heathland in the northeast of the country. The bid, intended for the construction of a holiday resort including a golf course and hot-air balloon rides, had attracted much attention both nationally and internationally. While the plot of land was both landlocked and barren, the transfer of a sizable portion of the country—amounting to 0.3 percent of the country's landmass—to a foreign national had generated much anxiety. At a time when Iceland was recovering from a devastating economic crisis, the prospect of selling part of its territory was seen as a desperate and dangerous move. The fact that the bid had been made by a Chinese citizen compounded these fears and raised additional security concerns that the transfer of land might give Beijing a "strategic foothold in the North Atlantic" (Jackson and Hook 2011).

Huang Nubo, described as a mountaineer and a poet, is said to have fallen in love with Iceland on his first visit in 2010, a passion originally awakened in his youth by a friendship with a kind Icelandic student (Trellevik 2013). As he explained in numerous interviews (Kim Blog 2011), his choice of location for the holiday resort was tied to this long-held fascination for the country. However, in Western news outlets much was also made of Huang's prior involvement with the propaganda department of China's Communist Party, especially when, after being turned down by Iceland, he attempted to purchase land near Tromsø in northern Norway (Eysteinsson 2015) and was rumored to be eyeing large plots of land on Svalbard (Lindbad 2014, Morgunblaðið 2014). For some commentators, his interest in the Arctic region had less to do with his personal fascination in the region than with China's own ambition to claim a stake in the Arctic—a region that is likely to become an important site of extraction of natural resources as new technologies develop and global temperatures continue to rise.

In their descriptions of Huang Nubo as a puppet of the Chinese state (Higgins 2014), Western media coverage of the story echoed a more general disquiet about China's meteoric rise and its ever-expanding economic and cultural footprint. This anxiety is perceptible in the treatment of China-related issues in the news. Along with the vast body of literature that has emerged in the last decade about China's rise (see Pan 2012), a sizable share of these academic and popular texts feature the words "power" and "threat" in their titles (Frayling 2014: 34). China thus appears to be located at a critical juncture between being an object of admiration and something to be feared.

A recent political video perfectly illustrates this ambivalence. Produced by the Americans for Prosperity Foundation and released during the 2010 midterm elections, and then again during Mitt Romney's presidential campaign (Citizens Against Government Waste 2010), the video depicts a Chinese professor addressing a hall of students in 2030 Beijing:

> Why do great nations fail? The Ancient Greeks [. . .], the Roman Empire, . . . the British Empire, . . . and the United States of America. They all make the same mistakes, turning back on the principles that made them great. America tried to tax and spend itself out of a great recession. Enormous so-called "stimulus" spending, massive changes to health care, government takeover of private industries, and crushing debt. Of course, we owned most of their debt. So now they work for us. (Yeats 2013: 267)

At this point, the whole audience erupts into laughter.

On the one hand, the 2030 China depicted in the video is successful and powerful. The professor is both eloquent and confident, and the students look affluent. Well-dressed and using the latest technology, they would not look out of place at an Ivy League university (Fig. 1.1). That China is now a world leader is implied by the fact that the video is in

FIGURE 1.1 "The Chinese Professor," Citizens Against Government Waste (2010).

Chinese with English subtitles, suggesting Chinese linguistic dominance. On the other hand, the Chinese future evoked here is clearly dystopic. The setting, from the giant Chinese flag and the poster of Mao down to the suit the professor is wearing, borrows from a panoply of totalitarian imagery reminiscent of North Korea (Fig. 1.2). The demeanor of the professor, who acts more like a Hollywood supervillain[1] than a university professor, emphasizes this.

In evoking traits such as cruelty and cunning, the video borrows from an established—and easily recognizable—cultural panoply associated with Oriental villains such as Dr. Fu Manchu or Dr. No (Clegg 1994, Frayling 2014, Mayer 2014). Just like Fu Manchu, the Chinese professor is highly educated, ruthless, and intent on world domination. The video's powerful message is further amplified by the audience of students

FIGURE 1.2 "The Chinese Professor," Citizens Against Government Waste (2010).

who look remarkably Western in their clothing and attitudes—note their relaxed postures in Figure 1.1—yet fully identify with the message delivered by the professor. The video here taps into the so-called "model minority" myth (Hsu 2015, Wu 2014), which portrays Asian migrant populations as communities that appear fully Westernized and acculturated yet remain deeply alien, loyal to China,[2] and ultimately inassimilable.

This specific cluster of stereotypes harkens back to the turn of the twentieth century, with the emergence of the notion of "Yellow Peril." The term was first used by Germany's Kaiser Wilhelm II in 1895 after he had a prophetic dream in which he saw the figure of a Buddha riding a dragon about to attack Europe. The term was popularized in English by Matthew Shiel (1865–1947), the author of *The Yellow Danger* (1898), a novel that featured Dr. Yen How, an Asian supervillain who would later provide the blueprint for another, more illustrious, Oriental supervillain—Dr. Fu Manchu, a fictional character in the series of novels by British author Sax Rohmer. Like Fu Manchu, Yen How embodied a set of core stereotypes that have proven particularly resistant and have lastingly been associated with Asians, both in Europe and in the United States. Cosmopolitan, highly educated, and extremely intelligent, he is also cruel, pragmatic, and intent on world domination.

These associations, which emerged at the turn of the twentieth century, were tied to specific historical events and were embedded in particular cultural contexts. In the United States, they were linked to the arrival of Chinese workers in California and to the economic competition that these migrants represented. Chinese immigrants also differed racially from the white majority and were perceived as alien, dangerous, and carriers of disease (Shah 2001: 28). In Russia, fears of a tide of Chinese inundating the Russian Far East emerged in the context of an imperial rivalry between Tokyo and St. Petersburg for the control of Northeast Asia, peaking in 1905 with Russia's humiliating defeat at the hands of the Japanese (Siegelbaum 1978)—the first time an Asian nation had triumphed militarily over a European power. While these events were not the first time the West had experienced anxiety vis-à-vis Asia—the thirteenth-century Mongolian invasion having proven especially traumatic—these two events acted as catalysts. They signaled that Asia had to be taken seriously, and they strongly undermined long-held Western assumptions of cultural superiority.

The "Yellow Peril" is patently a discourse tied to race and embedded in racial classifications originating in the West. The attribution of the color yellow to Asian populations, and indeed the separation of human groups into discrete races, in fact only emerged through the taxonomical attempts of eighteenth-century physicians, and was later reinforced and ossified by anthropologists (see Demel 1992, Dikötter 1992, 1997; Keevak 2011). Though recent, this discourse did not emerge in a cultural void, but instead built upon much older imaginations of Asia as mysterious, dangerous, and inherently alien. Associated with violent invaders such as Genghis Khan (Zhou 2006), with deadly diseases such as the bubonic plague (Watts 1997), and occasionally depicted as the location of hell in medieval cartography, Asia has in fact long been Europe's cultural Other (Osterhammel 1998, Said 1977). At times, this sense of unbridgeable otherness has also positioned Asia as an object of fetishistic fascination, for example during the Enlightenment period, when *chinoiseries*—objects and architectural models inspired by Chinese forms—evoked fantasies of the Orient as a site of sophistication and exoticism.[3]

If today the moniker of "Yellow Peril" sounds quite dated, even somewhat quaintly so, the recent meteoric rise of China as a global economic powerhouse appears to have given a second lease on life to this racist discourse. In 2014 alone, four academic studies were published on the theme of the "Yellow Peril" (Frayling 2014, Mayer 2014, Tchen & Yeats 2014, Witchard 2014) and, like in the essays in this volume, the subject of China is prominent in these studies. This efflorescence of studies suggests that the concerns indexed by Yellow Peril narratives remain current and that they continue to reverberate within Asian studies. It also suggests that the anti-Chinese sentiments currently heard in a variety of contexts are the echoes of older, sedimented narratives, albeit under a different name. By placing in direct contrast current and older anti-Chinese narratives, the books by Tchen and Yeats (2014) and Frayling (2014) make the continuity of this visual political language explicit. The numerous examples and illustrations they provide lend great support to their argument, and the similarities are often striking. The association of the Chinese—and Asians overall—with cunning and excessive rationality and pragmatism, as well as with disease and danger, is one that seems to span the entire twentieth century and to be well-entrenched in Western popular and political culture.

To an extent the essays in this book also speak to the numerous parallels and continuities that are seen between the emergence of the Yellow Peril ideology and the contemporary period. Thus, as Christos Lynteris (Chapter 2) discusses in relation to Severe Acute Respiratory Syndrome (SARS) and the H5N1 virus, older narratives that described Chinese migrants as carriers of diseases and epidemics (Shah 2001), or even the use of metaphoric epithets like the "Sick Man of Asia" to refer to China, may have disappeared but the underlying connection between China and disease has shown much resilience. In her chapter on Chinese migrant workers in Prato, Italy, Xiaojian Zhao also underlines the many discursive overlaps between contemporary Italian responses to these newcomers and the fears voiced by California residents at the turn of the twentieth century. In both settings, accusations of unfair economic competition and the cutthroat practices of the Chinese workers have dominated media coverage, and comparisons between the two reveal striking resemblances. David Walker's chapter on fears of Chinese geopolitical dominance over the Australian continent (Chapter 3), likewise, shows a clear continuity over the course of the twentieth century.

However, as these and the rest of the chapters convincingly demonstrate, these similarities also conceal vast differences, if only because the very object of the Yellow Peril discourse is positioned very differently with respect to the West. At the turn of the twentieth century, China had been constrained to sign unequal treaties with foreign powers such as Russia and Britain, and was struggling to retain full sovereignty. In the second decade of the twenty-first century, by contrast, China may well become the world's first economic power. Previously grounded in fears of its degeneracy, the spectral menace evoked by China is now one animated by fears of its excessive potency. Even in aspects that appear to constitute seamless continuations of specific narratives, such as "China as the birthplace of disease," the assumption cannot be made that the fears, motivations, and mechanics are the same. Further, as David Palumbo-Liu (1999: 287) has shown, even if they share features with generic Yellow Peril narratives, contemporary anxieties about Chinese money purchasing political influence have their own "particular texture and historical context" and are tied to the "modalities of transnational capitalism."

Tchen and Yeats's (2014) coinage of the term "Yellow Perilism" as a linguistically and culturally stable racist ideology thus appears somewhat hasty in that it homogenizes a very complex and mutable discourse, turning it into a transhistorical and transcultural phenomenon. Granted, contemporary Sinophobic discourse does come "prepackaged" insofar as it rests on a well-established cultural undercarriage, and, as the contributors to the volume show, depictions of Asians often remain colored by entrenched racial stereotypes such as mysterious and unfathomable (Fiskesjö), exploitative (Billé, Anthony and Dittgen, Zhao), and diseased (Lynteris). But Yellow Peril narratives are also cultural vectors of multiple kinds of anxieties that span the cultural (Billé), political (Fiskesjö), economic (Zhao), and affective (Qiu) realms. These anxieties are also heterogeneous, and the emergence of the term "Yellow Peril" in contexts as disparate as Italy, South Africa, Mongolia, or Nigeria cannot be assumed to be singular, to refer to the same fears, or to revolve around the same stereotypes. The discourse, even when used in reference to a single country like China, is thus inherently fractured and multiple.

It is with this multiplicity in mind that we decided to pluralize the title and to speak instead of "perils." In their chapters, the contributors ask what it means for the term to be used in countries like Russia or Mongolia that see themselves as Eurasian bridges between Europe and Asia (Billé); in South Africa (Dittgen and Anthony), a country still fiercely polarized along a Black/White dividing line; or in Nigeria (Qiu), which remained under British colonial rule for 160 years but is now a recipient of extensive economic, military, and political support from China. To what extent does the recent setting up of Chinese communities in Italy (Zhao), a country that has long been a locus of emigration but only recently a place of immigration (see Stella 2004), evoke fears resembling those that accompanied the emergence of Chinatowns in the United States a hundred years previously? How can we make sense of the use of the term "Yellow Peril" in Asian contexts such as Mongolia (Billé) or in culturally Chinese Hong Kong (Carrico)? And how are these narratives received in China itself and to what extent do they shape official policies (Urbansky, Fiskesjö)?

Which Asia?

In their analysis of the evolution and current reverberations of the Yellow Peril discourse, the chapters in the volume are all concerned specifically with China. This focus does not, however, make this collection simply a study of Sinophobic sentiments. The geographic convergence of this volume merely reflects the current place of China in global imaginaries as a rising economic powerhouse with military ambitions, notably in the South China Sea. While contemporary geopolitical dynamics play a large role in contemporary anxieties about China, it would be reductive to interpret them simply as the product of the current political and economic situation. As the contributions of this book show, they are deeply embedded in older narratives about Asia.

Many of the current anxieties about China are racialized insofar as they essentialize the Chinese as a group. In particular, descriptions of the Chinese as calculating, inscrutable, excessively hardworking, and lacking creativity (see Wu 2002: 68) constitute many interpretive filters and rationalizations of China's economic rise and geopolitical ambitions. These echoes of early twentieth-century Yellow Peril narratives do not mean they represent a seamless continuation of the same discourse, but neither are the similarities fortuitous, as the chapters by Walker and Lynteris make especially explicit. Attempting to disentangle current anti-Chinese discourse from these older narratives—and indeed from wider racialized imaginations of Asia—would feel somewhat disingenuous.

It is also important to bear in mind that the object of the Yellow Peril discourse is not stable, and that we are essentially dealing with a free-floating concept that has shifted throughout the twentieth century in line with the political and economic situation. During the Russo-Japanese War (1904–1905) and World War II (1939–1945), for example, many of the same fears currently attached to China focused in fact on Japan.[4] In the 1980s and 1990s, at the height of Japan's economic boom, anxieties about Japan's buying spree caused much anxiety in the United States and elsewhere (Pan 2012: 27). The predominant perspective then was of a Japan described both as a technologically developed nation and as a "closed society where individual initiative was completely stifled in service of a rigidly hierarchical and monolithic system" (Lee 1999: 206; see also Morris 2013). By contrast, the popular notion that the twenty-first century will be an Asian century is currently focused exclusively on China, with its promise of a vast market of 1.3 billion customers (Pan 2012: 56) but with the dreaded prospect of its gaining dominance economically and militarily.[5] These different emphases have been reflected in the realm of education as well, with the 1990s boom in Japanese studies gradually declining in favor of Chinese studies, leading to the current glut of China-focused scholars in many disciplines such as anthropology, for instance.

The nation playing a dominant role in Yellow Peril narratives thus appears to have reflected the dominant fears of a particular period and situation. The fact that Japan and China played that role over the twentieth century means that these shifts have occasionally required political U-turns and media campaigns to differentiate one group from another. *Life Magazine* famously ran a piece in December 1941 entitled "How to tell Japs from the Chinese," in which two "representative faces" are compared. The article listed "scientific" racial differences ("The Jap is squarely Mongoloid with flat, blob nose") along with cultural features ("Chinese wear rational calm of tolerant realists. Japs [. . .] show humorless intensity of ruthless mystics") and emphasized the differences between the two groups by choosing as representatives of each group a "Chinese public servant" and a "Japanese warrior." A similar distinction was made by Belgian cartoonist Hergé in the *Blue Lotus* (1934–1935), the fifth volume of *The Adventures of Tintin*, where he depicts the Chinese and Japanese characters completely differently. While the "Japanese are given long teeth and mostly look angry, suspicious, or malicious," the Chinese are depicted as "friendly people who have become the victims of Western and Japanese imperialists" (Goddeeris 2013: 233).[6] The exact opposite is seen in the November 1894 issue of the British magazine *Punch*, published during the Opium War, where the Chinese personages are routinely depicted as uneducated and speaking broken pidgin English, whereas Japanese characters are Westernized and speak unaccented English.

A multilayered palimpsest, the discourse of the Yellow Peril has been eminently slippery and mutable, its margins and mileposts shifting in line with the political situation. If some Asian groups have at times been described as better than the rest,[7] this higher status has remained fragile and subject to sudden reversals. Often Asian groups have been amalgamated into a single entity, with its internal components easily permutable. A recent Hollywood movie, for instance, originally featured the Chinese as the baddies until it was decided it might be a mistake to antagonize the lucrative Chinese market, and that it might be preferable to have the North Koreans play that role (Frayling 2014: 326–327). Clearly, which specific group was used did not matter as long as it could serve as the vehicle for "Yellow Peril" fantasies. Similarly, derogatory names for Asians have tended to be freely interchangeable. For instance, the term "gook" (from *hanguk* 한국 "Korea") was used by Americans during the Korean War to refer to both North and South Koreans, as well as to the Chinese (Lee 1999: 190). In the same way, ultimately, all Asian groups have been collapsed under the single category "yellow."

The mapping of Asians onto the color yellow has been particularly enduring. However, as many scholars have shown (Demel 1992; Dikötter 1992, 1997; Keevak 2011), this association is comparatively recent, dating from the beginning of the twentieth century at the earliest. The earliest accounts provided by European travelers and missionaries in Asia rarely focused on skin color; rather, they focused on the shape of the eyes of Asian populations, their relative hairlessness, or other physical features (Keevak 2011: 102). When they did mention color, missionaries in fact referred to the Chinese and Japanese as white. The color yellow, when used, tended to refer to Jews and other Semitic people, or occasionally to North Africans or even Indians (Keevak 2011: 45). Rather than descriptive, color terms were evaluative: the whiteness of East Asians—and in particular that of the Japanese (Kowner 2004)—indexed their perceived capacity to become Westernized and enlightened (Keevak 2011: 28).[8]

In his book *The Discourse of Race in Modern China* (1992), historian Frank Dikötter shows how racial categories originating in the West later became embedded in and were appropriated by the Chinese and other Eastern Asian countries. For the Chinese, the color yellow had positive symbolism (unlike white, which symbolized death), as it recalled the Yellow River (*Huang He*) and the Yellow Emperor (*Huangdi*). It also covered a much broader range of hues than in Europe, from broken white to light brown (Dikötter 1992: 56). For Chinese nationalists, this single category was a way to emphasize intra-Asian connections and racial loyalties. For the Japanese, however, this same single racial category was problematic as it placed them on a par with Chinese, Vietnamese, Indonesians, and other Asian groups that were seen as inferior and less "developed" (Keevak 2011: 134–135). As several contributions in this volume will make clear (Billé, Carrico, Urbansky), other Asian groups have sought to magnify existing differences between themselves and the rest of Asia.[9] This phenomenon has also been described in the Chinese diaspora, notably in the United States where acculturated American-Chinese fluent in

English are keen to dissociate themselves from "just off the boat" Chinese settlers who "might do something that will get every Asian into trouble" (Yu 2002: 191).

This multiethnic, historically layered, and geographically disper-sive Asia makes the circumscribing of the notion of "Asia" particularly tricky. As East Asia specialist Harry Harootunian (2000: 25) has famously argued, "one of the enduring ironies of the study of Asia is that Asia itself, as an object, simply doesn't exist." Potentially extending as far west as Turkey, "Asia" is a vast swath of land encompassing multiple ethnic groups, cultures, and language groups that share little, if anything at all, with each other. A similar elasticity has been witnessed with the adjec-tive "Indian," which, as Walker and Sobocinska (2013: 9) have noted, can potentially refer to "any number of people from the Americas to the Pacific Islands"—a slippage complicated further by "European coloniz-ers' tendency to brand any new acquisitions 'The Indies.'"

This very nebulous geographic, cultural, and racial entity also makes it difficult to use it productively as a theoretical framework. Numerous cultural theorists have nonetheless found Edward Said's seminal book *Orientalism* useful, despite the fact that Said's "Orient" referred to the Middle East rather than East Asia. To an extent, the stereotypes through which the region is framed do resonate with narratives about East Asia. The Jews' remarkable (but dangerous) intelligence and their alleged con-spiratorial machinations for world domination certainly echo Western concerns regarding East Asia's capacity to become a dominant global force. However, in spite of several overlaps, the two sets of stereotypes remain distinct, as will be discussed in the next section.

In a similar way, the concept of "Yellow Perilism" put forth by Tchen and Yeats (2014) and others before them (Okihiro 1994, Espiritu 2008, Palumbo-Liu 1999), while useful to weave together various strands of this racial discourse, ultimately offers only limited theoretical mileage. In attempting to make coherent a large set of stereotypes, "Yellow Perilism" also silences the numerous differences found between the different speak-ers and subjects of these narratives. As Michael Keevak in fact notes in the introduction to his analysis (2011: 3), "like most other forms of racial stereotyping," the concept of yellowness "cannot be reduced to a simple chronology and was the product of often vague and confusing notions about physical difference, heritage, and ethnological specificity."

If some of the core stereotypes about Asians appear to be shared across regions and speakers, many of them are also context-specific. The diasporic and dispersive nature of much of Asian culture (Shih 2007) means that relations with—but also within—Asia show a great deal of variance and are all but monolithic. This has unfortunately rarely been given the attention it deserves. The vast majority of publications on the "Yellow Peril" and anti-Asian prejudice continues to focus virtually exclusively on Asian experiences within the United States (Eng 2001, Lee 1999, Lui 2005, Okihiro 1994, Palumbo-Liu 1999, Shah 2001, Yu 2002, W. Wu 1982, F. Wu 2002), and to some extent in other anglophone countries such as the United Kingdom (Witchard 2014) and Australia (Walker 1999). All too often, analyses of stereotypes about Asians have assumed that the speaker is both Western and white—and frequently male. But the West does not have a monopoly on Sinophobic and anti-Asian narratives, as several of the contributions in this volume demonstrate. This means that stereotypes also show great variations, and are embedded differently in local cultures. This variance must be taken seriously as it shows the limitations of the West/Asian binary opposition that under-girds Said's thesis.

Even within anglophone culture, a subset that is somewhat culturally cohesive, stereotypes and attitudes often vary due to historical specifici-ties.[10] The coding of Asians as a "model minority" is thus one that makes little sense outside of the United States and the context of the melting pot. The US stereotype of the "Asian driver" who drives too slowly, does not indicate before turning, and has poor vision is also one that appears to be circumscribed to North America—though it may be gaining ground through Hollywood representations.

Further afield, cultural imaginations of China are even more frac-tured. In Russia, for instance, the well-established Western stereotype of the attractive and submissive Asian woman does not hold true and is in fact largely unknown. There, both historically and in the contemporary period, intermarriages have been virtually exclusively between Russian women and Asian men (Gamsa 2014).[11] While this disparity is due in part to the population and gender imbalance that prevails in the Russian Far East, this particular configuration also finds its roots in a complex and culturally specific cluster of assumptions linked to race and gender. In Russia, Chinese men are seen as hardworking, reliable, and sober, while Chinese women are thought to be capricious and to take poor care of themselves.[12] Conversely, in Chinese culture Russian men are often considered coarse and violent while Russian women enjoy the reputation of being some of the most beautiful women on earth.

In non-white parts of the world, like in Mongolia (Billé), South Africa (Dittgen and Anthony), or Nigeria (Qiu), representations of China are positioned in an even more complex way as they are inflected with a particular colonial history (Asia, Africa) and Cold War ideologies (Russia, Mongolia). Mongolia, an Asian country under the political and cultural leadership of the Soviet Union for the most part of the twentieth century, currently holds views of its southern neighbor that are largely consonant with those of Russia. Mongolian imaginations of China, rather than being based in direct interactions (the latter were prohibited between the 1960s and early 1990s) have instead been mediated by Russian narratives. As a result, contemporary Mongolian views of China remain inflected by a very European and Orientalist discourse that sees the Chinese (and Asians overall) as inscrutable, mercantile, and miserly (Billé 2015). In Nigeria, the Chinese have to an extent supplanted the white British colonial rulers and are perceived by the local population as new mentors holding the promise of enrichment and modernity. But in contrast to the British racial and cultural hierarchy, the Chinese have ushered in what Qiu refers to as "scalable modernity," a multitier system that feels less exclusive and offers different levels of access and participation.

Why this book?

If, as argued above, anti-Chinese and anti-Asian narratives are configured differently in different cultures, it seems perhaps counterintuitive to bring them all within this book under the same, though pluralized, "Yellow Peril" rubric. Yet there are a number of reasons why doing so may be worthwhile. First of all, soft power vehicles such as Hollywood movies tend to disseminate US views well beyond their originally intended audience.[13] Some of these stereotypes may be too culturally specific to really take hold elsewhere or to resonate in any meaningful way, but others can, and indeed do, as several contributions to this volume clearly show. The increasing global interconnectedness of world cultures, greatly facilitated by social media platforms such as YouTube and Facebook, means that the assumption that worldviews and prejudices are self-contained and discrete no longer holds true. The ethnographies described in this book, in spite of their international character, thus remain heavily inflected by Western, and especially North American, views. They constitute in this sense local reverberations and syntheses of global narratives of Asia that emerged in the West and continue to be transmitted through Western media. As the authors show, reception and adaptation of these global narratives eventually percolate into very diverse understandings of China and Asia overall, but the strong imprint imparted by the West, and Hollywood especially, forms the dominant cultural shorthand and interpretive prism.

Cultural views also become entangled further through a very extensive Chinese diaspora, as Shu-mei Shih (2007) has shown. The complex and unanticipated ways in which cultural trends refract and ricochet across oceans can be seen with the so-called "Chinese fortune cookie." Invented in the United States, the cookie did not appear in China until 1989, when American tourists began traveling to China and asking for them after their meals. Originally introduced in China as "American fortune cookies," they are an apt illustration of the ways in which cultural expectations and practices become ever more enmeshed on a global scale.[14]

Another advantage of bringing these different narratives together is that it sheds important light on the mechanism of this racial discourse in particular, and on xenophobia and racism in general. Stereotypes about Asia and Asians may have their own specificities, but they nonetheless also present several fascinating overlaps. While the contributors to *Yellow Perils* do not assume that these stereotypes share the same origins, significance, or reverberations, they seek to tease out their commonalities and examine why Yellow Peril narratives appear to resonate in so many disparate cultural contexts in such a specific way.

One particular cluster of stereotypes around which these racialized narratives appears to be revolving is that of excess. As mentioned earlier, the large population of China, at 1.3 billion people, regularly weaves into stories featuring both threat and economic opportunities. That demographics loom large in any discussion of China's place in the world might seem only natural given the country's enormous population. Yet the unspoken bias that fuses "population" and "threat" becomes particularly evident when one compares it with the media treatment of India. India's own demographic footprint, at 1.2 billion, comes a close second to China's, and India is in fact projected to become the world's most populous country by 2022, surpassing China. Yet, in spite of similar demographics and economic growth, India does not seem to attract the same superlatives, or to be embedded within the same narratives of fear and anxiety. India, like China, may be one of the new "rising powers," but there is no such thing as an "Indian Peril."

In addition to their population, the Chinese—and to some extent the Japanese before them—are also "excessive" in their behavior and relationships. Too populous, they are also too competitive, too driven, too ruthless. Increasingly numerous at top universities in the United States and elsewhere, Chinese students are seen as overly ambitious and competitive to the point of unfairness. As the student body president of the University of California, Berkeley, reportedly said, "Some students say that if they see too many Asians in a class, they are not going to take it because the curve will be too high" (Wu 2002: 48). In the business world, China's economic practices are routinely described as cutthroat and unethical, leading to an adverse impact on the environment and the climate, as well as to acquisitive exploitation in developing countries, especially Africa.

All these narratives point to Western anxieties relating to East Asia's competitive economic power. Very similar Yellow Peril fears in fact emerged in the 1980s with respect to Japan (Morris 2011: 18).[15] This sense of threat would seem to materialize, therefore, against an imagined East Asian capacity to emulate and to be competitive at a similar level. After all, what China is charged with is an excess of business acumen, ambition, and drive—qualities that are all highly praised in the West. This is noteworthy as it appears to deviate from the usual mechanics of racialized speech where xenophobic statements are a way of defining what the speaker is not: dirty, smelly, animalistic, immoral. While Chinese businesses practices have occasionally been described as immoral,[16] this immorality is premised primarily on excess rather than difference.

Jeffrey Wasserstrom has argued that the bifocal—i.e., positive *and* negative—fantasies that are currently projected onto China "reveal more about our own hopes and anxieties than they do about people living across the Pacific" (Wasserstrom 2007: xxiii). In his view, these images are not specific to China, and the fact that Yellow Peril narratives have indeed been free-floating as far as China, Japan, or even North Korea are concerned would appear to support this line of argument. It is nonetheless important to bear in mind that these narratives have not attached in the same way to India or to African or Middle Eastern countries. If

Chengxin Pan is correct in his assessment that these fears are in fact "derived less from China's rise or its uncertain intentions than from the self-righteous certainty about the universality of Western historical trajectory" (2012: 47), then it would seem that China and Japan occupy a privileged site with respect to the West.

I discuss in the section that follows the cultural positioning of Asia in the United States, a focus that may seem surprising given the international character of this book's contributions. It is important, however, to give due credit to the capacity of the US cultural force to shape global narratives, an imprint that can be traced in many of the chapters in this volume. Thus, the stereotypical representation of Asians as imitators finds a close echo in the new South African coinage of "Fong Kong" (Dittgen and Anthony), the comparison of the Chinese to a horde is actively deployed in the context of Italy (Zhao) and Hong Kong (Carrico), while their alleged mercantile ruthlessness informs media debates in settings as distant as Nigeria (Qiu) or Mongolia (Billé).

The force of US race representations in the media is clear from the pressure currently experienced by Hollywood to cast more Chinese actors in its movies, and the demand from Chinese audiences to see themselves represented through meaningful roles, not merely as cameos (Schwartzel 2016). An early example of a major Asian character on American television was Ling Woo, a lawyer played by Lucy Liu on Fox's *Ally McBeal*, While she was not wholly unproblematic,[17] Ling Woo vanquished stereotypes of Asian women as meek and submissive (Nakao 1999). Liu's representation of a young Asian female who was "neither submissive nor selfless" (Sun 2002: 661) was a hit among Asian-American viewers but also among audiences in East Asia, notably in Korea and China.

Similarly, American media representations of other racial groups are not circumscribed to a domestic audience but circulate well beyond the cultural West, including in non-white parts of the world. The emergence of hip-hop on the East Asian music scene has been accompanied by the adoption of cultural accoutrements coded as "black," such as clothing, "bling," and specific dance movements. In Mongolia, for example, the popularity of hip-hop—currently one of the most prevalent music types among the youth—was greatly facilitated by media representations portraying urban American black culture as "cool." The popularity of the band Kiwi, a trio made up of a Mongolian girl and two ethnically mixed Asian girls—one white, one black—has similarly greatly relied on a racially triangulated image of cosmopolitan modernity (see Billé 2015: 52).

This suggests that an analysis of Yellow Peril narratives, both within and outside of the United States, along a binary axis does not fully capture global dynamics of race representations. Indeed, comparisons of portrayals of blacks and Asians in the media reveals very different racial assumptions. Whereas much of anti-black narratives hinge around the notion that they are less cultured, less "evolved," and more "animalistic" than whites, this does not hold true as far as Asians are concerned today.[18] On the contrary, Asians are often depicted as highly intelligent, less sexual and physical (i.e., less animalistic), and rational to the point of complete emotional detachment. The latter stereotype is in fact so ingrained that it has proven very difficult to unseat. In his book on love and intimacy in a Chinese village, anthropologist Yunxiang Yan (2003) recounts his difficulties in framing the results of his research. He explains that in Western literature, the Chinese way of life is conventionally depicted as a corporate model in which overrationality prevails to the detriment of emotions. The view of Asians as highly intelligent (with typical representations of Asian students as nerdy math geniuses) is just as well-established, and with a long history. As early as the 1930s, at the height of scientific racism, Asians were ranked as almost equal to whites in term of intelligence.[19] The correlation that some scientists established between intelligence, brain size, and, inversely, size of genitalia, in fact appeared to give Asians a privileged, more "evolved" status (Palumbo-Liu 1999: 154), and this is in fact one of the points upon which anxieties relative to the Chinese—and East Asians generally—would seem to hinge.

As historian Christopher Connery wrote (1994: 34), as the Western present had previously been the East Asian future, now "if Japan was anywhere in time, it was in the future." This insight is in fact clearly visible in science fiction movies where futuristic representations frequently have a distinct Asian flavor. A good case in point is the 1982 classic movie *Blade Runner*, directed by Ridley Scott, where Chinese characters and advertisements in Japanese feature prominently in the dystopian landscape of post-apocalyptic Los Angeles. While many scholars have analyzed this particular melding of Asia and futurity (Palumbo-Liu 1999: 326; Wu 2002: 117), fewer have noted the parallel absence of blacks. The Asianness of *Blade Runner* and other science fiction movies is thus perhaps not simply a symptom of racial anxieties (though it is also that) but is also indicative of assumed racial hierarchies—with Asians at the top and blacks at the bottom. The privileged position occupied by Asians is also perceptible in the way intelligent humanoid aliens are routinely portrayed in ways consonant with ethnic representations of Asians, typically seen as hairless, lacking muscularity, smaller in stature, and frequently asexual (Eng 2002; Lui 2005; Ngyuen 2014; Okihiro 1994; Palumbo-Liu 1999). Unlike blacks, who are routinely vilified as criminal and brutish, Asians tend to be portrayed as an ethnic success story, having attained the status of model minority (Hsu 2015; Wu 2014). While these representations are far from benign and indeed inflict considerable discursive violence and mental anguish on their recipients (Wu 2002; Reece 2017), the position occupied by Asians, in the United States as well as in many other settings, is one of a group at the same time admired and maligned, with both superhuman and inhuman qualities.

From "yellow" to "off-white"

The ambivalent place of Asians with respect to the "unmarked" white category means they are not seen as opposites but are positioned at a tangent—as mirrors and similes. Asia may be the site of the future and of hypermodernity, but it remains nonetheless a place associated with copies rather than creativity. As Shu-mei Shih (2007: 44) has cogently argued, Asian postcolonial hybrid cultures are "usually seen by the center as but corrupted versions or poor cousins of metropolitan cultures and are seldom, if ever, seen as precursors."

The association between Asia and the culture of the copy is deeply embedded in a much older Orientalist discourse that has portrayed East Asians as replicators rather than innovators. Asian languages—and Chinese in particular—were described as "childlike," and "destitute of all grammatical forms" (Keevak 2011: 115), while Asian forms of modernity spurred by Europe's colonization of Asia were dismissed as copies that were "ludicrous, flattering and threatening all at once" (Okihiro 1994: 198). In the 1980s, Japan was routinely depicted as a nation that merely miniaturized Western inventions: unable to invent and be creative, its only contribution was allegedly to take a product and reduce its size.[20] Over the last decade China has become the nation primarily associated with duplication and copying, though very differently from the way

Japan had been (Bosker 2013).[21] This reputation is of course not wholly unfounded given the whole industry supporting the counterfeit products that have flooded the domestic and international markets (Aguiar 2012). These fake goods, or *shanzhai* in Chinese, span a wide range of items, from films, technology, and designer fashion, to art, architecture, and prescription drugs (Yu 2011).

This alleged "lack of creativity" also informs the way Asians are imagined to operate, akin to robots. As Frank Wu writes (2002: 68),

> We are familiar with Asian American sensations at the piano or the violin. They exhibit superlative technical prowess on the keyboard or with the bow, but nonetheless are criticized for being without passion, even bereft of a human soul. We know the notes and follow the score, but we have become too precise to be artists. We are automatons, frightening in our correctness.

Drawing a parallel with *Blade Runner*, Robert Lee even compares Asian Americans with replicants—those Artificial Intelligence robots that are virtually indistinguishable from humans yet are inalienably Other. Both represent perfectibility and perfect malleability but, as simulacra, are completely inauthentic (Lee 1999: 194–195). These replicants "look like humans, they talk like them, they even have feelings and emotions." They are perfect "skin jobs" (Giuliana Bruno, cited in Eng 2001: 35). The attention given to skin is of course not coincidental. In a strongly racialized society such as the United States, skin color has long both denoted and moored social hierarchy. The near-whiteness of Asians— so close to and yet different from the unmarked dominant group—must be read here in the wider context of a white/black dichotomy that bookends the racial spectrum. In the context of the United States, the "introduction of Asian race notions into a formerly bipolar racial imaginary of black and white" (Chen 2012: 107),[22] in what Claire Jean Kim (1999) has called "racial triangulation," means that relations between Asians and whites are inextricably tied to the position of blacks. As the writer Frank Chin perceptively noted: "Whites love us because we're not black" (Chin 1974, in Lee 1999: 145). Indeed, the very term "model minority" suggests Asians may serve as model for other ethnic minorities to emulate, notably for blacks who have "trailed behind" and "failed to integrate." In addition to the fact that they do not address historical injustices (Hsu 2015: 21), what all these statements do is aggravate racial tensions between African Americans and Asian Americans (Wu 2002: 67).

The moniker of "model minority" emerged through the Asian tradition emphasizing learnedness coupled with Asian immigrants' desire for education, thereby creating a strong positive image to resist attempts to debase their intelligence (Metrick-Chen 2013: 208). After decades of laws restricting Asian emigration, preferential access to "front gate" immigration made it possible for highly skilled Chinese and Japanese workers to enter and settle in the United States (Hsu 2015: 5). But as many Asian American scholars have shown, "economic success and class ascension do not necessarily erase racial distinctions" (Palumbo-Liu 1999: 3), and positive assessments of Asian success can very rapidly turn into negatives. The enmeshment of both aspects was noted by Frank Wu (2002: 68):

> To be intelligent is to be calculating and too clever; to be gifted in math and science is to be mechanical and not creative, lacking interpersonal skills and leadership potential, to be polite is to be inscrutable and submissive. To be hard working is to be an unfair competitor for regular human beings and not a well-rounded, likable individual. To be family oriented is to be clannish and too ethnic. To be law abiding is to be self-righteous and rigidly rule-bound. To be successfully entrepreneurial is to be deviously aggressive and economically intimidating.

For Gary Okihiro, this particular intertwining of positive and negative characteristics does not constitute an oscillation between two poles but denotes rather a circular relationship, whereby any slight deviation in either direction is liable to turn the "model minority" into a "Yellow Peril" and vice versa. In his analysis, "'model' Asians exhibit the same singleness of purpose, patience and endurance, cunning, fanaticism, and group loyalty characteristic of Marco Polo's Mongol soldiers" (1994: 199). This "model" quality is thus less a sign of successful integration than a mask concealing a radically alien nature.

The trope of the mask is a recurrent one in Yellow Peril narratives and is closely linked with stereotypical representation of East Asians as mysterious and impenetrable. Like the "perfect skins" of the replicants in

Blade Runner, this mask is the cover of acculturation and Westernization East Asians are believed to be operating behind. Though not about Asia specifically, the 1962 movie *The Manchurian Candidate* played with this imagery. Outwardly patriotic but in reality a sleeper agent controlled by a foreign power, the eponymous character is the son of a prominent right-wing political family who becomes an unwitting[23] assassin in an international communist conspiracy. That the film's narrative closely reverberates Yellow Peril anxieties has been particularly evident at a number of political junctures. The March 1997 cover of *National Review* magazine, for example, famously depicted Bill and Hillary Clinton and Vice President Al Gore as "Manchurian candidates": the trio were buck-toothed, yellow-faced, and clad in caricatured Asian costumes (Yeats 2013: 268). That the editors felt that the use of such a racialized cartoon would be an apt illustration for an article on alleged political corruption speaks volumes about the survival and persistent force of this tradition of racial grotesques (Lee 1999: 1).

Such examples provide a discursive context in which news stories such as those detailing Chinese businessman Huang Nubo's Arctic investments become immediately legible. His self-description as a poet and romantic fails to convince as it comes preceded by countless narratives of Asian deceit and treachery. This cluster of racial characterizations in fact informs media analyses of China overall. As Chengxin Pan convincingly demonstrates (2012), once a particular paradigm becomes dominant, all news stories then tend to be interpreted through that particular prism. If over the last several decades China has been depicted by the US media in different ways—in turn as a society of disciplined automatons, as a politically ruthless regime, and more recently as an economic miracle—the core assumptions have not much evolved beyond early twentieth-century views. China (and to a large extent Japan) remains a "riddle wrapped in a mystery inside an enigma," in the words of American political analyst and commentator William Kristol.

The well-entrenched belief that the Chinese have a master plan, and that they are able to patiently work toward their goal, is another stereotype that has proven resilient and has continued to inform analyses of China. The blueprint for these skilled Asian politicians is of course the figure of Fu Manchu, who is highly educated and speaks the purest English.[24] Fu Manchu is not a mindless brutal ruler—far from it. While he is cruel, he is primarily an astute statesman who kidnaps highflying financiers from all over Europe and, like in *The Manchurian Candidate*, controls them by "turning them into stereotypical Chinese people with the aid of his magic mushrooms" (Frayling 2014: 15).

The danger inherent in Fu Manchu—and by extension in Asia in global imaginaries—is in fact his capacity to bring together "esoteric Eastern knowledge and Western scientific knowledge" (Hevia 1998: 210–211). The danger this poses is "far more disturbing than the classic European fantasy of barbarian invasions from the East" in that it has the "potential to undermine the structure of empire and of global white supremacy, and could conceivably topple the British and other Western empires like a row of dominoes" (ibid.). Less a radically alien Other than a liminal character astride two worlds, Fu Manchu is able, just like the Asian model minority, to harness and exploit the West's very strengths. In fact, as Urmila Seshagiri (2006: 182) has cogently analyzed,

> Dr. Fu-Manchu himself becomes the "juggernaut" of modernity: his complete control over time, space, technology, languages, and social systems makes him a monstrous reflection of the very Western civilization he threatens to subsume, and his racial alterity makes literal the alienating, unknowable character of modern urban life.

This particular ambivalence extends the contributions of this volume well beyond an overview of current global Sinophobic narratives. The lateral position occupied by anti-Asian cultural and racial stereotypes with respect to the hegemonic dominance of white Euro-American culture means that these analyses also provide a prism through which to understand the position of various groups respective to central Western narratives of development and modernity. This tangential positioning is akin to the concept of the "off-modern" proposed by Svetlana Boym (2001: xvi-xvii) to "explore sideshadows and back alleys rather than the straight road of progress" and to allow to "take a detour from the deterministic narrative of twentieth-century history." The imaginary personage that animates Yellow Peril narratives similarly traces the global reverberations of Western narratives of development and modernity and their resonance and limitations in places as far afield as Nigeria, South Africa, Mongolia, and Hong Kong.

Chapter outline

Chapter Two, by Christos Lynteris, foregrounds the discourse of pathology and disease as a historically established vector of anti-Chinese sentiment, and as a source of infectious disease epidemics in the Western imagination. From smallpox and bubonic plague in the past, to SARS and avian flu today, China's cities and landscapes have been depicted in both the lay and the medical press as the breeding grounds of infectious pathogens that have devastated humanity. In many cases, especially in the past, this identification of China as the source of diseases has led to a consequent pathologization of Chinese bodies and items, in the context of overseas communities and Chinatowns, with severe effects on migration policies and host population attitudes toward Chinese immigrants. Lynteris' chapter explores the development and transformation of these "epidemic imaginaries" over the past 250 years, underlining how the focus on different pathogens has linked and in turn fostered different forms of Yellow Peril ideology in different political and socioeconomic contexts.

The third chapter, by David Walker, explores the multiple representations of invasive Asia in late nineteenth- and early twentieth-century Australia. Tracing the origins of Australian anxieties to the writings of Charles H. Pearson, an Oxford-educated historian who immigrated to the Australian colonies and became a prominent politician and educator, Walker argues that Australia's geographical location in the Asia-Pacific region created a fertile cultural setting for a survivalist imaginary that positioned Asia as a growing threat to European civilization and depicted Australia at the forefront of this new civilizational challenge. Once viewed as a remote outpost of the British Empire, Australia could now be seen as central to the greatest geopolitical challenges of the twentieth century, a theme picked up by the American race theorist Lothrop Stoddard in his influential bestseller, *The Rising Tide of Color*, first published in 1919.

Xiaojian Zhao's ethnographic exploration of racial tension in Italy is the topic of the fourth chapter. In her contribution, Zhao traces the conditions that gave rise to anti-Chinese hostility in Prato, Italy's historical capital of the textile industry. In the early 1990s, when thousands of Chinese migrated to the city, they were welcomed by the locals as a valuable resource. The textile industry was declining at the time, due largely to a lack of interest on the part of the younger generation. The Chinese arrived at an opportune juncture. They subcontracted work from the sewing and knitwear factories and bought equipment and properties from discontinued enterprises. Utilizing a network of friends and relatives among their fellow migrants as well as people who had stayed in China (the majority in Wenzhou, Zhejiang province) and taking advantage of China's participation in the global economy, Chinese entrepreneurs rapidly grew more successful and powerful, as many self-employed subcontractors eventually became competitive independent producers. Although the growth of Chinese enterprises revitalized Prato's economy, anti-Chinese sentiments also emerged. In her chapter, Zhao also explores the responses of the Chinese migrants to these tensions, and their survival strategies.

The following chapter, by Romain Dittgen and Ross Anthony, focuses on another site of recent Chinese immigration. Over the past decade, China has invested significant diplomatic energy into promoting its engagement within Africa with the paradigm of "South–South" cooperation, forwarding concepts such as "brotherly assistance," "win-win," "harmonious development," and president Xi Jinping's recently launched "African Dream." Chinese official rhetoric is often at pains to stress the equality of its engagement and frequently emphasizes— often by way of comparison to former European colonial powers—its outright rejection of hegemonic control within Africa. In this chapter, Dittgen and Anthony examine the attitudes of Chinese migrants toward African locals vis-à-vis these large-scale Chinese state–driven narratives. Unlike large Chinese companies and State-Owned Enterprises (SOEs) in Africa, where the state has a far more direct influence on their behavior, far less influence is wielded upon small-scale traders—despite the fact that the Chinese government might suggest otherwise. The way in which the attitudes of these groups square up to official rhetoric addresses the "Yellow Peril" question from the other side; the question then becomes "In what ways does 'the Chinese presence' at both the level of state rhetoric and local-level actors contribute to, mitigate, or transform this stereotype?" Using South Africa as a case study, Dittgen and

Anthony's contribution brings a deeper understanding of the Chinese engagement in Africa and places the "Yellow Peril" phenomenon in a more global context.

Staying within an African context, the chapter by Yu Qiu further complicates the common East/West dichotomy with an ethnographically rich study of Sino-Nigerian social and romantic entanglements. She shows that the contemporary position of the Chinese in Nigeria replicates in some ways that of the white (*oyibo*) British colonial master, thereby embedding the Chinese newcomers in a preexisting racial and social hierarchy. This entangles both groups in relations of dependency and mentorship that the Chinese do not necessarily understand or accept. At the same time, these new social formations are creating emerging contact zones between a limited yet growing number of Chinese and young Nigerian graduates and urban entrepreneurs who look for common grounds with the Chinese people by learning about business strategies and entrepreneurial ethics from them. For these young Nigerians, the "scalable modernity" of Chinese practices opens exciting avenues of economic opportunities and social independence.

Chapter Seven, by Franck Billé, looks at the ways in which the European racist discourse of the Yellow Peril mutated, was internalized, and was ultimately appropriated by the Mongols as a marker of difference. The association of China with threat has a long history in Mongolia, and is closely connected to the country's incorporation into the Qing empire from the seventeenth century until 1911. Throughout the twentieth century, anti-Chinese sentiments were actively fostered by the Soviet Union: China was routinely described as an imperialistic nation intent on invading Mongolia, prevented from doing so only by the Soviet Union. Not only aggressive, China was also portrayed as culturally backward, dirty, and nonmodern, while the Soviet Union represented the pinnacle of high culture and urban modernity. Throughout the twentieth century, as Mongolia became increasingly aligned politically and culturally with the Soviet Union, it actively sought to expunge all its cultural links to Asia, and to redefine itself as a Eurasian nation. In postsocialist Mongolia, this worldview remains dominant, and the Mongolian public discourse is saturated with media articles, graffiti, popular songs, and rumors pointing to alleged malevolent Chinese intentions. Billé argues that the Mongolian version of the "Yellow Peril" constitutes both an internalization of Russian ideas of Asia and a policing discourse emphasizing distance from China and Asia overall. Ostensibly about the Chinese, it is in fact an internal discourse by and for Mongols, as well as a claim of membership in the cultural "West."

Blurring the line further, Kevin Carrico's chapter examines reverberations of the Yellow Peril discourse in culturally Chinese parts of Asia. Carrico analyzes in particular the emergence of Yellow Peril discourses in Hong Kong, where a series of political, educational, and cultural controversies, from stalled political reform to patriotic education to public defecation, have heightened tensions with Mainland China in recent years. His chapter examines the origins and implications of resulting discourses of ethno-racial difference, from the appearance of the derogatory term "locust" for Mainlanders to a recent issue of the University of Hong Kong student paper *Undergrad* promoting local consciousness and self-determination for the "Hong Kong nationality." Carrico's analysis traces the formation of ethnic distinctions in the process of political, social, and cultural conflicts, on the one hand deconstructing the assumed unity of "Chinese culture," while on the other hand highlighting the origins and often unsavory consequences of growing ethnic and sub-ethnic conflicts in China today.

Chapter Nine, by Magnus Fiskesjö, probes the complex sets of narratives of fear and fearmongering that have accompanied the setting up of Confucius Institutes in Europe and America over the last decade. The Confucius Institutes form part of a strategic Chinese government campaign to try to increase China's "soft power" around the world, but unlike other comparable ventures, such as those of the Alliance Française or the Goethe Institutes, the Chinese government's strategy has been to embed their sponsored institutes and classrooms inside host country institutions. Underlying suspicions about a Chinese political agenda and enduring concerns about the academic integrity of host universities suddenly turned into vocal complaints after the attempt by some Confucius Institute agents to censor the program of the biannual meeting of the European Association of Chinese Studies in Portugal in July 2014. Retracing the debates, which culminated in several universities in Canada, the US, and Sweden canceling their hosting of Confucius Institutes, Fiskesjö examines the ways in which Western opposition to these institutes reverberate deeply sedimented cultural ideas of China, and the claims by the Chinese government that critics of the Confucius

Institutes are motivated by Sinophobia. To better understand these dynamics, Fiskesjö argues in his chapter for the usefulness of a grammar of identity and otherness going beyond a simple opposition between "East" and "West."

The final chapter, by Sören Urbansky, looks at the reverberations of the discourse of Yellow Peril in China itself, from its emergence in the late nineteenth century until the present day. Its emergence in the United States, Germany, and Russia had different but interconnected causes. In the United States, it was predominantly a reflexive reaction to the massive influx of Chinese immigrants. In Germany, in absence of regular contact with Chinese people, it evolved as a geopolitical doctrine, based on civilizational and racial categories. In Russia, the ways of stereotyping in Germany and the United States amalgamated and were reinforced by a distinct fear of losing the Russian Far East as a result of Chinese immigration. Countless Western publications on the color metaphor for race reflected these fears. Yet also among Chinese intellectuals, politicians, and scholars, these debates about the "Yellow Peril" discourse (*huanghuo lun*) left their traces. Until recently, historians neglected the writings by Lu Xun and Sun Yat-sen, and the numerous publications in the Chinese press. Urbansky's chapter explores perceptions of the "Yellow Peril" myth in China from the late nineteenth century to the present by analyzing major themes and major shifts in the Chinese debate. Whereas early reflections in *Dongfang zazhi* and other newspapers often simply added comments to translated Western writings on the "Yellow Peril," contemporary articles in *Renmin Ribao* and other media outlets evolve around the "China Threat Theory" (*zhongguo weixielun*). The examination of changes of perception in a *longue durée* perspective exposes not only how China was perceived in the West but also reveals the perceptions of the Chinese themselves and how they see China's place in the world.

Notes

1 The title of the video—"The Chinese Professor"—evokes a long filmic history of highly intelligent but deranged "mad professors," an allusion that is made unequivocal when he laughs.
2 The infamous case of Los Alamos physicist Wen Ho Lee, who was accused of spying for the Chinese government, was analyzed at length by Frank

Wu (2002: 176–190). Wu shows that, in spite of flimsy evidence, Lee's criminal prosecution was due to racial profiling. The assumption whereby China would look for an ethnic Chinese as their inside source ultimately hinged on the belief that, however assimilated an Asian American may be, their loyalties would remain primarily to China rather than their host societies.

3 On Sinophilia, see Witchard (2014).

4 Yellow Peril narratives are composed of clusters of stereotypes. As a result, while there is easy slippage from one nation to another, there is rarely a direct equivalence or translation. Hygiene, for instance, has been one of the lynchpins of anti-Chinese speech, something we see reverberated from the early twentieth century to the present (Lynteris, this volume); by contrast, it is never a focus of anti-Japanese speech.

5 The majority of studies of the Yellow Peril have focused on the anglophone world, but European cultures share, by and large, the same set of stereotypes. A book published in 1973 by French politician Alain Peyrefitte, *Quand la Chine s'éveillera . . . le monde tremblera* [When China awakes . . . the world will shake], also combines the notion of threat with a sense of awe and admiration.

6 Interestingly, Hergé's depictions of the Chinese were a stark departure from contemporary European stereotypes that portrayed China as "barbaric, overpopulated, and inscrutable" (Assouline 2009: 48). In the *Blue Lotus*, Hergé actually pokes fun at these Western stereotypes through the comic characters of the two incompetent detectives Dupond and Dupont (in English "Thomson and Thompson").

7 In the early 1990s, Japan was considered a modern nation, different from the rest of the continent (Walker 2013: 76). For others, such as the early supporters of a Eurasian Australia, the Chinese and Japanese, as "representatives of ancient and venerable civilizations," had been "unfairly classified as inferior" and were in fact "equals or near equals to Europeans" (Collins 2013: 102–103). For novelist Jack London, both the Chinese and the Japanese were equally threatening. The "menace" to the Western world, in his eyes, came from "millions of yellow men" (the Chinese) finding themselves under the management of "the little brown man" (the Japanese) (in Wu 2002: 13–14).

8 Interestingly, the same situation is found in contemporary South Africa where the category "Black" refers only to South African blacks. Nigerians working and living in the country, as "expats" and therefore educated and well-off, fall under the "White" category.

9 A similar phenomenon has also been described for contemporary Korea (Shin 2013: 386) and Japan (Miller 2004), where cosmetic practices such

as skin bleaching and blepharoplasty (double eyelid surgery) are tied to racial hierarchies and the desire to create distance from the rest of Asia.

10 Political leanings can also make important differences. As Agnieszka Sobocinska has shown (2013), in the same postwar period, two groups of Australians had diametrically opposed views of Asia. Soldiers serving with the British Commonwealth Occupation Forces in Japan had very colonial and patronizing attitudes, while participants in the Volunteer Graduate Scheme in Indonesia saw locals as their equals.

11 This appears to be the case not only with Chinese men, but also with Mongolian and autochthonous Siberian men, such as Buryats, in the Russian Far East.

12 Under the rubric of personal care, the issue of shaving (or lack thereof) is a point frequently commented on (Franck Billé's fieldwork interviews with Russian interlocutors in Blagoveshchensk, Russia, in spring 2014).

13 While Hollywood representations have been instrumental in creating overlaps, anti-Chinese and anti-Asian narratives already existed around the world, often in striking similar patterns. Many of them emerged around Chinese diasporas, in contexts as distinct as the United States, Australia, or Russia.

14 These processes are of course not unique to the Chinese diaspora. A very similar process was witnessed with the "Hawaiian pizza," which is now found on menus in Italy.

15 *Time Magazine* in fact published an article in 2011 paralleling 1980s Japan and contemporary China's economic menace to the West (Schuman 2011).

16 Recall, for instance, the milk scandal of 2008 involving the adulteration of milk products and infant formula with melamine, or the 2007 contamination of pet food with wheat gluten. The pursuit of economic profit also led some unscrupulous Chinese entrepreneurs to sell fake eggs made of gelatin, paraffin, and other chemicals (LaFraniere 2011). The Chinese have also of course been vilified as dirty (Lyntcris, this volume; see also Billé 2015, Shah 2011).

17 The character played by Lucy Liu, while it was seen as empowering by many viewers, also relied on a stereotype—that of the "dragon lady" (see Prasso 2005, Shah 1997), a term inspired by the characters played by Chinese-American actress Anna May Wong.

18 The perception of Asians has changed considerably over time. This is especially true for Chinese immigrants in the United States, whose urban diaspora communities were perceived as threat to the hygiene, health, and moral values of their white environment a century ago (Shah 2001).

19 In 1931, psychology professor Thomas R. Garth calibrated the relative positions of minorities on America as follows: "The racial I.Q.'s are, by

way of résume: whites, 100; Chinese, 99; Japanese, 99; Mexicans, 78; southern Negroes, 75; northern Negroes, 85; American Indians, full blood, 70. If one says that what is fair for one is fair for another, then regardless of environmental difficulties, the Chinese and Japanese score so nearly like the white that the difference is negligible" (in Palumbo-Liu 1999: 151).

20 Western emphasis on Japan as a culture of the miniature—such as bonsai trees—might be interpreted as an attempt to "reduce" and "minimize" Japan's very real economic and cultural impact. Japan's own development of the cultural miniature through the notions of the "cute" and the "kawaii" (可愛い) might similarly be read, in part, as an active appropriation and co-opting of this Orientalist discourse.

21 Other aspects were eerily similar, such as the deviousness associated with mimicry. In the 1980s Japan was believed to have the best spies in the world; the current view of China as adept at industrial espionage is also prevalent.

22 As discussed above, North American racial hierarchies disseminated by Hollywood have successfully imprinted media audiences worldwide.

23 He has been brainwashed and is unaware of his actions.

24 The figure of Fu Manchu himself did not come from images of China but in fact from the super-villains of recent British literature—the heirs of the scowling villains of the Gothic novel and the Byronic hero-villain, together with the mysterious conspiracies of French *romans-feuilletons* (Frayling 2014: 234). Similarly, much of the popular visual imagery of China came from pantomime and music halls in pre-cinema days: "Reminiscences by visitors to China sometimes noted that this was how they actually *saw* Peking when first they arrived. They discovered that the pantomimes were *really* about England in fancy dress" (Frayling 2014: 150).

References

Aguiar, José Carlos G. 2012. "They come from China: Pirate CDs in Mexico in transnational perspective," in *Economic Globalization from Below*, eds. Gordon Mathews, Gustavo Lins Ribeiro and Carlos Alva Vega. London: Routledge.

Assouline, Pierre. 2009 [1996]. *Hergé, the Man Who Created Tintin*. Oxford: Oxford University Press.

Billé, Franck. 2015. *Sinophobia: Anxiety, Violence, and the Making of Mongolian Identity*. Honolulu: University of Hawai'i Press.

Bosker, Bianca. 2013. *Original Copies: Architectural Mimicry in Contemporary China*. Honolulu: University of Hawaiʻi Press.

Chen, Mel Y. 2012. *Animacies: Biopolitics, Racial Mattering, and Queer Affect*. Durham, NC: Duke University Press.

Citizens Against Government Waste. 2010. "Chinese Professor," accessed online on February 8, 2016 at https://www.youtube.com/watch?v=OTSQozWP-rM

Clegg, Jenny. 1994. *Fu Manchu and the "Yellow Peril": The Making of a Racist Myth*. Oakhill, UK: Trentham Books.

Collins, Kane. 2013. "Imagining the Golden Race," in *Australia's Asia: From Yellow Peril to Asian Century*, eds. David Walker and Agnieszka Sobocinska. Crawley: University of Queensland Press.

Connery, Christopher L. 1994. "Pacific Rim Discourse: The U.S. Global Imaginary in the Late Cold War Years." *boundary* 221: 1 (Spring): pp. 30–56.

Demel, Walter. 1992. "Wie die Chinesen gelb wurden: Ein Beitrag zur Frühgeschichte der Rassentheorien," *Historische Zeitschrift* 3, Vol. 255, pp. 625–666.

Dikötter, Frank. 1992. *The Discourse of Race in Modern China*, London: Hurst & Company.

Dikötter, Frank. 1997. *The Construction of Racial Identities in China and Japan*. London: Hurst & Company.

Eng, David L. 2001. *Racial Castration: Managing Masculinity in Asian America*. Durham, NC: Duke University Press.

Espiritu, Yen Lee. 2008. *Asian American Women and Men: Labor, Laws, and Love*. Lanham, MD: Rowman & Littlefield.

Eysteinsson, Ægir Þór. 2015. "Huang Nubo hættir við stórtæk jarðakaup í Norður-Noregi," *Kjarninn*. February 7.

Frayling, Christopher. 2014. *The Yellow Peril: Dr. Fu Manchu & the Rise of Chinaphobia*. New York: Thames & Hudson.

Gamsa, Mark. 2014. "Mixed Marriages in Russian-Chinese Manchuria" in *Entangled Histories. The Transcultural Past of Northeast China*, eds. Dan Ben-Canaan, Frank Grüner, and Ines Prodöhl. New York: Springer, pp. 47–58.

Harootunian, Harry. 2000. *History's Disquiet: Modernity, Cultural Practice, and the Question of Everyday Life*. New York: Columbia University Press.

Higgins, Andrew. 2014. "A rare Arctic land sale stokes worry in Norway," *The New York Times*, September 27.

Hsu, Madeline Y. 2015. *The Good Immigrants: How the Yellow Peril Became the Model Minority*. Princeton: Princeton University Press.

Jackson, Robert, and Leslie Hook. 2011. "Iceland rejects Chinese investor's land bid," *The Financial Times*, November 25.

Keevak, Michael. 2011. *Becoming Yellow: A Short History of Racial Thinking.* Princeton, NJ: Princeton University Press.

Kim, Claire Jean. 1999. "The Racial Triangulation of Asian-Americans," *Politics and Society* 27:1 (March), pp. 105–138.

Kim blog (Kínversk-Íslenska Menningarfélagid 冰中文化交流协会). 2011 (December 16). "Viðtal við Huang Nubo í Morgunblaðinu," http://kim .blog.is/blog/kim/entry/1211783, accessed on February 8, 2016.

Kowner, Rotem. 2004. "Skin as a Metaphor: Early European Racial Views on Japan, 1548–1853," *Ethnohistory* 51:4 (fall), pp. 751–778.

LaFraniere, Sharon. 2011. "In China, Fear of Fake Eggs and 'Recycled' Buns," *The New York Times*, May 7, accessed online on February 23, 2016, at http://www.nytimes.com/2011/05/08/world/asia/08food.html?_r=0

Lindblad, Knut-Eirik. 2014. "Her har han nettopp solgt en bit av Norge til Kina," *Nordlys*, May 16.

Mayer, Ruth. 2014. *Serial Fu Manchu: The Chinese Supervillain and the Spread of Yellow Peril Ideology.* Philadelphia: Temple University Press.

Miller, Laura. 2004. "Youth Fashion and Changing Beautification Practices," in *Japan's Changing Generations: Are Young People Creating a New Society?,* eds. Gordon Mathews and Bruce White. London: Routledge, pp. 83–98.

Morgunblaðið, 2014. "Vill kaupa jörð á Svalbarða," May 16. Accessed online on February 5, 2016, at http://www.mbl.is/frettir/innlent/2014/05/16/vill _kaupa_jord_a_svalbarda

Morris, Narrelle. 2013. *Japan-Bashing: Anti-Japanism since the 1980s.* London: Routledge.

Nakao, Annie. 1999. "Asian-American Actress a Hit On 'Ally McBeal'," *The Chicago Tribune*, March 8, accessed online at http://articles .chicagotribune.com/1999-03-08/features/9903080026_1_ling-woo -jeff-yang-asian-americans on January 13, 2017.

Ngyuen, Tan Hoang. 2014. *A View from the Bottom: Asian American Masculinity and Sexual Representation.* Durham, NC: Duke University Press.

Okihiro, Gary Y. 2014. *Margins and Mainstreams: Asians in American History and Culture.* Seattle: University of Washington Press.

Osterhammel, Jürgen. 1998. *Die Entzauberung Asiens: Europa und die asiatischen Reiche im 18. Jahrhundert.* München: Beck.

Pan, Chengxin. 2012. *Knowledge, Desire and Power in Global Politics: Western Representations of China's Rise.* Cheltenham: Edward Elgar.

Prasso, Sheridan. 2005. *The Asian Mystique: Dragon Ladies, Geisha Girls, and Our Fantasies of the Exotic Orient.* New York: PublicAffairs.

Reece, Robert L. 2017. "How Trump's Latest Affirmative Action Move Uses the Asian 'Model Minority' as a Prop: And Undercuts Black Scholars Like Me in the Process," *vox.com*, August 4, https://www.vox.com/first-person /2017/8/4/16094648/affirmative-action-trump-sessions-asian-american, accessed on August 15, 2017.

Said, Edward. 1977. *Orientalism*. London: Penguin.

Schuman, Michael. 2011. "Will Asia 'buy up' America?" *Time Magazine*, August 30, accessed online on March 7, 2016, at http://business.time. com/2011/08/30/will-asia-buy-up-america

Schwartzel, Erich. 2016. "Hollywood Under Pressure to Put More Chinese Actors in the Spotlight," *The Wall Street Journal*, September 19. Accessed online at http://www.wsj.com/articles/hollywood-under-pressure-to-put -more-chinese-actors-in-the-spotlight-1474304341 on January 13, 2017.

Shah, Nayan. 2001. *Contagious Divides: Epidemics and Race in San Francisco's Chinatown*. Berkeley: University of California Press.

Shah, Sonia. 1997. *Dragon Ladies: Asian American Feminists Breathe Fire*. New York: South End Press.

Shiel, Mathew P. 1898. *The Yellow Danger*. London: Grant Richards.

Shih, Shu-mei. 2007. *Visuality and Identity: Sinophone Articulations Across the Pacific*. Berkeley, CA: University of California Press.

Shin, Gi-Wook. 2013. "Racist South Korea? Diverse but not Tolerant of Diversity," in *Race and Racism in Modern East Asia*, eds. Rotem Kowner and Walter Demel. Leiden: Brill, 369–390.

Siegelbaum, Lewis H. 1978. "Another 'Yellow Peril.' Chinese Migrants in the Russian Far East and the Russian Reaction before 1917," *Modern Asian Studies* 12:2, pp. 307–330.

Stella, Gian Antonio. 2004. *L'Orda: Quando gli Albanesi eravamo noi*. Milan: Rizzoli.

Sun, Chyng Feng. 2002. "Ling Woo in Historical Context: The New Face of Asian American Stereotypes on Television" in *Gender, Race, and Class in Media. A Text-Reader*, eds. Gail Dines and Jean M. Humez. Thousand Oaks: Sage, pp. 656–675.

Tchen, John Kuo Wei, and Dylan Yeats. 2014. *Yellow Peril! An Archive of Anti-Asian Fear*. London: Verso.

Trellevik, Amund. 2013. "Noen kjøper luksusbiler. Jeg lager poesifestivaler," *Finnmark*, August 27.

Walker, David. 1999. *Anxious Nation: Australia and the Rise of Asia 1850–1939*, St Lucia: University of Queensland Press.

Walker, David. 2013. "Rising Suns" in *Australia's Asia: From Yellow Peril to Asian Century*, eds. David Walker and Agnieszka Sobocinska. Crawley: The University of Western Australia, pp. 73–95.

Wasserstrom, Jeffrey N. 2007. *China's Brave New World: And Other Tales for Global Times*. Bloomington: Indiana University Press.

Watts, Sheldon J. 1997. *Epidemics and History: Disease, Power and Imperialism*. New Haven: Yale University Press.

Witchard, Anne. 2014. *England's Yellow Peril: Sinophobia and the Great War*. London: Penguin.

Wu, Ellen D. 2014. *The Color of Success: Asian Americans and the Origins of the Model Minority*. Princeton: Princeton University Press.

Wu, Frank H. 2002. *Yellow: Race in America Beyond Black and White*. New York: Basic Books.

Yan, Yunxiang. 2003. *Private Life under Socialism: Love, Intimacy, and Family Change in a Chinese Village 1949–1999*. Stanford, CA: Stanford University Press.

Yeats, Dylan. 2013. "Chinese Professors," in *Yellow Peril! An Archive of Anti-Asian Fear*, eds. John Kuo Wei Tchen and Dylan Yeats. London: Verso, pp. 267–271.

Yu Hua. 2011. "山寨 Copycat" in *China in Ten Words*. London: Duckworth Overlook, pp. 181–202.

Zhou, Xiaojing. 2006. *The Ethics and Poetics of Alterity in Asian American Poetry*. Iowa City: University of Iowa Press.

CHAPTER 2

~

Yellow Peril Epidemics

The Political Ontology of
Degeneration and Emergence

CHRISTOS LYNTERIS

IN THE SUMMER OF 2013, a ground-breaking exhibition entitled *A Journal of the Plague Year* opened in Hong Kong. Featuring world-leading artists like Ai Weiwei, it has since traveled to San Francisco (spring 2015) and beyond on a world tour whose "each iteration departs from and remains strongly connected to an exploration of the events that affected Hong Kong in the spring of 2003" (Kadist 2015). The exhibition explores the "layered memories" of the 2003 Severe Acute Respiratory Syndrome (SARS) crisis and the traumatic suicide of pop idol Leslie Cheung during the same year (Wong 2013). In doing so, its California curators explain, it "confronts fear of contamination (both physiological and cultural) and the projections and prejudices that emerge from societies that encounter alterity" (Kadist 2015). Most interestingly, the exhibition appears to be well informed by current historical research. The San Francisco exhibition press release reads,

> Stemming from its colonial past, Hong Kong has internalized a history of epidemics and representation as an infected land waiting to be conquered from nature, disease, and oriental habits in order to be made healthy, modern, and profitable. Culminating in the discovery of the bacteria causing the plague during an 1894 epidemic in Hong Kong, these narratives contributed to a dubious association of the disease with Asia, and heightened the

infamous "yellow peril" racist discourse in Europe and America at the time. For example, the 1900–04 plagues epidemic in San Francisco's Chinatown (part of the same epidemic wave affected Hong Kong) together with the virulent racism in California further intensified the association between disease and Asian populations. (Kadist 2015)

This is not the first art exhibition to tackle the issue of the so-called Yellow Peril (see, for example, Wong 1990). Still, it is the first to frame it within an explicitly epidemiological framework introduced by Adrian Wong's now famous *Sak Gai* (*Chicken Kiss*) photograph (2007), which depicts the artist kissing an animal that is widely considered as a potential origin of influenza viral spillover to humans.[1] Drawing parallels between nineteenth- and early twentieth-century Yellow Peril narratives and the recent racialization of SARS is a powerful political weapon in the struggle against Sinophobic renderings of pandemic threat. In the report "Yellow Peril Revisited: Impact of SARS on the Chinese and Southeast Asian Canadian Communities," coordinated by the Chinese Canadian National Council's National Office, Leung and Guan (2004) invested in the same strategy. Pointing out how, in the late nineteenth century, "Chinese settlements and expansions were regarded with the same hysteria as an infectious disease spreading across Canada" (ibid., 6), Leung and Guan noted that in official statements regarding the Chinese presence in Vancouver in 1885, "the city is an allegory for the human body while Chinatown is the disease, the foreign substance threatening to engulf and destroy the whole body" (ibid., 6–7). This entanglement of the urban and the corporal was equally present in media "visual strategies" that "fuelled SARS panic" by entangling images of Chinatown streets and masked Asian-looking individuals (ibid., 9). The temptation hence arises, not only for academics or artists but also for the very people involved in the recent association of China with infectious diseases, to attempt to understand the recent racialization of epidemic crises, such as SARS, in terms of the epidemic imaginary that formed part of nineteenth-century Yellow Peril discourse. There is a temptation to trace the origins of today's dynamic and as-yet-indeterminate biopolitical configuration in terms of what appears to be, by now, well known, concretely objectionable, and universally rejected.

This "explor[ation of] the connections between historic epidemics and xenophobia" (Martinez 2015) introduces us, however, to a familiar fallacy, which in a time of danger may, subtly yet persistently, appear analytically luring and politically useful: what Michel Foucault has famously decried as the passion for origins. Drawing on Nietzsche's notion of genealogy, Foucault (1977: 142) noted that "this search is directed to 'that which was already there', the image of a primordial truth fully adequate to its nature, and it necessitates the removal of every mask to ultimately disclose the original identity." Abandoning the metaphysics of truth inherent to the "ideality of the origin" (ibid., 145) is a necessary step to mounting critical genealogies of any relation and formation of power. Indeed, as an operation that unfolds against the grain of seeking the secret of how "the past actively exists in the present" (ibid., 146), Foucault's genealogical approach runs parallel to and in entanglement with anthropological approaches, which seek to examine socio-cultural practices and forms beyond apparent similarities or structural homologies. The methodological premise of this chapter, then, is that it is necessary to employ this approach rigorously in order to understand both nineteenth-century and twenty-first-century approaches to China, as well as to Chinese spaces, bodies, and culture, as implicated in infectious disease epidemics across the globe.

In their discussion of the SARS outbreak in Toronto, Roger Keil and S. Harris Ali have argued that in order to understand the entangled process of identifying Chinese bodies and spaces with the particular epidemic, we should not simply examine how this may reflect "historical patterns of stigmatization of Chinese populations" (2008: 160). Equally important, they claim, is to examine how this is interconnected with two further processes involving the identification of China: first as an emerging global power, and, second, as the origin of infectious diseases. Comparing SARS-related responses to the discourse surrounding HIV and Ebola, Keil and Ali point out that the former was seen as resulting from the out-of-control development of China, with "commentators insist[ing] on inscribing the SARS-origin story into the lore of rapid (and threatening) Chinese modernization" (ibid., 162).

In this chapter, I want to take this argument further so as to explore what I identify as a key element of contemporary discourses that configured China as the origin of epidemics and Chinese bodies as privileged carriers of global biological peril. By examining the entanglement of popular culture representations and epidemiological discourses as registers that inform and propel each other in complex and often politically determined ways, this chapter will argue that, for all their common attributes, the association of China with the threat of infectious disease at the turn of the nineteenth century and the apparently similar association today should not be read in terms that rely or put emphasis on their continuities. Rather, our anthropological and historical gaze should focus on a single, critical discontinuity that, I will maintain, renders the two phenomena distinct in terms of their political ontology. In short, this chapter will demonstrate the contrast between nineteenth-century and modern perceptions of China as a source of infectious diseases. On the one hand, at the turn of the nineteenth century, the fear of Chinese bodies and spaces as sources and carriers of disease were related to ideas of China as a land of "degeneration" and "decay." On the other hand, in recent years, a new fear has arisen, one related to an idea of China as a land of "emergence."[2]

Nineteenth-century plagues

As David Scott (2008: 9) has discussed, in the course of the nineteenth century China emerged in what we may broadly call the Western imperialist imagination as the "Sick Man of Asia." This "sickness" of China comprised in the Qing Empire's perceived lack of and resistance against modernity, both in technological terms and in the form of largely disadvantageous international trade treaties. Following a flourishing tradition of cultural and racial othering, this was imagined as revolving not so much around a governmental plan of political economic autonomy as on what came to be seen in Europe and North America as a constituent part of the "Chinese character": slavish attachment to the past. Still, as Larissa Heinrich (2008: 16) has argued, in the course of the nineteenth century "China became in the popular imagination of the West not only the 'Sick Man of Asia' but, more specifically, the 'original home of plague', as well as a perceived source of the cholera in Europe (also known as 'the pestilence of the East') and for some—no-coincidence—the 'cradle of small-pox.'" In other words, with several variations between North American, British, French, and Australian epidemic imaginaries, the "sickness" of China was imagined to be one associated not simply with a slow, chronic civilizational ailment but also with a process of contagious pathogeny, or more precisely, as I will demonstrate below, with the interrelation of these two disease-related processes.[3]

In the course of the nineteenth century, epidemic imaginaries relating to the different infectious diseases were inter-entangled around the symbolic form of China. If, following Heinrich (2007), the image of China as the "cradle of smallpox" was fostered in the course of the nineteenth century as a result of what colonial doctors saw as the resistance of the Qing to endorse Jennerian vaccination in place of variolation, bubonic plague's association with China was, by comparison, a nineteenth-century latecomer, coinciding with the peak of Yellow Peril discourse. Plague made its appearance in Hong Kong in March 1894. Bearing devastating effects upon the Crown Colony, where it persisted for three decades, the disease proceeded to spread across the world, with the so-called third plague pandemic acquiring, for the first time in the history of the disease, true global proportions. Cities, harbors, and villages across all inhabited continents were infected, with over 12 million people recorded as dying of plague during the course of the pandemic. The disease struck major urban centers like San Francisco, Cape Town, Sydney, Porto, Glasgow, Alexandria, Bombay, and Harbin, and established itself across large parts of the world, where it is still endemic today. The pandemic of what was soon seen to be a modern form of the Black Death (itself an early nineteenth century term) fueled the fear of China and the Chinese as sources and spreaders of disease across the globe. This process of pathologization was articulated around four main focal points: China as the original source of plague, Chinese urban space and forms of habitation as the "breeding grounds" of the disease, Chinese bodies as plague transmitters, and Chinese culture as a pathogenic catalyst. Historians of medicine and Chinese studies scholars have explored in detail several aspects of these four imaginaries. Here I will examine these briefly, not with the ambition to cover their full ground or provide an authoritative summary, but to underline the neglected yet pertinent question of degeneration, which by connecting them allowed for the much broader entanglement of nineteenth-century Yellow Peril imaginary with the fear of epidemics.

The imagination of China as the original home of plague arose out of turn-of-the-century efforts to configure the disease as a scientifically knowable and actionable category. As already mentioned, the first outbreak of plague to capture international attention occurred in Hong Kong in the spring of 1894. This outbreak did not only constitute, in medical eyes, Hong Kong as the starting point of the global pandemic that was to follow; it also created a prehistory of the pandemic. Based on the writings of colonial officers and doctors stationed in or visiting Southwest China, British authorities in Hong Kong speculated that the true origin of plague was not the South Chinese coastal area of Canton and Hong Kong, but instead the remote province of Yunnan. Based on a wide range of native and colonial sources, it was gradually surmised that plague somehow began during the Panthay Rebellion in China's Southwestern province (1856–1873) (Benedict 1996). Providing thus the unfolding pandemic with a more or less mythic prehistory, this narrative associated the disease with the endemic decline and disorder reigning in the Qing Empire, a theme to which I will return later in this chapter. Moreover, by depicting China as the original home of plague, it simultaneously projected an image of it as the potential source for the return of the Black Death. The diachronic implications of this can be seen in the international press coverage of the 1910–1911 Manchurian plague epidemic. Spreading south from the Russian–Chinese border in what appeared for a few months to be an unstoppable, all-consuming course, this airborne form of plague led to an explosion of publications across the globe. What captured the public's imagination was that this might, finally, be the outbreak that would lead to a pandemic of apocalyptic proportions. Articles, like the three-page-long feature in the British illustrated newspaper *The Sphere*, "A Real Yellow Peril—The Terrible Scourge of Plague in the Far East," fanned fears that this might be the beginning of a new Black Death that could consume Europe and Asia. In this way China was configured not simply as the land where the ongoing plague pandemic originated, but also as the potential source of a global pandemic apocalypse.

The source of this double pandemic (the real ongoing one and the imagined apocalypse) was seen to be not simply China as a country but Chinese space, both in China and abroad. Nineteenth-century doctors from both contagionist and anticontagionist traditions, in Ackerknecht's sense of the terms (2009), pictured the urban terrain as closely associated with infectious diseases. Either as the source of epidemics (in the sanitarian tradition) or as the conduit of human-to-human infection (in the contagionist tradition), the urban environment "mirror[ed] or echoe[d] illness and health sympathetically, creating a pathological ecology" (Heinrich 2008: 61). In the case of the third plague pandemic, this confluence of the two traditions has been explored in detail by Mary Sutphen (1997) in her examination of the Hong Kong and Calcutta plague outbreaks of 1894 and 1899. In the case of Hong Kong, the idea that forms of Chinese habitation were in one way or another responsible for the outbreak provided a common, practical ground between rival etiological schools. This anxious consensus led to the resumption of a large area of the working-class neighborhood of Taipingshan, which was seen as the main source of the outbreak.

What is important to note here is that up until 1905 no scientific agreement existed regarding the mode in which plague spread. Before the endorsement of the rat-flea hypothesis (first postulated in 1898 by Paul-Louis Simond, but only slowly accepted by medical and public health authorities), the answer was sought often in the soil. This was seen as the place where the plague bacillus persisted during periods when plague was absent from the city. There it was imagined to lurk, until, regaining its virulence, it struck again in a process known as true recrudescence. This idea fostered problematizations of the urban environment in terms of the "breeding grounds" of plague. And no other urban environment was seen as fitting this property more than Chinese urban and housing forms.

Two cases stand out in the global history of modern plague as paradigmatic of this medical attitude: the Honolulu and San Francisco Chinatowns. As Mohr (2005) has discussed, the association of Honolulu's Chinatown with the outbreak in the city in 1899 led to its almost complete incineration, in an operation that public health officers believed would cleanse the city of the "breeding grounds" of the disease. In the case of San Francisco, the association of Chinese urban space with infectious diseases was catalytic in the formation of local discourses on the Yellow Peril. As Shah (2001, 1) has shown, Chinatown was seen as a "laboratory of infection." The image of salaciousness, as scholars like Barde (2003), Risse (2012), and Shah (2001) have discussed, predated the plague outbreak of 1900 and formed what we can call a noso-symbolic substratum of anti-Chinese attitudes during the epidemic, a term that is not meant to draw on Foucault's category of noso-politics but rather to evoke the power of disease (*nosos*, in Greek) as a symbolically constituted and at the same time symbol-constituting experience. In the words of Susan Craddock (1995: 957), who has examined the spatial metaphors of smallpox in nineteenth-century San Francisco, what emerged was no less than "an almost complete metonymy of place and disease" that led to the "transformation of Chinatown into a pustule of contagion threat-ening to infect the rest of the urban body." This was an image of Chinese migrants living in damp, cramped, opium smoke–filled cellars dripping with insalubrious fluids and teeming with putrefying material, in other words, a paradigmatic image of matter-out-of-place (Douglas 1993): a space where objects, waste and effluvia, humans and animals, air, water, and earth merged and melted into one another in an indistinguishable mass of putrefaction and pollution. Shah (2001: 18) has argued that "[t]he creation of 'knowledge' of Chinatown relied upon three key elements: dens, density and the labyrinth," all images that would be systematically employed by doctors and the lay press in depicting Chinese urban space during the plague outbreak. Moreover, seen as the "breeding grounds" of plague, San Francisco's Chinatown was meticulously photographed by the public health bureau's officer, J. M. Williamson; 178 of his photo-graphs were bound together in an album functioning as a visual archive of Chinese urban and housing as plague incubators (Risse 2012). This was a photographic archive that promoted the image of San Francisco's Chinatown as a disease-ridden and infectious neighborhood.

Yet it was not only Chinese spaces that were targeted as sources or conduits of disease in the course of the third plague pandemic. The bodies of Chinese migrants were also framed within the same noso-symbolic apparatus. To take once again the example of San Francisco, as Shah (2001: 155) has demonstrated, Walter Wyman's idea that plague was an "Oriental disease, peculiar to rice eaters," was widespread and would persist in the popular imagination even after the establishment of the rat-flea etiology in 1905. In the same way that this rendered the torching of Honolulu's Chinatown as a legitimate anti-plague measure, it also helped to foster the idea that racial segregation, by means of strict quarantine of all the Chinese within San Francisco's Chinatown, could save the city (and possibly America itself) from the epidemic. Here, as in Honolulu, or in fact in Hong Kong, Manchuria (Lynteris 2013), and the Transvaal (Anon., 1904), the imaginary embodiment of plague by the Chinese as "Oriental bodies" was predicated upon an entanglement of racial and class categories that led to the identification of the Chinese as a race of "coolies." A characteristic, and historically ignored, example of the racial and class entanglement underlying the fear aroused by Chinese bodies is found in the contention by US Army doctor James Joseph (1918a) that the influenza pandemic of 1918 was actually pneumonic plague carried to the

West from Northeast China on the backs of "Chinese coolies." Besides scholarly works published by King (1918b), this opinion was also voiced in the lay press at the time, with reporters claiming that the source of the pandemic was Chinese coolies (fighting alongside the French) in the Western Front who had been captured by the Germans. According to this theory, "it seems possible that the *bacillus pestis* may have been present in a non-virulent state in the Chinese coolies and assumed new virulence, vigor and somewhat different form when transplanted into virgin soil" (ibid., 1). Once again, here we have the image of a phantom pathogen, lurking in Chinese "breeding grounds." This time, however, the pestilent substratum in question is not the walls or soil of Chinese houses but the bodies of the Chinese themselves, collectively seen as a race of coolies, or, in an extreme example published in the Australian press, depicted as a Chinese-faced, plague-carrying horde of rats (Anon., 1900).

What was seen as both pathological and pathogenic was not, however, simply China, Chinese urban space, or Chinese bodies, but also the Chinese cultural condition. Heinrich (2008: 70), in his examination of the pathological portraits by Lam Qua, famously depicting Chinese patients bearing deforming tumors and fibromata, says that "we see both the creation and pathologization of an image of Chinese identity based on certain Chinese 'characteristics': insensibility to pain, the inadequacy of native medicine, a cultural inability to perform either amputation or autopsy, a belief in the spirits of the dead, and superstition in general." This visual trope thus identified as the cause of illness not simply specific practices or habits, but Chinese culture as such. In the case of plague, a characteristic example comes from the work of Broquet (1902), who, writing about plague in Guangzhouwan in South China, tells us that the local Chinese population believed the disease to be a punishment brought upon them by the imperial Ming ancestors, a retribution for not rising up against the Manchu usurpers of the throne. Framing Chinese culture as riddled by an ancestor-focused, fatalistic attitude, colonial authors hence attributed plague to the assumed stagnation of the Chinese civilization, and its tendency to resist change and progress.

Four aspects thus composed the core of disease-related Yellow Peril discourse at the turn of the nineteenth century. Though several scholars have noted these aspects, one crucial narrative thread running across these epidemic imaginaries has not been examined. This, I want to argue, was the image of degeneration, decline and decay associated with late-imperial China; an image that was produced both inside and outside China and that became internalized and elaborated into a biopolitical strategy by ruling elites at the end of the Qing era and by the nationalist state in the course of the Republic.

Decline, degeneration, and decay

Notions of Chinese pathology drew on Western imaginaries of Qing China as an obsolete empire, representing an aged, stagnant civilization in decline. This preconception, already in place at the beginning of the century, was later further enhanced by Social Darwinist perceptions of race and racial struggle that depicted the Chinese as a numerically vast but qualitatively moribund race. As Dikötter (1992) and Heinrich (2008) have argued, the ferocity of this racial discourse may best be understood by examining diverse Western perceptions of China as a vast repository of human relics, "freaks" and "wildmen," that became objects of medical and lay fascination and exploitation around the world. Such was the demand for these living spectacles of Chinese backwardness that, following an article published in the *Chinese Medical Missionary Journal*, at the end of the nineteenth century there existed practices of actually constructing "wildmen" (MacGowan 1893). These involved the abduction and skinning alive of Chinese individuals followed by grafting animal skins onto their bare flesh, an operation that, if successful, led to the creation of "wildmen" who were then used to extract money from doctors interested in studying them as well as from circus audiences throughout China. This somatization of imaginary backwardness also manifested itself in less brutal but perhaps more pervasive ways, such as the photographic practice, analyzed by Heinrich (2008: 98), of associating pathological symptoms with cultural traits by imaging cure through their simultaneous "removal." Hence, for example, Jeffreys and Maxwell's iconic first edition of *The Diseases of China* (1910) features a "before-and-after" image of a tumor-removing operation, which depicts medical success through the removal not only of an enormous facial fibroma but also of the queue of the male Chinese patient, a bodily trait symbolizing, in the eyes of the authors, Chinese cultural stagnation and decay. Similarly, Carol Benedict (1996: 166) has noted how "plague marked China as a hygienically 'backward' country that continued to incubate a medieval disease in the modern era." More than that, however, I would like to argue that plague was seen as arising out of the decay of the Qing Empire. Not simply a medieval relic but the active product of stagnation and decline, plague was associated, as we have already seen, with political disorder in the southwest corner of the empire (i.e., the Panthay Rebellion) and, hence, with the increasing decline of the Qing imperial system. It was also associated with what different Western observers (such as the French, American, Portuguese, and British) saw as the social and material decay of Chinese cities, as well as with the imagined racial degeneration of the Chinese as a whole. Finally, it was associated with the perceived decay of Chinese civilization—its supposed inability or resistance to adapt to modernity, its alleged fatalism and traditionalism that hampered reform and change. The Yellow Peril, at least in its noso-symbolic form, was hence tied to the imagination of dynastic decline, racial degeneration, urban decay, and civilizational stagnation.

What made this problematization of China politically efficacious was the fact that it was not simply an external, imperialist strategy but, as scholars like Polachek (1992) have shown, an internal discourse that had flourished since the beginning of the nineteenth century. Initially part of Ming restorationist vocabulary, following the Opium Wars and the mid–nineteenth-century rebellions this discourse experienced a radical shift. As Dikötter (1998: 60) has argued, the Taiping Rebellion (1850–1864) in particular necessitated "the militarization of powerful lineages [that] reinforced folk models of kinship solidarity, in turn forcing more loosely organized associations to form a unified descent group under the leadership of the gentry." In the context of reform politics of the late nineteenth century, this concern with descent and lineage would be impregnated with Malthusian and Social Darwinist ideas. This led so-called new intellectuals [*zhishi jieji*] to problematize the strength of the empire not as an administrative-military unit but as a race with an emphasis on the physical-sexual reproduction of its individual elements: "the scientific category of 'race' and the administrative category of 'population' were heralded as objects worthy of systematic investigation" (ibid., 61). Based on fears of lineage extinction [*miezu*], the reformers would construct a fear of race extinction [*miezhong*]. This fear went hand in hand with a radical (and, for the first time, properly biopolitical) shift in centuries-old methods of self-strengthening. For the first time, the individual body would be tied with the body politic of the population so that the wealth and health of the population was considered dependent on the "regulation of human reproduction and the disciplining of individual behavior for the sake of the nation" (ibid., 62). As Heinrich (2008: 10) has argued, this led to colonial ideas about China as the Sick Man of Asia being "absorbed into China's own vision of itself, into its own rhetoric: the vision of a weak, fundamentally diseased self we see so clearly and in such gory detail in literature of the Republican period."[4]

This entanglement of Western and Chinese reformer discourses, in their own irreducible plurality, fostered epidemic images of China, Chinese urban spaces, Chinese bodies, and Chinese culture as the common denominators of decay and degeneration. As diseases associated with China were seen from afar, and increasingly by Chinese reformers and nationalists, as deriving from a civilizational and racial decline, an important shift in the perception of decay and degeneration took place. Rather than simply afflicting China and the Chinese themselves, this was now seen as a process that rendered them highly contagious and made them a threat for the health of humanity as a whole.

I will now move to examine the epidemic imaginary surrounding China and the Chinese in contemporary times, an imaginary based on a radically different political ontology than the one evinced in degeneration-centered fears at the turn of the nineteenth century.

SARS, wet markets, and superspreaders

The 2002–2003 outbreak of what came to be known as Severe Acute Respiratory Syndrome (SARS) was caused by a coronavirus (SARS-CoV) that had not previously been observed to infect humans. The disease was first reported in Shunde, in the Chinese province of Guangdong, in November 2002, but became evident to the international medical world only after the Chinese government informed the WHO in February 2003. The disease spread to 14 countries outside the People's Republic of China, infecting 8,273 individuals out of which 775 died of the disease (and 60 more of other causes). Beyond the danger it posed to global health, SARS was seen as also threatening the global economy, with "major banks such as Morgan Stanley and Goldman Sachs [. . .] warning that the epidemic could tip the whole of Asia, and subsequently the world, into a 'global slowdown'" (Washer 2004: 2567). This was then a fear that functioned both on the local and on the global level, or to be precise on the perceived links between the two, with disease contagion portrayed as threatening humanity not only in terms of public health but also in terms of a global economic contagion (Peckham 2013).

However limited, the spread of SARS across the globe led to a wave of discrimination and stigmatization against Chinese individuals and businesses across the Western world.[5] Russell Leong, writing for the *Amerasia Journal*, reported that

> Chinatowns in New York, London, San Francisco, and Los Angeles, among other urban centers, find their restaurant businesses decimated due to a lack of customers who fear the SARS virus might be transmitted by Chinese and other Asians. Chinese tourists and customers, regardless of national origin, are refused accommodations in hotels and in some restaurants throughout the world. (2003: vii)

In California and Britain, respectively, this discriminatory attitude was reportedly reflected even at the most prestigious educational institutions, with UC Berkeley attempting to bar summer students arriving from areas infected by SARS (ibid., vii) and Eton barring pupils returning from East Asian countries (Washer 2004: 2568). What underlined these attitudes was a perception of China as the place of origin and the Chinese as hosts (Leung and Guan 2004) of SARS-CoV. Ho-fung Hong (2004) has discussed the global reach and impact of seeing SARS as a "Chinese plague," recounting how Chinese delegates were stopped from attending trade fairs, how Chinese students were barred from attending graduations, and how Hong Kong delegates attending the Special Olympics in Ireland were quarantined for 10 days in Macau before being allowed to attend the Games. In Toronto, where the disease broke out in April 2003, the impact of this attribution was so great that, as we have already seen, a large-scale study of the phenomenon was commissioned by the Chinese Canadian National Council's national office. Similarly, Laura Eichelberger (2007: 1284) has examined the production of SARS-related blame and "medical scapegoating" in New York City's Chinatown, which recorded "a tremendous drop in business and tourism." Though individuals from other afflicted countries like Vietnam also faced discrimination (hence leading Verghese (2003) to claim that narrative on the Chinese plague had given way to one on the "Oriental plague"), the main impact of this attitude was borne by individuals seen as being Chinese.

During the epidemic, and, to use Charles Briggs' term its "mediated communicability" (2010), images that had been integral to the articulation of the nineteenth-century Yellow Peril noso-symbolic apparatus were mobilized to create a vision of Chinese-/China-specific insalubriousness. Analyzing representations of SARS in British newspapers, Peter Washer (2004: 2566) notes,

> There were further descriptions of the poor hygiene standards of the Chinese, and a new aspect started to be mentioned: spitting. "This is a common habit in southern China, where most people cough and sneeze without covering their faces. Pools of saliva are frequent sights in restaurants, trains and buses. Epidemiologists say such practices, combined with overcrowding and pollution, plus a history of viral outbreaks jumping from pigs and poultry to humans, make Guangdong province one of the world's most dangerous breeding grounds for infectious viruses." (Sheriden, 2003)

Yet, rather than putting emphasis on the continuity of this narrative with nineteenth-century Yellow Peril discourse, we should note here a crucial difference. This pertains not to what usually comes under sociological scrutiny, the imagined mode of disease *transmission*, but instead to the supposed mode of disease *generation*. To better understand this difference, it is worth focusing on what has stood as an important image in both nineteenth- and twenty-first-century epidemic imaginaries: urban animal markets.

In the case of nineteenth-century discourse, Chinese animal markets were not seen as paradigmatically different to Western ones. Whether in London or in Hong Kong, these were seen as places of filth, putrefaction, and noxious smells and effluvia—they stood, in the eyes of the bourgeoisie, for working-class ignorance and disorder or, in socialist discourse, for capitalist greed (Stallybrass and White, 2007). They were, moreover, spaces where disease arose and spread through processes of putrefaction and decay. These associations were more pronounced in the case of China and Chinatowns across the globe, as they were anchored not only in supposed class unruliness and notions of matter-out-of-place (Douglas 1993) but also, as we have already seen, in an imagined cultural stagnation and racial decline. The "Chinese character" of fatalism or apathy led, in Western eyes, to insalubrious market practices and a general neglect of hygiene.

On the other hand, in the case of SARS we have an unprecedented exceptionalization of the Chinese animal and poultry market. Singularized as prototypically South Chinese, these so-called "wet markets" were seen not simply as spaces from which old diseases arise and spread, but as foci where new diseases emerge. Whereas in the case of nineteenth-century biopolitical discourse Chinese towns and Chinatowns were spaces where ancient horrors like bubonic plague and smallpox lurked and re-awakened, in contemporary discourse the diseases arising in China are paradigmatically novel. Diseases hitherto unknown to humans, new forms of life, and at the same time new forms of death are configured as enemies of humanity potentialized by a specifically Chinese environment of exchange. In these primarily urban spaces, the co-existence of wild and domestic animals, the proximity of humans and non-human animals, and the supposed cramped conditions are seen as catalysts of viral mutations into forms that can "jump" the species barrier and infect humans.

As I discuss elsewhere (Lynteris, 2016b), the visualization of the Chinese wet market as "pandemic ground zero" developed at the time of the SARS outbreak around the depiction of civet cats. These animals, which were considered at the time to be the source of the epidemic, embodied the ambiguities and perils supposedly harbored by the rise of postsocialist China. Civet cats were seen as taxonomically messy animals that emerged out of the dark inland Empire of China, were marketed as "intimate commodities" (Jackson 2008) in the species-mixing markets of South Chinese cities, and consumed in the form of the conspicuous dragon-and-tiger dish by the rising Chinese plutocracy (Zhan 2005). Through a complex process that attributed the epidemic to the entanglement of zoonotic and cultural vectors, these animals stood for the emergence of Chinese power and wealth and for the threat these allegedly posed to global health and security.

As Priscilla Wald (2008) has shown, equally important for the SARS "outbreak narrative" was the figure of the superspreader, who came to account for the failure of epidemiological models in making sense of the rapid spread of the pathogen. Superspreaders were believed to be individuals with an extraordinary ability to spread the virus to others. If a "typical" person was expected to spread SARS to four of his or her contacts, so-called superspreaders were considered able to contaminate at least eight individuals (Zhuang et al. 2004). As a *New York Times* article from the peak of the outbreak put it, these "people are hyperinfective, spewing germs out like teakettles, while others simmer quietly like stew pots" (MacNeil and Altman, 2003). The importance of the superspreader in the pathologization of Chinese bodies in the course of the SARS outbreak lay with what we could call its mythic impact: the establishment of an epidemic imaginary that associated Chinese bodies with super-infective propensities (the two prototypical superspreaders, the individuals associated with the Metropole Hotel and the Amoy Gardens so-called super-spreading events, were Chinese). Creating thus an extraordinary image of the Chinese body as an organism or human type possessing superspreading potentialities, this epidemiological shortcut provided an important reference point for Sinophobic discourses and practices around the world.

If the image of the South Chinese wet market functioned as a symbolic condenser of narratives regarding China as a space where new viruses emerge, the image of the superspreader functioned as a prototype of the Chinese as a contagious human type. In the years following SARS this association of epidemic disease with Chinese bodies and spaces was quickly transferred beyond the confines of the specific disease to include the threat of an avian flu pandemic. In the article "Avian flu: the new Yellow Peril," Sylvie Déthiollaz writes: "Although the flu virus is found all over the world, some regions, like Asia and China in particular, are prime reservoirs because of the life style and especially the population's promiscuity with animals, which encourage mutations and the development of new strains." This noso-symbolic complex on the one hand reflects the idea that the West is "needlessly threatened by the unclean world beyond our borders" (Aronson 2010: 3), yet, more profoundly, I believe, is part and parcel of a new experience of the East, and China in particular, as the source of emerging forms and processes, that ultimately lie beyond the control of our techno-scientific power or knowledge.

Emergence

Both SARS- and avian flu–related outbreak narratives form part of what Sheldon Ungar (1998: 43), in his study of the mid-1990s Ebola media coverage, first called the "mutation-contagion package." This comprised five key ideas that, between them, wove the imaginary of viral emergence.

Read against scientific literature that has emerged in the two decades since the publication of Ungar's paper, I would like to elaborate on these. The first concerned the image of "microbes on a rampage" (ibid., 43) that represents viral agents as all-consuming forms of life whose aim (rather than simply function) is to infect as many individuals as possible in an apparent quest for global dominance. The second involved the image of "microbes as cleverer than us" (Ungar 1998: 44). This idiom configured emerging viruses in the guise of stealthy, murderous geniuses—"killer viruses," in Wallis and Nerlich's sense of the term (2005)—that are able to mutate almost at will in response to the obstacles medicine erects against them. The third aspect of this narrative involved the image of "engineering microbial traffic" (ibid., 44), which represents emergent viruses as agile "species-jumpers," always awaiting the opportunity to infect new pools of hosts. The fourth aspect consists of the image of "microbes know[ing] no boundaries," with Stephen Morse's notion of "instant-distant infections" promoting the idea of global collapsed space (ibid., 44). Finally, the fifth element of this narrative involves the notion that we are "waiting for the next pandemic," which I will explore further below.

This is a narrative that, as shown by the cover of the *New Scientist* (9 May 2015), titled "The New Plague: We're one mutation away from the end of the world as we know it," has not diminished but rather acquired new proportions in the two decades following Ungar's article. Elaborating on this discursive paradigm, Washer's landmark study of SARS news coverage has shown how the former was portrayed as a mystery pathogen about to cause the so-called "next pandemic": "a frequently recurring theme was that SARS could mutate into a more infectious and potentially more lethal form" (2004: 2568). The notion of the "next pandemic," alongside its popular science synonym "the coming plague" (Garrett 1995), refers to a global catastrophe of Biblical proportions that is, supposedly, about to threaten humanity with extinction. This is more often than not seen as a "plague" that will be caused by flu, with SARS functioning as a pandemic herald. This is clearly evident in the influential letter to the *British Medical Journal* by Zambon and Nicholson (2003: 669), who claimed that SARS "should be considered a rehearsal for the next pandemic of influenza." Adding to this imaginary, as Hong (2004: 35) has noted, at the time of SARS readers of the *New York Times* (May 12 2003) were reminded that China was the original home not only of SARS but also "most likely" of the flu pandemic of 1918. Even Arthur Kleinman and James Watson, scholars known for their sober and robust research, were tempted into the "next pandemic" narrative, claiming that "in retrospect, SARS is probably best seen as a harbinger of future events that might be catastrophic for the global system as we know it today" (2006: 1). There is no space here to cover or analyze in depth the imaginary of the "next pandemic."[6] What is important to stress, however, is that this threat to global health and human survival is seen as related to what since 1989 has come to be known as infectious disease emergence.

Emergence, Nicholas King (2005) has argued, entered the epidemiological vocabulary as a result of the 1989 "Emerging Viruses" conference chaired by Stephen S. Morse. Seen as a process accelerated through globalization, viral emergence was destined to assume in the course of the following decades center stage not only in medical and biological discourse but also in the mass media, primarily through the popularization and amplification of the term in the works of Richard Preston (1992, 1994) and Laurie Garrett (1995). Through their bestselling books, as well as via films like *Outbreak* (1995), scientific anxieties over new pathogens such as Ebola came to be entangled with a popular fascination about human extinction and "nature" taking revenge on humanity. In the maelstrom of these outbreak narratives, the notion of emergence has functioned as a way of encapsulating the connection of these viral, asymmetric threats with the new, unstable, and unpredictable post–Cold War global political and economic condition. New economic and political forms and forces springing out of the end of the Cold War have come to be seen as both potent and dangerous. Positioned at a liminal state between the old and the new, the entity that seems to distill the potentiality and peril of this process of emergence is postsocialist China. Coming out of the "cold"— its closed-doors, command economy, mass-line past—and yet not having made a clean, liberal cut with it, China is often portrayed today as a land where new economic and social forms are constantly emerging, but also as a country where this emergence is not transparent, due to the continuing hold of power by the Communist Party. In the past decade SARS has been an important point of reference as regards this double process of emergence and its discontents, reflecting what Jeon (2012) has analyzed in much broader terms as Western anxieties over Chinese global influence. Seen as arising out of the deregulation, opening-up, and entrepreneurial explosion in the Chinese South, SARS is thought to have been allowed to spread and threaten global health because of the Communist

Party's predilection to secrecy. Through this noso-symbolic complex China is portrayed both as what gives rise to new "indeterminate entities" (Caduff 2014: 300) and as what keeps this emergence secret, hence allowing new pathogens not only to emerge but to assume globally threatening proportions.

Conclusion

Understanding the noso-symbolic aspects of Yellow Peril discourse today, as well as at the turn of the nineteenth century, requires focusing our analytical gaze on the distinct political ontologies of fear and accusation that target and, at the same time, configure China and Chinese spaces, bodies, and cultures. This initially requires us to go beyond the apparently common-sense, positivism-inspired argument that as diseases like bubonic plague or SARS derived from China, the outbreaks resulting from them needed to be made sense of in terms of their origins. For it is the very imagination of the origins of a disease (be these geographical or species-related) that forms the core of the epidemiological configuration of these outbreaks as a process not simply of association but of identification. Hence, rather than plague or SARS being diseases simply associated with China as a geographical location, they were rendered into diseases inextricably identified with China as a political, cultural, and racial entity.

In these terms, the nineteenth-century association of China with infectious disease epidemics unfolded in the much wider context of what we may call the classical period of Yellow Peril discourse. Although this discourse was never unified, but in fact assumed dynamic, fragmented, and multilayered forms, as far as the way in which the fear of epidemics featured in these narratives and practices, this was underlined by a common emphasis on identifying China and the Chinese as sources and spreaders of disease. This configuration, as I have shown in this chapter, was informed by an epidemic imaginary that invested in notions that disease derived from processes of decay and degeneration seen as central to the political and biosocial condition of the late Qing Empire. By contrast, twenty-first-century narratives and practices revolving around the fear and accusation of China and the Chinese as sources and spreaders of infectious diseases are underlined by the pathologization of a diametrically different condition: the emergence of postsocialist China as a world-leading economic and political power. What we thus have here is not simply a permutation or variant of the self-same Yellow Peril, but rather the constitution of a new Sinophobia; of a new complex of fear predicated on a distinct political ontology.

Whereas in the case of the turn of the nineteenth century, the noso-symbolic production of the Other was based on an imagination of China as a moribund society and the Chinese as a race in decline, in the case of twenty-first-century Sinophobia, the production of Otherness is based on the imagination of China as a source of wealth and power, and, at the same time, on the imagination of China as the realization of the West's own fantasy of unrestrained capitalist production and exploitation. While in the first case disease was seen as the result of stagnation and putrefaction, in the second case it is considered as an outcome of an excess of life, productivity, and novelty. If the extent to which this reversal is entangled in shifting self-perceptions and configurations of the "West" as a unified civilizational field during these distinct historical periods cannot be overlooked, equally important in further investigations of Yellow Peril–related epidemic imaginaries is to explore the function and impact of these perceptions in China itself today.

What is most pertinent to the comparative analysis attempted in this chapter is the recognition that although reference to nineteenth-century Yellow Peril discourse when analyzing twenty-first-century Sinophobic discourses and practices related to epidemic threats may form a potent polemical tool, it does so at the peril of disregarding crucial discontinuities between the two phenomena, hence running the risk of a political convenience: treating contemporary disease-related Sinophobic attitudes as mere relics of a bygone era, rather than as the products of new political, economic, and cultural dynamics.

Notes

I would like to thank the editors for inviting me to contribute a chapter to the present volume. Research leading to this publication was funded by a European Research Council Starting Grant (under the European Union's Seventh Framework Programme/ERC grant agreement no. 336564) for the project Visual Representations of the Third Plague Pandemic at the Centre for Research in the Arts, Social Sciences and Humanities (CRASSH) of the University of Cambridge.

1   The term *spillover* commonly refers to the transmission of a virus or bacterium from one animal species to another (including from non-human animals to humans), following a mutation of the microbe in question that allows this so-called "species jump" to take place for the first time.

2   As this chapter adopts a comparative rather than a genealogical approach, the examination of these particular periods necessarily leaves out of this chapter a discussion of the fate of disease-related Yellow Peril discourses in the years between the establishment of the Chinese Republic and our times. For a discussion of Western perceptions of disease in China and Chinatowns during the Republican period, see Rogaski (2004) and Shah (2001).

3   On the convergence of these narratives across these locations as regards Chinese attitudes towards plague corpses, see Lynteris (2018).

4   My own research of the Manchurian pneumonic plague outbreak of 1910–1911 has demonstrated how this internalized discourse reflected itself in the accusation of Shandong migrant workers (so-called "coolies") for the spread of the disease by China's leading anti-plague officer, Dr. Wu Liande (Lynteris 2013).

5   On the topic of stigma, which I will not discuss in this chapter, see Person et al. 2004; Kleinman and Sing 2006.

6   For discussion of some of its visual aspects, see Lynteris (2016a).

References

Ackerknecht, Erwin H. 2009 "Anticontagionism between 1821 and 1867: The Fielding H. Garrison Lecture." *International Journal of Epidemiology*, 38: 7–21.

Ali, S. Harris, and Roger Keil. 2008. "SARS and the Restructuring of Health Governance in Toronto." In *Networked Disease: Emerging Infections in the Global City*, edited by S. Harris Ali and Roger Keil. Malden, MA: Blackwell Publishers, pp. 55–69.

Anonymous. 1904. "Transvaal Infected by Diseased Chinese." *Los Angeles Herald*, 31, no. 220 (6 May 1904): 4.

Anonymous. 1911. "A Real Yellow Peril—The Terrible Scourge of Plague in the Far East." *Supplement to The Sphere* (February 18 1911): i–iii.

Aronson, Stanley M. 2010. "Racism and the Threat of Influenza." *Medicine and Health, Rhode Island*, 93, no. 1 (January 2010): 3.

Barde, Robert. 2003. "Prelude to the Plague: Public Health and Politics at America's Pacific Gateway, 1899." *Journal of the History of Medicine*, 58: 153–186.

Benedict, Carol. 1996. *Bubonic Plague in Nineteenth Century China*. Stanford: Stanford University Press.

Briggs, Charles. 2010. "Pressing Plagues: On the Mediated Communicability of Virtual Epidemics." In *Plagues and Epidemics: Infected Spaces Past and Present*, edited by D. Ann Herring and Alan C. Swedlund. Oxford: Berg, pp. 39–60.

Broquet, C. 1902. *Un Foyer de peste bubonique dans la Chine méridionale*. Paris: Jean Gainche.

Caduff, Carlo. 2014 "Pandemic Prophecy, or How to Have Faith in Reason." *Current Anthropology*, 55, no. 3 (June 2014): 296–315.

Craddock, Susan. 1995. "Sewers and Scapegoats: Spatial Metaphors of Smallpox in Nineteenth-century San Francisco." *Social Science & Medicine*, 41, no. 7: 957–968.

Déthiollaz, Sylvie. 2004. "Avian Flu: The New Yellow Peril?" *Prolune* 12 (May 2004), web.expasy.org/prolune/pdf/prolune012_en.pdf

Dikötter, Frank. 1992. *The Discourse of Race in Modern China*. London: Hurst & Co.

Dikötter, Frank. 1998. *Imperfect Conceptions: Medical Knowledge, Birth Defects and Eugenics in China*. New York: Columbia University Press.

Douglas, Mary. 1993. *Purity and Danger: An Analysis of the Concepts of Pollution and Taboo*. London: Routledge.

Eichelberger, Laura. 2007. "SARS and New York's Chinatown: The Politics of Risk and Blame During an Epidemic of Fear." *Social Science & Medicine*, 65: 1284–1295.

Ewald, Paul W. 1988. "Cultural Vectors, Virulence and the Emergence of Evolutionary Epidemiology." *Oxford Surveys in Evolutionary Biology*, 5: 215–245.

Foucault, Michel. 1977. "Nietzsche, Genealogy, History." In *Language, Counter-Memory, Practice: Selected Essays and Interviews*, edited by D. F. Bouchard. Ithaca: Cornell University Press, pp. 139–165.

Garrett, Laurie. 1996. *The Coming Plague: Newly Emerging Diseases in a World Out of Balance*. London: Penguin.

Heinrich, Larissa. 2007. "How China Became the 'Cradle of Smallpox': Transformations in Discourse, 1726–2002." *Positions: East Asia Cultures Critique*, 15, no. 1 (Spring 2007): 7–34.

Heinrich, Larissa. 2008. *The Afterlife of Images: Translating the Pathological Body between China and the West*. Durham: Duke University Press.

Hung Ho-fung. 2004. "The Politics of SARS: Containing the Perils of Globalization by More Globalization." *Asian Perspective*, 28, no. 1: 19–44.

Jackson, Paul. 2008. "Fleshy Traffic, Feverish Borders: Blood, Birds and Civet Cats in Cities Brimming with Intimate Commodities." In *Networked Disease: Emerging Infections in the Global City*, edited by S. Harris Ali and Roger Keil. Malden, MA: Blackwell Publishers, pp. 281–296.

Jeon, Joseph Jonghyun. 2012. *Racial Things, Racial Forms: Objecthood in Avant-Garde Asian American Poetry*. Iowa City: University of Iowa Press.

Kadist. 2015. "A Journal of the Plague Year." http://www.kadist.org/en/programs/all/2104

King, James Joseph. 1918a. "The Origin of the So-Called 'Spanish Influenza.'" *Medical Record*, 94 (October 12 1918): 632–633.

King, James Joseph. 1918b. "Did the Influenza Plague Really Come from China?" *The Ogden Standard* (November 16, 1918): 1.

King, Nicholas B. 2004. "The Scale Politics of Emerging Diseases." *Osiris*, 19: 62–76.

Kleinman, Arthur, and James L. Watson. 2006. "Introduction: SARS in Social and Historical Context." In *SARS in China, Prelude to Pandemic?*, edited by Arthur Kleinman and James L. Watson. Stanford: Stanford University Press, pp. 1–16.

Kleinman, Arthur and Sing Lee. 2006. "SARS and the Problem of Social Stigma." In *SARS in China, Prelude to Pandemic?*, edited by Arthur Kleinman and James L. Watson. Stanford: Stanford University Press, pp. 173–195.

Leong, Russell C. 2003. "Chaos, SARS, Yellow Peril: Virulent Metaphors for the Asian American Experience?" *Amerasia Journal*, 29, no. 1 (2003): v–viii.

Leung, Carriane, and Jian Guan. 2004. "Yellow Peril Revisited: Impact of SARS on the Chinese and Southeast Asian Canadian Communities." www.gwu.edu/~ieresgwu/assets/docs/ponars/pm_0094.pdf

Lynteris, Christos. 2013. "Skilled Natives, Inept Coolies; Marmot Hunting and the Great Manchurian Pneumonic Plague (1910–1911)." *History and Anthropology*, 24, no. 3 (August 2013): 303–321.

Lynteris, Christos. 2016a. "The Epidemiologist as Culture Hero: Visualising Humanity in the Age of 'the Next Pandemic.'" *Visual Anthropology*, 29, no. 1: 36–53.

Lynteris, Christos. 2016b. "The Prophetic Faculty of Epidemic Photography: Chinese Wet Markets and the Imagination of the Next Pandemic." *Visual*

Anthropology, Special Issue: Medicine, Photography and Anthropology, 29, no 2: 118–132.

Lynteris, Christos. (2018) "Suspicious Corpses: Body Dumping and Plague in Colonial Hong Kong." In *Histories of Post-Mortem Contagion: Infectious Corpses and Contested Burials*, edited by Christos Lynteris and Nicholas Evans. London: Palgrave Macmillan, pp. 109–134.

MacGowan, D. J. 1893. "The Artificial Making of Wild Men in China." *Chinese Medical Missionary Journal*, 7, no. 2: 79–81.

Martinez, Alanna. 2015. "Inspired by the 2003 SARS Epidemic, the Contemporary Art Exhibition 'A Journal Of The Plague Year' Has Traveled from Hong Kong to San Francisco to Reveal the Lasting Social Impacts of Epidemics." *Observer* (April 1, 2015), http://observer.com/2015/04/a-traveling-exhibition-that-confronts-xenophobia-at-every-stop/

McNeil, D. G., and L. K. Altman. 2003. "How One Person Can Fuel an Epidemic." *New York Times* (April 15 2003), http://www.nytimes.com/2003/04/15/science/how-one-person-can-fuel-an-epidemic.html

Mohr, J. C. 2005. *Plague and Fire: Battling Black Death and the 1900 Burning of Honolulu's Chinatown*. Oxford: Oxford University Press, 2005.

Peckham, Robert. 2013. "Infective Economies: Empire, Panic and the Business of Disease." *The Journal of Imperial and Commonwealth History*, 41, no. 2 (April 2013): 211–237.

Person, Bobbie, Francisco Sy, Kelly Holton, Barbara Govert, Arthur Liang, and the NCID/SARS Community Outreach Team. 2004. "Fear and Stigma: The Epidemic within the SARS Outbreak." *Emerging Infectious Diseases*, 10, no. 2 (February 2004): 358–363.

Petersen, Wolfgang. 1995. *Outbreak*. Warner Bros. Pictures.

Polachek, James M. 1992. *The Inner Opium War*. Harvard East Asian Monographs, 151, Boston: Harvard University Press.

Preston, Richard. 1992. "Crisis in the Hot Zone." *New Yorker* (October 26, 1992): 58–81.

Preston, Richard. 1994. *The Hot Zone*. New York: Doubleday.

Risse, Guenter. 2012. *Plague, Fear and Politics in San Francisco's Chinatown*. Baltimore: Johns Hopkins University Press.

Rogaski, Ruth. 2004. *Hygienic Modernity: Meanings of Health and Disease in Treaty-Port China*. Berkeley: University of California Press.

Scott, David. 2008. *China and the International System, 1840–1949: Power, Presence, and Perceptions in a Century of Humiliation*. New York: SUNY Press.

Shah, Nayan. 2001. *Contagious Divides: Epidemics and Race in San Francisco's Chinatown*. Berkeley: University of California Press.

Stallybrass, Peter and Allon White. 2007. "The City: The Sewer, the Gaze and the Contaminating Touch." In *Beyond the Body Proper: Reading the Anthropology of Material Life*, edited by Judith Farquhar and Margaret Lock. Durham: Duke University Press, pp. 266–286.

Sutphen, Mary. 1997. "Not What, but Where: Bubonic Plague and the Reception of Germ Theories in Hong Kong and Calcutta." *Journal of History of Medicine and Allied Sciences*, 52: 81–113.

Ungar, Seldon. 1998. "Hot Crises and Media Reassurance: A Comparison of Emerging Diseases and Ebola Zaire." *The British Journal of Sociology*, 49, no. 1 (March 1998): 36–56.

Verghese, Abraham. 2003. "The SARS Epidemics: The Metaphor of Blight." *Wall Street Journal* (May 13, 2003), http://www.wsj.com/articles/SB105278837343638600

Wald, Priscilla. 2008. *Contagious: Cultures, Carriers, and the Outbreak Narrative*. Durham: Duke University Press.

Wallis, Patrick, and Brigitte Nerlich. 2005. "Disease Metaphors in New Epidemics: the UK media framing of the 2003 SARS epidemic." *Social Science & Medicine*, 60: 2629–2639.

Washer, Peter. 2004. "Representations of SARS in the British Newspapers." *Social Science and Medicine*, 59: 2561–2571.

Wong, Adrian. 2007. "A Fear Is This." Exhibition 1a Space Gallery, To Kwa Wan, Hong Kong S.A.R., http://www.adrianwong.info/selected/?a_fear_is_this

Wong, Paul. 1990. *Yellow Peril Reconsidered*. Vancouver: On Edge.

Wong, Phoebe. 2013. "After the Plague." *Asia Art Archive*, 3, http://www.aaa.org.hk/FieldNotes/Details/1215?lang=eng

Zambon, M., and K. G. Nicholson. 2003. "Sudden Acute Respiratory Syndrome May Be a Rehearsal for the Next Influenza Pandemic." *British Medical Journal*, 326: 669–670.

Zhan, Mei. 2005. "Civet Cats, Fried Grasshoppers, and David Beckham's Pajamas: Unruly Bodies after SARS." *American Anthropologist*, New Series, 107, no. 1 (March 2005): 31–42.

Zhuang Shen, Fang Ning, Weigong Zhou, Xiong He, Changying Lin, Daniel P. Chin, Zonghan Zhu, and Anne Schuchat. 2004. "Superspreading SARS Events, Beijing, 2003." *Emerging Infectious Diseases*, 10, no. 2 (February 2004): 25–260.

CHAPTER 3

~

Day of Judgment

Australia and the Rise of Asia

DAVID WALKER

B Y THE LATE NINETEENTH CENTURY there were two competing understandings of Australia's geopolitical position. According to one view, Australia was a remote, underpopulated continent positioned on the outer fringe of the British Empire (Blainey 1966). Its indigenous population was small and judged to be among the least developed people on earth. Their lowly condition was thought to reflect the harsh climate and aridity that characterized so much of the country. There was a degenerationist narrative at play in this account of Australia, namely that this was a continent that, over time, would stunt the character and racial aptitudes of its settler population, dragging them down to the miserable status attributed to the indigenous people.

An alternative view saw Australia not at the fringe of world affairs, but at the center of an impending struggle for supremacy between East and West. Charles H. Pearson's *National Life and Character: A Forecast*, a seminal and widely reviewed book published in 1893, spelled out the key elements in this new reading of Australia's future (Pearson 1893).[1] Europe, Pearson argued, had reached the limit of its expansion and the American frontier was now largely closed. While Europe faced stasis, Asia, particularly China, would continue to expand into tropical regions deemed unsuited to European settlement. Once considered remote, Australia was now strategically situated in the very heart of the Pacific, a sought-after territorial prize. Australia was considered the last continent available for the expansion and renewal of the otherwise static "higher races." Pearson made another arresting observation. When viewed from his home city of Melbourne, Australia, the world looked different than when viewed from London. Europe appeared to shrink appreciably in size and significance, while Asia looked much larger and more powerful. Australians, he suggested, were the first Europeans to be exposed to the shrinking of the European world.

The new Commonwealth of Australia was created on January 1, 1901, at a time when "Yellow Peril" speculation was rife (Walker 1999).[2] For over a century, Australians had struggled to define their place in the world. As a British settler society, Australia was connected to Europe both culturally and historically, but was geographically part of Asia. The first impulse of the new Commonwealth was to separate itself from Asia by legislating strict prohibitions on non-European immigration. Popularly known as the "White Australia Policy," the intention was to build a racially homogenous nation (Brawley 1995). This was commonly presented as a bold experiment in nation-building, based on the unifying principle of "one dear blood" (Curthoys 2003: 8–32).[3] A persistent threat to this prospect of a golden future for a new race of white Australians was nearby Asia. There was a regular drumbeat of anxious speculation that invasive Asia—poor, overcrowded, and supposedly desperate for new territories—would overrun sparsely settled Australia. For some, this would complete an inevitable historical sequence. In the language of the day, just as "white" had dispossessed "black," so too would "yellow" replace "white."

The idea that Asia would do to white Australia what white Australia had done to the indigenous population was a central theme in *The Coloured Conquest*, published in 1903, an up-to-the-minute tale of Asian invasion that drew upon the growing awareness of things Japanese following the signing of the Anglo-Japanese Treaty in 1902 (Roydhouse 1903). Japan, Britain's new ally in the Pacific, sent a training squadron to Australia. From its first appearance, early in May 1903 to its departure five weeks later, the squadron attracted immense interest as it visited the major ports in the country (Walker 1999: 83–97). The reader of *The Coloured Conquest* encounters the narrator, Frank Danton, and his fiancée, the lovely Mabel Graham, as they visit the squadron during its stay in Sydney. There is considerable enthusiasm for the visitors. Indeed, the attention that young women shower upon the Japanese troubles Frank. His concern intensifies when an indiscreet Japanese officer shows an inappropriate interest in Mabel. In a show of antipodean manliness, Danton knocks this rogue to the ground, declaring that he would shoot Mabel rather than see her become a plaything of the Japanese. Despite Danton's bravado, the Japanese invade an unprepared Australia. They soon establish "Fair Lily Colonies" where the comeliest European women, including the unlucky Mabel, are forced to cohabit with Japanese. As the last surviving white man (echoing the theme of the dying tribes of Aboriginal Australia), Danton is left to write the story of the conquest of white Australia. It was common in invasion narratives to impute both a sexual and a territorial motivation to the Asian invader. On the Australian side, the truest race patriot was the white bushman from the dry interior of the continent. Australian women were more suspect, considered too prone to fraternize with the enemy. An all-too-urban cosmopolitanism supposedly blinded flighty Australian women to the geopolitical dangers confronting the nation (Walker 2005a: 89.1–89.11).

While the emergence of the invasion novel might appear to indicate a population fearful of the rise of Asia, this oversimplifies the picture. The invasion novel and the spy thriller were popular in Britain and North America (Burton 2016; Clarke 1992). In Australia, the dramatic spectacle of an endangered continent vulnerable to Oriental villainy offered new plots, treacheries, and blood-curdling horrors for the mass reading public that had grown from the 1880s in the wake of free public education. While stories of escaped convicts, dying explorers, and the trials and tribulations of the pioneers referenced a receding past, the invasion story was modern and gripping, and addressed the future (Dixon 1995). *The Coloured Conquest*, then, could hardly have been more up to date in themes and contemporary references. The invasion genre opened the way to an exploration of taboo subjects, including interracial sex and the new freedoms created by city living. Just as the enduring popularity of murder mysteries did not prove the popularity of murder so much as the imaginative possibilities and multiple plots that the genre created for writers, in a similar way, the invasion narrative drew upon contemporary geopolitical discourse while also opening the way for daring flights of imagination and new plots ranging from the plausible to the ridiculous. The unifying theme was the looming Asian future and the social and cultural capital needed to meet this challenge. One implication was that it was not possible to understand Australia's future without also knowing Asia.

If many European societies have had a history of speculation about the rise of Asia, Australia is unusual in imagining that its very survival as a nation was threatened by it from the first moment nationhood was proclaimed. Asia was an unwelcome onlooker at the birth of the Australian Commonwealth. In this sense, survivalist anxieties about the threat posed by invasive Asia are inseparable from the idea of the Australian nation itself and its prospects as an independent white democracy in the Pacific. This was Australia's existential threat. It was also a threat that for decades was politically manipulated to strengthen ties with Britain and later with the United States. Only kith and kin, it was argued, would save Australia in the event of an attack from the north (Lockhart 2012: 269–297).

A more nuanced debate about the need for Australia to find its place in the Asian region began to emerge during the 1930s. Prime Minister Robert Menzies in particular urged Australians to rethink their place in the Pacific world. In April 1939, in his first radio broadcast on becoming prime minister, Menzies pointed out that what was the Far East in Britain was the Near North for Australia (*Argus* 1939: 1). Australians, he said, would have to start thinking of themselves as citizens of a Pacific nation.

In calling upon Australians to rethink their nation as a Pacific power, Menzies was not seeking to diminish ties with Britain and the British Empire. A devoted monarchist, he was determined that Australia would remain within the British fold. Voters clearly agreed with him: Menzies became Australia's longest-serving prime minister, serving first from 1939 to 1941 and again in a record-breaking second term from 1949 to 1966 (Martin 1993). In arguing that Australia was a Pacific nation, he sought only an expanded international role for his country. Australia, he insisted, needed a respected international voice. While it seemed unlikely that Australia could ever influence European affairs, it did seem possible that it might develop an understanding of Asia. A recurrent metaphor from this period onward was that Australia might act as a "bridge" to Asia.

The pursuit of such a goal required a shift in public rhetoric away from inflammatory "Yellow Peril" language to more conciliatory references to Australia's "neighbors." In seeking a closer understanding of Asia, Menzies was nonetheless aware that Australians remained very nervous about Asia's proximity. They continued to boast that Australia was more British than Britain itself. Even in the 1950s, Australia congratulated itself on being 98 percent British (Malouf 2003: 12). The immigration restrictions underpinning "White Australia" were not changed until the immigration reforms of the early 1970s (Tavan 2005). While economic and cultural ties to Britain faded across the twentieth century, there was no appetite to cut ties with the monarchy to become a republic (Ward 2001; McKenna 2008: 261–287). Additionally, from the late 1930s onward, Australia drew closer to the United States for defense and security, signing a formal treaty in 1951. Australia remained attached to its "white" kith and kin, still fearing isolation in the Asian region. For all the "neighborly" talk, old anxieties persisted about overflowing Asia and the "rising tide of color," a metaphor popularized by the American race theorist Lothrop Stoddard in the 1920s (Stoddard 1920). If there was to be a "rising tide," no continent seemed more vulnerable than Australia. In the late 1920s, Stoddard had warned that America would have to come to the rescue if Australia was to be saved for the white races. Stoddard freely acknowledged the important role Pearson's *National Life and Character* had played in forming his central thesis.

The Australian response to Asia always shifted between two opposing ideas: apparent threats from rising Asia versus rich opportunities that close proximity might create. Until the Second World War, threats seemed much more powerful and believable than opportunities. A small European population inhabiting an entire continent close to an Asian world made for arresting prophecies of doom. Often, warnings were accompanied by criticisms of Australian insularity. Those Australians were far too focused on the pleasures of the day. They were sport-obsessed, hedonist, and altogether too comfortable. In this way, imagined threats from rising Asia were entangled with judgments about the character and intelligence of Australians. Were they capable of settling and defending their unique and strategically located continent? Had they been given a nation-building (and race-building) task beyond their capacities? Knowing Asia was often seen as a test that Australians consistently failed. They seemed not to know enough about the nations to their north or to know the wrong things. Asia, for its part, served as a source of multiple threats. Apart from the security threat, failure to keep pace with changing Asia led to assertions that Australians were a poorly educated, second-rate people. Failure to understand the complex cultures of Asia opened the way for criticisms of Australia as a fool's paradise.

Yellow Peril narratives created opportunities to evaluate the strengths and limitations of the nation. In the Australian context, such stories invariably served a domestic, nation-building agenda. Invasion stories created a moral geography of the new nation whose tropes persisted well into the twentieth century. Despite differing plots and changing Asian adversaries, a common theme included a critique of the modern city-dweller as poor material for patriotic purposes. The city, as the highest expression of "getting and spending,"[4] emerges from the invasion narrative as a parasitic swamp that feminized its men and masculinized its women. This seemed a weak foundation on which to build a strong nation (Walker 1999: 127–140). By the 1890s, Australia was already a highly urbanized society. Contemporaries were inclined to condemn this development as a moral failing, evidence of a population addicted to comfort. They failed to see it as resulting from an economy focused on the import and export activities of its port cities (Davison 1995: 40–74).

The Australian suburbanite was portrayed as timid, small-minded, and quite unequal to the settlement tasks facing the nation. These supposed failings called into question the legitimacy of the colonizing project itself. Australians seemed to be a selfish people determined to keep others out of a continent they were either unwilling or unable to develop by themselves. One of the striking features of the Australian response to Asia is the manner in which a watchful Asia was thought to be judging the performance of white Australia.

A British journalist visiting Australia just prior to the First World War told a story about an English visitor who had seen the future of Australia in a dream (Nicol 1909). He described his vision to an excited Australian audience: he saw ports crowded with ships from around the globe. [Loud applause.] He saw large, prosperous cities populated by a disciplined, industrious population. [More loud applause.] Most remarkable of all, the vast continent, once so sparsely settled, was now dotted with bustling towns, villages, and farming communities. [Thunderous applause.] This was exactly the future Australians wanted. But the speaker had not finished. He held up his hand to quell the excitement. He paused. Upturned faces awaited the next wonderful revelation. The speaker continued. At no point in his dream, he finally revealed, had he seen a single white face. The transformation was an Asian achievement, not a white Australian one, a demonstration of Asian intelligence, ingenuity, and perseverance. The story ends with the speaker rushing from the hall pursued by an outraged audience. What was a diverting dream for the visitor was a disturbing nightmare for white Australians.

The story highlights a persistent theme—continuing to the present—in Yellow Peril speculation. While there was a good deal of comment about Asian vices and deficiencies, especially in relation to the Chinese, the deeper concern was that Australia's potential Asian adversaries would prove to be cleverer, more patiently watchful, more adaptable, and more disciplined than white Australians. In a word, Asia would eventually outsmart Australia. Thus, another common theme in Asian invasion stories was that Australians had to update their knowledge of Asia. Too many white Australians, it was argued, had based their judgments on the lowly coolie laborers they had encountered across the country. The invasion stories presented a different picture of clever, resourceful, and sometimes visionary Chinese and Japanese leaders, patiently playing a long game of tactical advantage. They may also have been predatory, cruel, and unscrupulous, but they were not to be underestimated. The message was clear enough: rising Asia presented a formidable intellectual challenge to youthful Australia. In defending the White Australia Policy, Alfred Deakin, one of the most highly regarded political leaders (and prime minister on three occasions before the First World War), argued that one of the reasons for opposing Japanese immigration was the challenge presented by Japanese capacities. Australians would struggle to compete with such a people (Norris 1981: 248–256). Historians have been inclined to view Deakin's comment as an aberration or a lapse, but when viewed in historical context his comments address a deep unease about the cultural and intellectual power of Asia. This was exactly the intended message of the British journalist: Australia could only flourish if transformed by Asian ingenuity.

This belief also spoke to the ambiguous nature of the Australian continent itself. Late nineteenth- and early twentieth-century theories of race and climate maintained that the strongest and most resilient races were the product of cold climates, whereas tropical zones were regarded as diseased and likely to cause Europeans to degenerate (Huntington 1915). The northern third of Australia lies within the tropics, while the center of the continent and much of what is now Western Australia is desert. The most habitable and densely populated southeastern coast has a Mediterranean climate. Only the island of Tasmania has a climate approximating that of the United Kingdom. The British colonizing project had transferred a cold-climate people to a warm climate that was poorly suited, according to prevailing climate theories, to white settlers. The problem was most acute for tropical Australia. There was a sustained debate continuing down to the 1930s about the future of white settlement in Northern Australia, the region most exposed to Asia (Price 1939). It was widely argued that even if whites could survive and even prosper in the tropics, the region was much better suited to Asian settlement. No matter how the continent was described, it seemed as much Asian as European. Was Australia, then, climatically and geographically destined to become an Asian possession, not a European one?

If Australia could be thought of as special for its strategic location in the Pacific, it was also special in being a continent surrounded by ocean. The promise of a continent providentially set aside for the renewal of the European race was intensified by the idea that Australia was effectively quarantined from the disease and dysfunction of the Old World. Britain's entrenched class divisions could be resisted in egalitarian Australia. In a society that took pride in honest labor, there would be no room for an effete class of idle rich. Character would be the measure of the Australian citizen, not birth, class, or wealth, with the important proviso that only those of European birth would qualify as immigrants. Likewise, Australia would be kept free of the diseases that seemed so prevalent across Asia. Contradicting those who feared racial degeneration in generations to come, a sharp contrast was drawn between diseased Asia and healthy Australia. While some insisted that Australian heat was harmful to Europeans, vocal climate patriots insisted that Australian heat was energizing, quite unlike the debilitating heat of Asia (Bedford 1911).

While the dominant argument in the case against Asian immigration continued to be the unfair competition that threatened from "cheap Asian labor," the degrading influence attributed to diseased Asia ran a close second. In fact, the two arguments were intertwined. Critics of Asian immigration maintained that Australia could never become the healthy, egalitarian, new world democracy it aspired to be if working hours and conditions were reduced to those prevalent across Asia. As the response to outbreaks of smallpox in the late nineteenth century demonstrate, Chinese workers were the first to be blamed for importing smallpox into Australia (Watters 2002: 331–343). A well-known cartoon of the time depicts an octopus with a disagreeable Chinese face (see Figure 3.1). Each of its tentacles bears the name of one of the diseases or vices attributed to the Chinese: leprosy, smallpox, opium addiction, gambling games, and, for good measure, robbery, bribery, and cheap labor (May 1886). Had there been more tentacles, room might also have been found for sexual predation, miscegenation, and homosexuality. Well into the twentieth century, the "white" aspect of "White Australia" stood for an oasis of endangered purity in a dirty and diseased Asian world (Anderson 2006). Whenever negative assessments of the character, intelligence, or cultural capacities of Australians were raised, the counter-argument was that Australia, while far from perfect, was for the most part a healthy, even blessed, land (Brady 1915).

While all Asian countries were eligible for "Yellow Peril" status, some seemed more perilous than others. China and Japan, the countries thought most likely to invade, were at the forefront of Australia's concern. For Australians, the Orient was never identified with Edward Said's Islam and the Middle East (Said 1878; Benjamin 1997). Although India retained

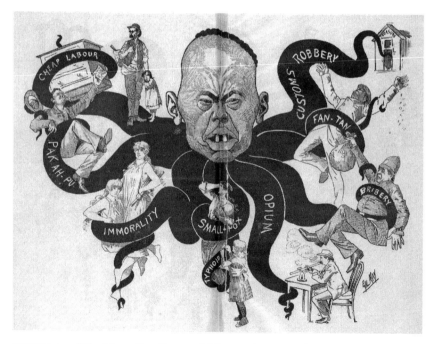

FIGURE 3.1 "The Mongolian Octopus," Library of New South Wales.

a considerable place in the colonial imaginary, it was characterized as the "antique Orient," a phrase used by Alfred Deakin, who had visited India and written two books on his experiences—*Irrigated India* and *Temple and Tomb in India* (Deakin 1893a; Deakin 1893b). Deakin both loved and hated India, with its spiritual traditions and "contaminating color." Nonetheless, he speculated about a fruitful association between India and Australia, encouraging his readers to think of Australia as "Southern Asia." India seemed less likely to invade than China or Japan (Sengupta 2012: 50–72). The reason, no doubt, was the reassuring presence of the British in that country, who could be relied upon to keep the Indians in their place. In a similar way, Australia's closest Asian neighbor, the Netherlands East Indies [now Indonesia], was also seen as non-threatening, since the Dutch were keeping their native subjects under control. Japan, by contrast, had the distinction of having never been colonized. It was the first Asian nation in the modern era to defeat a European power in the Russo-Japanese war of 1904–1905, and had emerged very quickly as a significant military and naval power in the Pacific. This made it a promising candidate for Yellow Peril speculation in Australia (Meany 1976). And finally, although China might have seemed weak, as it was being dismembered by European powers, the core of the Chinese threat had always been its huge population. As Pearson noted, China's annual increase in population was alone sufficient to "inundate" Australia. For those with invasion fears, East Asia looked more threatening than India or Southeast Asia.

Through the 1940s, war and decolonization revived and sharpened many of the old Australian anxieties about being an encircled continent far removed from the protection of kith and kin. When Japan swept down through Southeast Asia following the bombing of Pearl Harbor in December 1941, the much-foretold invasion of empty Australia appeared imminent. The fall of Singapore in February 1942 came as a terrible shock (Day 1992; Curran 2011). Australians had been reassured time and again that Singapore under the British was impregnable. Just weeks before Singapore fell, one of Australia's most popular writers and radio broadcasters, Frank Clune, repeated all the old assurances. Singapore was secure, not least because the racial prowess of the "white man" must far outweigh any Asian adversary (Clune 1941). There had been worried speculation through the 1930s about the military build-up in Japan, but this was often turned aside by dismissive references to the inferior fighting prowess of the "yellow man." As far as Clune was concerned, "white" would always defeat "yellow."

One failing often attributed to the Japanese was their poor vision, which allegedly prevented them flying at night. Moreover, it seemed unlikely that their guns, ships, submarines, and aircraft could ever match the sophistication of Western military hardware. These comforting stereotypes quickly collapsed. When Japanese aircraft bombed the northern port of Darwin and their submarines entered Sydney Harbor, it appeared that the "colored conquest" of Australia had begun. While historians have now shown that the invasion of Australia was not part of Japan's military planning, mere facts have never been able to dislodge this belief from the popular imagination (Stanley 2008). The reason lies in the sustained power of the "Yellow Peril" narrative. From the 1880s onward, it was foreseen as inevitable that there would be a struggle for supremacy between East and West with Australia as the prize. That Japan would claim the Netherlands East Indies as the final prize had no place in Australia's "Yellow Peril" imaginary. When invasion fears spread throughout Australia following the fall of Singapore, a widely circulated poster showed the dreadful consequences of reversing the racial order. It depicted a white Australian ex-serviceman pulling his Japanese master around in a rickshaw against the backdrop of Flinders Street Station, the main railway station in Melbourne, Victoria (Figure 3.2). This seemed the ultimate betrayal of white Australia (Northfield c. 1942).

The difficulty of keeping pace with change in Asia is neatly captured by Frank Clune's literary career. An accountant by training, Clune harbored no literary pretensions. His business was to make money from writing and broadcasting. There was money to be made in Asian travelogues mixed with potted histories and personal encounters. His first book on Asia, jauntily titled *Sky High to Shanghai*, was published in 1939, the year Prime Minister Menzies had urged Australians to embrace their destiny as a Pacific power (Clune 1939). Clune spread a hopeful message about the role Australia could play in the Near East. There was an inevitable leadership role for the white man in the emerging markets of Asia. Clune never imagined that the established order of European dominance and Asian deference was about to change (Sobocinska 2014).

Clune was certain that British dominance would continue in India and Singapore and that the Dutch would remain in full control in the Netherlands East Indies. Yet only a decade later, this reassuring picture of an Asia dominated by Europe was rudely overtaken by decolonization (Lake and Reynolds 2008). Right across Asia, European powers were in retreat. Clune was bewildered, outraged, and frustrated. His intoxicating glimpse of what it was to be revered and waited upon as a "white man" in the East had gone, never to return. Clune lost his benevolent interest in this Asia and gave up writing about it.

Through the 1950s, as Asian decolonization became the new reality, Clune feared the decline of the white races. He denounced all sugges-tions that Australia's restrictive immigration policies should be changed. He saw conspiracies everywhere, and believed that the United Nations was now working hand in glove with the colored races to bring down the West. In addition, he felt that the feminizing influence of working and voting women had weakened the race-building resolve of Australian pol-iticians. In his private correspondence, Clune's language became particu-larly bitter. In 1947, when Australia's Asian population still remained very small, Clune asserted, "We've enough Brindle Bastards in this country" (Clune 1947). These sentiments, which were quite widely shared, would be constantly repeated by Clune in years to come.

In 1955, when it became known that the newly independent nations of Asia and Africa would meet together in the Indonesian city of Bandung, there was much speculation about how the colored world was ganging up on the hated West (Goldsworthy 2001, Percival Wood 2012). In Australia, Bandung was seen as a direct racial challenge, a provocation. In Western attempts to understand the Bandung conference, the focus turned not to the unequal distribution of the world's resources, but rather to the psychological defects that supposedly characterized the "Asian mind." One of Australia's most senior diplomats in the 1950s, Walter Crocker, a man with considerable experience of Asia and Africa, emphasized the "emotionalism" of the colored races. There was much speculation that the immature "mind of the East" lay behind the drive for decolonization (Walker 2005b: 40–59). Whatever the driver, a new and more powerful Asia had emerged. The unquestioned colonial dominance that Clune admired had gone for good.

Asia's postwar rise coincided with profound changes in the British world. This had long-term implications for questions of iden-tity and belonging. As Britain sought to find its place in a new Europe, Australians were forced to again re-examine their place in the world. What larger community would Australia be part of (Ward 2001)? The

FIGURE 3.2 "A United 'Fighting Mad' Australia."

answer, although often an uncomfortable one in the 1950s and 1960s, was that Australia had no choice but to be part of Asia. In the 1950s and 1960s Australia still clung to the still-popular White Australia Policy. It was widely believed that any liberalization, any introduction of a quota system for limited Asian immigration, would signal the end not only of "White Australia," but of Australia itself. Since January 1, 1901, the idea of Australia had been predicated on racial homogeneity. Australia might celebrate many other qualities—egalitarianism, a fair go for working people, youthful optimism, a love of the outdoors, glorious beaches— but the unifying principle on which the nation had been built was racial.

One of the great social and political achievements of postwar Australia was to transition from a country where race and whiteness formed the basis of identity, belonging, and national strength (even survival) to a country that advocated strength through racial diversity. Australia began this process in the late 1940s with a new approach to postwar immigration (Macintyre 2015). The logic of this program, which commenced at a time when the memory of the threat of Japanese invasion was still strong, was to create a nation with sufficient population to properly defend its borders. The original plan was to preserve Australia's racial identity by bringing in British migrants. When the expected flow from Britain failed to arrive, the program was expanded to include immigrants from Italy, Greece, and Southern Europe. Racial boundaries shifted slightly. The face of white, Anglo-Celtic Australia was changing but remained within a European framework. Asia was still largely excluded. The popular rationale for the new program, which was crucial in obtaining support from the powerful labor movement, was the need to "populate or perish."

Perishable Australia proved an enduring and versatile theme. It suited the needs of twentieth-century visitors called upon to venture an opinion on Australia's future. When British press baron Lord Northcliffe visited Australia in 1921, he sounded familiar warnings about "defenseless" and "empty" Australia and its dangerous proximity to hungry Asia, so close that "you can almost smell the East on your northern winds" (*Sydney Morning Herald* 1921: 13). Northcliffe repeated Stoddard's warnings about the "rising tide of color," noting how Stoddard's book was so sought after in Australia that booksellers were unable to meet the demand. (It was also in vogue across America, and the subject of some deft satire. In *The Great Gatsby*, for example, Scott Fitzgerald has a portentous Gatsby make a muddled reference to Stoddard's book.) *The Rising Tide of Color* was the perfect book for a busy man to cite. No need to read it; the title said it all. Northcliffe's message to Australia could not have been better designed to arouse "Yellow Peril" anxieties. His public addresses spoke of a continent larger and richer than he had imagined. Although it was situated next to poor, desperate, and envious Asia, insular Australians seemed oblivious to the danger. Northcliffe was certain that leaders in nearby Asia had a better understanding of the wealth of the Australian continent than most Australians. There could be no more tempting prize, and it was virtually unguarded.

In the late 1920s, the British journalist Fleetwood Chidell picked up this theme in his book *Australia—White or Yellow?* (Chidell 1926). The title had been a popular one, given in 1888 to a story of Chinese invaders: "White or Yellow. A Story of the Race-War of 1908" (Lane 1888). The dire warning was repeated again in the late 1950s by the British writer and philosopher Malcolm Muggeridge, who declared that within a generation Australia would face a life-or-death showdown with rising China (Muggeridge 1958: 5). At the time, Australian journalist and author Donald Horne observed that it was a commonplace to hear people confess, "Australia did not have a chance" (Horne 1958: 228). Sooner or later Asia would prevail. In 1964, Horne pursued this theme in *The Lucky Country*, his influential analysis of postwar Australia (Horne 1964). In Horne's view, Australia's luck lay in having enough wealth and resources to prosper despite its poor political leadership and a mediocre education system. But his cheeky starting point offered a portrait of white Australia just before its imminent and inevitable transformation by Asia. Horne was out to provoke his readers: he knew very well that it broke all the rules to treat the subject so lightly. Horne had detected the stirring of a change of attitude in Australia's relationship with Asia and, in fact, less than a decade after the publication of *The Lucky Country*, a new Labor government would overturn the White Australia Policy, recognize the People's Republic of China, and make multiculturalism the centerpiece of a new immigration policy.

From the 1970s, Australia's transition to policies of Asian engagement and multiculturalism gained momentum. What should have been a difficult transition was, paradoxically, made considerably easier by Asia's rise. There was too much benefit to be had from trade. In 1957, against vocal opposition, the Menzies government signed a trade agreement with

Japan, which, to fuel its rapid industrialization, needed Australian raw materials, particularly its coal, iron ore, and wool. By the next decade, Japan had replaced Britain as Australia's major trading partner. Moreover, this economic change had not been accompanied, as some had feared, by any pressure to accept large numbers of Japanese immigrants. Between the 1950s and 1980s, trade with Japan lifted Australia's export performance very dramatically. It became easier to argue that there was more to gain than lose in Australia being part of Asia.

It was not all plain sailing, however. As the pace of economic, social, and cultural change quickened through the 1980s and 1990s, with reduced tariffs on local industries, the floating of the Australian dollar, and exposure to international competition in a globalizing world, anti-immigration and anti-Asian sentiment found a new champion in Pauline Hanson. She was elected as a member of the Federal Parliament in Canberra and went on to create and lead the One Nation party. Hanson's message drew upon the persistent appeal of "Yellow Peril" anxieties (Jakubowicz 1997). Her brand of anti-politics was widely reported at home and abroad. She warned that Australians were in danger of being "swamped by Asians," that living standards would fall and unemployment rise. The old Australia would disappear, she asserted, replaced by something alien and polyglot (Hanson 1996). At its peak in 1998, support for One Nation climbed to 8.43 percent of the primary vote for the Australian House of Representatives (online source 2016). Her xenophobic stand on immigration and refugees was soon echoed in the policies and rhetoric of the two major parties: the Liberal National Party Coalition and the Australian Labor Party.

From this Hansonite period onward, refugees arriving in Northern Australia by boat seeking asylum have been characterized as "illegal immigrants," or, more often, as "illegals." They are now banished to offshore detention centers in Papua New Guinea and Nauru with little hope of ever settling in Australia (Marr and Wilkinson 2004). While the fear of boat arrivals has been exploited by both sides of the political spectrum as politicians jostle to demonstrate their security credentials, it is hard to resist the conclusion that the arrival of boatloads of non-Europeans on Australia's isolated northern coastline plays directly into the deeply held, foundational anxiety of a fledgling Commonwealth fearing "colored conquest." Constant references to vulnerable northern borders have been used to justify the costly and controversial militarization of the seas between Australia and Indonesia (Balint 2012: 345–365). When critics of these harsh policies point out that the number of asylum seekers reaching Australia is relatively small, especially when compared to current figures for migrants fleeing to Europe from the Middle East, the typical response echoes arguments heard a century earlier: while the numbers now might be small, today's trickle will become tomorrow's flood.

As powerful as invasion anxieties can be, they are not reflected in Australia's current relationships with Japan and China, the key historical foci for "Yellow Peril" speculation. Neither Japan nor China generates boatloads of asylum seekers arriving in Northern Australia. Rather, refugees come via Indonesia from the Middle East, Afghanistan, and Sri Lanka. Japan, during the last twenty years, has emerged as Australia's security partner in the Asia-Pacific region and, despite a flatline economy, it remains Australia's third-largest trading partner. Through the 1990s, as the Japanese economy slowed, Deng Xiaoping's rise to power led to China's historic opening to the West, ushering in economic transformation on an unprecedented scale. China became the new powerhouse of twenty-first-century growth and replaced Japan as Australia's major trading partner. Australia enjoyed a remarkable boom in commodity prices, handsome budget surpluses, and an economy that was the envy of its Western counterparts. Even as recession swept through Western economies following the Global Financial Crisis of 2008–2009, the Australian economy continued to grow. While timely fiscal policies played their part, it was widely understood that Australia had benefited greatly from its trading relationship with China. While some Australians feared the rise of Chinese power, others were confident in Australia's balancing act, preserving both its major security alliance with the United States and its vital trading relationship with China. But if either party pushed back, would Australia face an awkward choice (White 2012)?

By the late twentieth century, updated stories of Asian invasion had largely disappeared from Australian popular culture. In the United States, they remained a flourishing genre until the events of September 11, 2001, changed the security landscape and perceptions of who was the main enemy. In the four years just before 2001, three big names hit the bestseller lists: Clive Custler with *Flood Tide*, Stephen Canell with *Riding the Snake*, and Tom Clancy with *The Bear and the Dragon* (Walker 2005c: 136–155). Floods, snakes, and dragons were core tropes for the Yellow

Peril industry. Each novel detailed Chinese plans to weaken and ultimately dismember the United States. Custler went so far as to reference Dr. Fu Manchu, the prototype of the Oriental mastermind, as a forerunner of the malevolent Chinese protagonist in *Flood Tide*. It was an explicit link to the "Yellow Peril."

These American offerings have no clear parallel in Australian popular culture of this period. Although Australians certainly express concerns that Chinese money is distorting real estate prices in Australia's major cities and worry when large tracts of agricultural land are sold to Chinese entities, many other Australians stand to gain from China's new wealth with marked growth in Chinese tourism, Chinese students entering the fee-paying education sector, and Chinese interest in Australia's service industries.

One fascinating indication of how far debate has shifted over the course of the last 120 years is the decision in 2015 to grant a 99-year lease over the Port of Darwin to a Chinese company despite its links to the People's Liberation Army. Then-President Obama took the unusual step of raising US concerns about this decision in public, not behind closed doors. He noted the lack of prior consultation with the United States on an issue seen as important to the Australia–US alliance. Given Australia's history of invasion fears and anxieties about the Chinese streaming into Australia through the "empty north," it is remarkable that in 2015, so little concern was shown about a long-term Chinese presence in Darwin's port. The old adversary had become the new trading partner.

Australia and China now share a defense relationship built on the annual Australia–China Defense Strategic Dialogue, which has continued over the last twenty years. Related activities include reciprocal visits of senior military personnel, ship visits, and bilateral and multilateral military exercises. In 2016, Australia and China conducted a joint adventure training exercise, known as *Pandaroo*, on Australia's east coast, and the two countries joined the United States to conduct *Kowari*, an environmental survival skills exercise, in the Northern Territory. Australia, China, New Zealand, and the United States also participate in the annual humanitarian assistance and disaster relief exercise known as *Cooperation Spirit*. Additionally, Australia and China cooperate in other multilateral exercises under the Association of Southeast Asian Nations (ASEAN) Defense Minister's Meeting-Plus framework. Australia's leading role in the search for missing Malaysia Airlines flight MH370 in the Southern Indian Ocean has reinforced the practical benefit of China–Australia defense cooperation.

Declining demand for iron ore is now of far greater concern than any perceived threat of invasion. Australia's politicians assure the public that China and much of Asia is becoming middle class, a development that, it is argued, will underpin Australia's economy well into the twenty-first century. It is no less remarkable that Japan was one of three countries, along with France and Germany, that tendered for the supply of a new fleet of submarines for the Australian Navy. While France won the contract, there is little evidence that old fears of invasive Japan influenced the decision.

Nevertheless, Pauline Hanson's election to the Australian Senate in 2016 with three colleagues from her One Nation party has again brought to the fore fear and antipathy toward migrants, although her emphasis has now shifted from Asians to Muslims; other populist issues are now canvassed, including climate change skepticism and anti-vaccination positions. As many as 30 percent of Australian voters in the July 2016 general election backed One Nation or parties with similar ideologies (Cassidy 2016). While a majority of Australians still favor multiculturalism (Hancocks 2016), they do not necessarily readily accept the full diversity of Asian migrants now entering the country from nations ranging from China to the Maldives. By 2016 the ethnopolitical nationalism apparent among many European countries was also being celebrated on the populist end of the Australian political spectrum, through apprehension about food security, environmental pressures, ownership of key productive assets, and urban enclave development (Tan 2016).

Australians began the twentieth century clinging to their White Australia policy and fearing that rising Asia might swamp their fledgling nation. They entered the twenty-first century knowing that Asian markets sustained their prosperity and that a multicultural policy underpinned their democracy.

Notes

1 Charles H. Pearson was an Oxford-educated historian who had immigrated to Australia, where he became a prominent politician and educator in the colony of Victoria. Theodore Roosevelt and Lord

Curzon were among those who reviewed the book. Kaiser Wilhelm was also alleged to have read it at the time he coined the term "the Yellow Peril." While Roosevelt, writing in the *Sewanee Review* (August 1894), considered Pearson to be a man of melancholy and pessimistic disposition, he nonetheless called *National Life and Character* "one of the most notable books of the century."

2 Federation, or the creation of the new Commonwealth, in 1901 saw six colonies become centrally governed "states." Defense of Australia was one of the key responsibilities of the new national government.

3 In a sonnet called "Federation," written in the 1890s by William Gay, the phrase "one dear blood" was used to capture the principle of racial homogeneity on which Australia was founded.

4 The phrase comes from a sonnet by the Romantic poet William Wordsworth, written c 1802:

The world is too much with us; late and soon,
Getting and spending, we lay waste our powers:
Little we see in Nature that is ours;
We have given our hearts away, a sordid boon!

References

Anderson, Warwick. 2006. *The Cultivation of Whiteness: Science, Health, and Racial Destiny in Australia*. Durham: Duke University Press.

Anon. 1921. "Lord Northcliffe's Warning. 'Only Numbers will save you.'" *Sydney Morning Herald*, October 1, p. 13.

Anon. 1939. "New Leader Talks to Nation: Common front for Defence Plans," *The Argus*, April 27, p. 1.

Anon. "Pauline Hanson's One Nation," http://australianpolitics.com/parties/one-nation. Accessed online, February 16, 2016.

Balint, Ruth. 2012. "Epilogue: The Yellow Sea." In *Australia's Asia: From Yellow Peril to Asian Century*, edited by David Walker and Agnieszka Sobocinska, pp. 345–365. Crawley: University of Western Australia Publishing.

Bedford, Randolph. 1911. "White, Yellow or Brown?" *Lone Hand*, July 1.

Benjamin, Roger. 1997. *Orientalism: Delacroix to Klee*. Sydney: The Art Gallery of New South Wales.

Blainey, Geoffrey. 1966. *The Tyranny of Distance: How Distance Shaped Australia's History*. Melbourne: Sun Books.

Brady, E. J. 1915. *Australia Unlimited*. Melbourne: George Robinson.

Brawley, Sean. 1995. *The White Peril: Foreign Relations and Asian Immigration to Australasia and North America, 1919–78*. Sydney: University of New South Wales Press.

Burton, Alan. 2016. *Historical Dictionary of British Spy Fiction*. London: Rowman & Littlefield.

Cassidy, Barrie. 2016. "One Nation: Voting Patterns Show Pauline Hanson's Impact Runs Deep," http://www.abc.net.au/news/2016-09-23/barrie-cassidy-one-nation-influence-runs-deep/7868466. Accessed online August 30, 2016.

Chidell, Fleetwood. 1926. *Australia—White or Yellow?* London: William Heinemann.

Clarke, I. F. (1992) [1966]. *Voices Prophesying War: Future Wars, 1763–3749*. Oxford: Oxford University Press.

Clune, Frank. 1939. *Sky High to Shanghai*. Sydney: Angus and Robertson.

Clune, Frank. 1941. *All Aboard for Singapore: A Trip by Qantas Flying Boat from Sydney to Malaya*. Sydney: Angus and Robertson.

Clune, Frank. 1947. "Letter to A. Calwell," 1 December, Frank Clune Papers, National Library of Australia, MS4951/1/677.

Curran, James. 2011. *Curtin's Empire*. Cambridge: Cambridge University Press.

Curthoys, Ann. 2003. "Liberalism and Exclusionism: A Prehistory of the White Australia Policy." In *Legacies of White Australia: Race, Culture and Nation*, edited by Laksiri Jayasuriya, David Walker, and Jan Gothard, pp. 8–32. Crawley: University of Western Australia Press.

Davison, Graeme. 1995. "Australia—The First Suburban Nation." *Journal of Urban History* 22, no. 1: 40–74.

Day, David. 1992. *Reluctant Nation: Australia and the Allied Defeat of Japan, 1942–45*. Oxford: Oxford University Press.

Deakin, Alfred. 1893a. *Irrigated India: An Australian View of India and Ceylon, Their Irrigation and Agriculture*. London: W. Thacker and Co.

Deakin, Alfred. 1893b. *Temple and Tomb in India*. Melbourne: Melville, Mullen and Slade.

Dixon, Robert. 1995. *Writing the Colonial Adventure: Race, Gender and Nation in Anglo-Australian Popular Fiction, 1875–1914*. Cambridge: Cambridge University Press.

Goldsworthy, David, ed. 2001. *Facing North: A Century of Australian Engagement with Asia, Volume 1: 1901 to the 1970s*. Melbourne: Department of Foreign Affairs and Trade, Melbourne University Press.

Hancocks, A. 2016. *Multiculturalism Discussion Paper*. Melbourne: Scanlon Foundation. http://scanlonfoundation.org.au/wp-content/uploads

/2016/02/DiscussionPaperMulticulturalismFINAL.pdf. Accessed online November 1, 2016.

Hanson, Pauline. 1996. "Appropriation Bill (No. 1) 1996–97 (First Speech)." *Australian House of Representatives Hansard.* Canberra: Australian Government.

Horne, Donald. 1958. "Has Australia Got a Chance?" *The Observer,* May 31, p. 228.

Horne, Donald. 1964. *The Lucky Country: Australia in the Sixties.* Ringwood, Victoria: Penguin.

Huntington, Ellsworth. 1915. *Civilization and Climate.* New Haven: Yale University Press.

Jakubowicz, A. 1997. "In Pursuit of the Anabranches: Immigration, Multiculturalism and a Culturally Diverse Australia." In *The Resurgence of Racism; Howard, Hanson and the Race Debate,* edited by G. Gray and C. Winter. Melbourne: Monash Publications in History, 24.

Lake, Marilyn, and Henry Reynolds. 2008. *Drawing the Global Colour Line: White Men's Countries and the Question of Racial Equality.* Carlton: Melbourne University Press.

Lane, William ["Sketcher"]. 1888. "White or Yellow? A Story of the Race War of 1908." *Boomerang,* February 18–May 5.

Lockhart, Greg. 2012. "Absenting Asia." In *Australia's Asia: from Yellow Peril to Asian Century,* edited by David Walker and Agnieszka Sobocinska, pp. 269–297. Crawley: University of Western Australia Publishing.

Macintyre, Stuart. 2015. *Australia's Boldest Experiment: War and Reconstruction in the 1940s.* Sydney: Newsouth Publishing.

Malouf, David. 2003. "Made in England: Australia's British Inheritance." *Quarterly Essay,* 12.

Marr, David, and Marian Wilkinson. 2004. *Dark Victory: How a Government Lied Its Way to Political Triumph.* Sydney: Allen & Unwin.

Martin, Allan William, assisted by Patsy Hardy. 1993. *Robert Menzies. Volume 1, 1894–1943: A Life.* Carlton: Melbourne University Press.

May, Phil. 1886. "The Mongolian Octopus—His Grip on Australia." *The Bulletin,* August 21.

McKenna, Mark. 2008. "Monarchy: from Reverence to Indifference." In *Australia's Empire,* edited by Deryck Marshall Schreuder and Stuart Ward, pp. 261–287. Oxford: Oxford University Press.

Meany, Neville. 1976. *The Search for Security in the Pacific, 1901–1914.* Sydney: Sydney University Press.

Muggeridge, Malcolm. 1958. "Mr. Muggeridge looks at Australia." *Daily Telegraph,* May 7, p. 5.

Nicol, Alex M. 1909. "How to People the Commonwealth: A Dream and a Reality." *Australia Today*, December 1.

Norris, R. 1981. "Deakin, Alfred (1856–1919)." In *Australian Dictionary of Biography, Volume 8: 1891–1939*, edited by Bede Nairn and Geoffrey Serle, pp. 248–256. Canberra: Australian National University.

Northfield, James. 1942. "A United 'Fighting Mad' Australia Can Never Be Enslaved." State Library of Victoria Pictures Collection, Accession number: H97.24/2.

Pearson, Charles H. 1893. *National Life and Character: A Forecast*. London and New York: Macmillan and Co.

Percival Wood, Sally. 2012. "Retrieving the Bandung Conference . . . Moment by Moment." *Journal of Southeast Asian Studies*, 43, no. 3: 523–530.

Price, A. Grenville, additional notes Robert G. Stone. 1939. *White Settlers in the Tropics*. New York: American Geographical Society.

Roydhouse, Thomas Richard, [Rata]. 1903. *The Coloured Conquest*. Sydney, N. S. W. Bookstall Co.

Said, Edward W. 1978. *Orientalism: Western Conceptions of the Orient*. New Delhi: Penguin Books.

Sengupta, Ipsita. 2012. "Entangled: Deakin in India." In *Australia's Asia: From Yellow Peril to Asian Century*, edited by David Walker and Agnieszka Sobocinska, pp. 50–72. Crawley: University of Western Australia Publishing.

Sobocinska, Agnieska. 2014. *Visiting the Neighbours: Australians in Asia*. Sydney: NewSouth Publishing.

Stanley, Peter. 2008. *Invading Australia: Japan and the Battle for Australia, 1942*. Sydney: Penguin Group Australia.

Stoddard, Lothrop. 1920. *The Rising Tide of Color against White World Supremacy*. New York: Charles Scribner's Sons.

Tan, Su-Lin. 2016. "Pauline Hanson Could Dent Asian Investments in Australia," *Australian Financial Review*, July 4.

Tavan, Gwenda. 2005. *The Long Slow Death of White Australia*. Melbourne: Scribe Publications.

Walker, David. 1999a. *Anxious Nation: Australia and the Rise of Asia, 1850–1939*. St Lucia: University of Queensland Press.

Walker, David. 1999b. "Lilies and Dragons." In *Anxious Nation: Australia and the Rise of Asia, 1850–1939*, pp. 127–140. St Lucia: University of Queensland Press.

Walker, David. 1999c. "Pacific Visitors." In *Anxious Nation: Australia and the Rise of Asia, 1850–1939*, pp. 83–97. St Lucia: University of Queensland Press.

Walker, David. 2005a. "Godless Heathen: China in the American Bestseller." In *East by South: China in the Australasian Imagination*. Edited by Charles Ferrall, Paul Millar, and Keren Smith, pp. 136–155. Wellington: Victoria University Press.

Walker, David. 2005b. "Nervous Outsiders: Australia and the 1955 Asia-Africa Conference in Bandung." *Australian Historical Studies* 37, no. 125: 40–59.

Walker, David. 2005c. "Shooting Mabel: Warrior masculinity and Asian invasion." *History of Australia*, 2, no. 3: 89.1–89.11.

Ward, Stuart. 2001. *Australia and the British Embrace: The Demise of the Imperial Ideal*. Carlton South: Melbourne University Press.

Watters, Greg. 2002. "The SS *Ocean*: Dealing with Boat People in the 1880s." *Australian Historical Studies*, 33, no. 120: 331–343.

White, Hugh. 2012. *The China Choice*. Collingwood: Black Inc.

CHAPTER 4

∽

Chinese Entrepreneurship in Prato, Italy

XIAOJIAN ZHAO

I N LATE 2009, Prato, a quiet Italian city in the heart of Tuscany about sixteen miles from Florence, began to capture the attention of the international media. The historical capital of Italy's textile industry had earned a reputation for quality products and craftsmanship. But at this time, the town was at the forefront of the anti-Chinese hostility that was emerging in Italy and Europe. Beginning in late June, law enforcement agents repeatedly raided garment factories run by Chinese migrants. By the end of the year, 233 Chinese enterprises had been searched and 209 had been shut down (Wen 2010). On January 19, 2010, the government launched a full-scale operation, dispatching local police, firefighters, and tax collectors with the assistance of more than 150 armed national police and military guards. This special operation blocked the entire street of Via Rossini on the outskirts of Prato's downtown area and conducted a blanket-style search of Chinese factories. In one day, the authorities interrogated more than 200 Chinese business owners and workers and rounded up 70 undocumented individuals, shutting down more than 300 factories (Wen 2010).

The next day, the operation moved to another Chinese business district. As a helicopter circled above, officers confiscated 500 machines and closed 28 businesses; more than 190 migrants were interrogated (Bo 2010; Zhang 2015). The police also sealed off real estate and ordered the Chinese owners to leave their homes. Those who had no legal work permit were forced to leave Italy within five days (Liu 2010). Raiding Chinese factories soon became a routine business of the local police (Dinmore 2010).

84

Several times a week, Linda Iervasi, head of the immigration division of the Prato police, would suddenly appear in the Chinese districts with her team of police officers. Factories that hired undocumented workers or used informal practices would be shut down immediately (AFP 2010). These operations brought a substantial amount of revenue for the municipal government. In 2009, businesses that used Chinese-language signs were fined a total of 40,000 euros (Wen 2010). For the first ten months of 2010, fine payments from Chinese enterprises generated 180,000 euros (Liu 2010). In June 2010, prosecutors filed charges against 24 individuals and 100 businesses for money laundering, prostitution, counterfeiting, and misuse of the "Made in Italy" label (Donadio 2010).

Such a show of force could hardly be understood as simply an effort by local officials to enforce migration laws and labor regulations even though raids and incidents against Chinese migrants and their businesses had also taken place, to a lesser degree, in Milan, Rome, and other places in Italy and Europe (Kington 2007; Meichtry 2011; Suibian 2013). This chapter examines Chinese migration and entrepreneurship in the context of the development of Prato's textile industry, where "the fear of the coming Chinese age," as Frank N. Pieke points out, "connects seamlessly with the fear of migration" (Pieke 2004, 1). Chinese migrants to Prato arrived at a critical time, when the increasingly integrated global economy challenged regional and national boundaries and when the city's textile industry was declining in the midst of an economic recession. The newcomers took the jobs that few locals wanted and helped revitalize Prato's economy; this was largely recognized and appreciated. But feelings changed as the migrants carved out a niche in the textile industry by adopting a new production model, which had a mixed reception among the locals. As local business owners began to see themselves as victims of globalization, they associated their economic problems with open borders and migration. Anti-Chinese sentiment thus became a powerful force in their ideas about preserving their traditional way of living and everything else that was meaningfully Italian about their way of life.

Strangers in the "Italian Manchester"

Known as "Italian Manchester," Prato is an industrial city in Tuscany, where handcrafted wool, textile, and leather goods have been produced since the thirteenth century. After the unification of Italy in the nineteenth century, Prato established itself as a prominent industrial center, attracting migrant labor from other regions. The city experienced significant economic growth after World War II, as demand for high-quality textile products increased. Although advancements in production technology, the development of synthetic fiber, and improved logistics posed constant challenges, factories in Prato were able to maintain their artisan tradition by producing quality and durable goods for customers who were willing to pay high prices. In the 1970s, the textile industry expanded by adding a new line of knitwear products. In the 1990s, a few local businesses also produced fast fashion (Ceccagno 2009).

But overall, changes in this ancient Italian town took place slowly. Until recently, Prato's traditional methods of production were kept intact. Local residents were proud of their strong artisan tradition and quality products. When major producers in Europe and the United States outsourced their production to developing countries, factories in Prato resisted the temptation and continued to manufacture locally. To many, the textile industry represents the essence of the city's rich culture and tradition in the same way that Renaissance arts and architecture represent the culture of Florence and Rome. The city's Textile Museum (Museo del Tessuto), housed in a nineteenth-century textile factory filled with exhibits of antique and contemporary fabrics, hand-weaving tools, and spinning wheels, is one of the city's top tourist attractions (Magrini, undated). By the late 1980s, however, industry integration and global manufacturing made it more and more difficult for locally produced products to compete. Established European and American companies, including some Italian companies, lowered their prices by producing abroad. At the same time, some non-Italian producers, especially those in China, had steadily narrowed the quality gap (Rhoads 2003). Efforts to cut down production costs locally met with strong resistance, as subcontractors found it more and more difficult to recruit workers from the younger generation. Moreover, new varieties of cheap fabrics and trendy versus classic clothing styles began to dominate the fashion market, reducing the demand for expensive and durable goods. The recession of the early 1990s hit Prato hard, leading to a loss of 3,550 small businesses. Some 15,000 Italian workers left the trade. Empty factory buildings and abandoned machinery were clear signs of a troubled economy (Denison et al. 2009).

The Chinese arrived at an opportune time, when the lack of local interest in employment in the textile industry created a favorable climate for newcomers in search of work. Manufacturers needed workers to assemble the products, while those who had gone out of business needed to get rid of their machinery and equipment. Landlords of vacant business buildings were especially eager to find new tenants. The newcomers utilized resources abandoned by local factories and took jobs few others wanted (Ottati 2014, 1252). Although Prato had experienced little foreign immigration until then, local residents did not find the faces and accents of the Chinese strange. There was no sign of hostility at first. The foreignness of the newcomers seemed largely unnoticed or ignored.

The Chinese immigrants were a "blessing" to Prato's economy, as the city's mayor, Marco Romagnoli, acknowledged, saying that "The city would be bankrupt without the Chinese, who are buying houses, cars and fabric, creating new jobs and filling old jobs. And Prato's citizens are reaping their share of the profits, charging astronomical rents for dark, poorly ventilated and dilapidated factory buildings without toilets" (Ehlers 2006). In the mid-1990s, the city government developed programs to assist the migrants. The Social Policy Office of Prato established a research center for documentation and service to the Chinese community, which was designed to help the migrants with economic planning and problem solving. It also provided information on business opportunities (Denison et al. 2009, 5–6). The newcomers could also seek assistance with housing issues at a public meeting place. The migrants, for their part, facilitated cross-border trade and exchange: in 2003 Prato and Wenzhou entered a twin-city agreement, which led to a number of exchange projects and collaborations between Prato and the migrants' region of origin in areas of cultural preservation, health, tourism, and workplace diversity (Denison et al. 2009, 5–6). Economic opportunities and the friendly reception from the locals encouraged the inflow of new migrants. Within two decades, Prato emerged as one of the biggest concentrations of Chinese population in Europe (Ridgwell 2010).

Making it in Italy—Chinese style

Most of the new migrants originated from the Wenzhou district of Zhejiang province on the southeast coast of China, where mountain terrains separate the region from its neighbors. There, geographical isolation had fostered a distinct regional dialect, and the shortage of arable land had led to a unique economic pattern based on commercial crops and trade. During the early 1900s, those who ventured overseas sold carved stone art pieces and various kinds of small merchandise on the streets of European cities. According to a report by the renowned Chinese journalist Zou Taofen, the peddlers sold their products out of their suitcases (Qingtian huaqiaoshi bianxie zu 2007, 26). Fei Xiaotong, a prominent Chinese anthropologist, recalled his early encounter with a Wenzhou trader in England in 1937. According to his account, some ten thousand peddlers in Berlin, Paris, and other European cities were natives of the Wenzhou-Qingtian region (Fei 1999, 455).

From the 1950s to the late 1970s, the Chinese economy was tightly controlled by the state. The government launched political campaigns against capitalism and cracked down on most private enterprises. All industries were to be run by either the state or local collectives. Geographic isolation, however, enabled the Wenzhou people to evade government regulation and continue their entrepreneurial tradition. During the decade of the Cultural Revolution (1966–1976), when private enterprises were completely wiped out in most regions of China, the Wenzhou natives built extensive networks of underground manufacturing, marketing, and transportation; tens of thousands of unlicensed vendors were actively engaged in trade (Wang et al. 1997; Kuhn 2008, 335–337).

Once China's transition to a market-oriented economy began in the late 1970s, the Wenzhou natives were poised to expand their trade and production. Between 1978 and 1998 the region's industrial production value increased more than 120 times, from over 1.1 billion to 138.4 billion yuan. With an annual production of 2 billion pairs, Wenzhou was the number one producer of leather shoes in China. The region also produced sunglasses, cigarette lighters, clothing, electronic devices, and countless types of small goods—all sold in markets throughout China and in some regions overseas (Zhou 2013). What set the Wenzhou economy apart from others was its communal approach to business endeavors. Small and often family-run factories were known for their efficiency and flexibility; clustered together and linked to one another, they built extensive business networks and formed shared economies of scale, closely tied to their own distributors and vendors. By the 1980s, the region's agricultural population had shifted to manufacturing, commerce, transportation, and other services; over a thousand stores, for example, were selling electronic devices produced in the city of Liuzhou. Based on market information furnished by distributors and vendors within their own networks, the Wenzhou entrepreneurs never limited themselves to what they were already good at producing. Their flexibility in adapting to market-oriented production has been celebrated as the "Wenzhou character" (Fei, 1999, 461).

Wenzhou natives were highly mobile in the last three decades of the twentieth century. They seized domestic opportunities first in the early years of Chinese economic reform and spread out to at least 14 provinces by the late 1980s. In the nation's capital, Beijing, thousands of Wenzhou entrepreneurs formed a dominant force in a thriving enclave known as Zhejiang Village. They manufactured and sold a wide range of garments and footwear, offering urban consumers a variety of fashion choices at affordable prices. In the late 1990s, the Zhejiang Village reached a population of 96,000 residents, most of whom were either from Wenzhou or working for Wenzhou bosses. The 2010 Chinese census shows that over 1.2 million Wenzhou natives resided in other cities both large and small, especially in Shanghai, Beijing, Guangzhou, and Hangzhou. Meanwhile, household factories in Wenzhou continued their own production of textile and leather goods, accessories, and electronic devices, providing jobs for a huge influx of young workers from rural regions of neighboring provinces (Wang et al. 1997).

The late 1970s also marked China's re-entry into the global community after 30 years of isolation, creating new opportunities for Chinese people to find their ways across national borders. Following in the footsteps of the region's early migrants, the Wenzhou exodus was Europe-bound at first. Italy had a special appeal, as the migrants greatly admired its artisan tradition. In Tuscany and in Campi Bisenzio (between Prato and Florence), some migrants worked under subcontractors in leather and textile goods production. Being able to play a part in some of the world's most recognized fashion houses such as Versace, Gucci, and Armani was appealing, and many workers gained valuable business knowledge and experience in their adopted country.[1]

When Prato's textile industry declined, the Wenzhou migrants seized the opportunity. They moved in from nearby regions, bought abandoned machinery, and leased factory spaces at good bargains. Most newcomers became self-employed, subcontracting jobs from local contractors.

Opportunities to work and to start their own businesses encouraged the migrants to send for their family members, relatives, friends, and fellow villagers from elsewhere in Europe and China. The Chinese population in Prato increased from 169 in 1990 to 4,806 in 2001 and 10,080 in 2006 (Ottati and Cologa 2015, 33; Denison et al. 2009). By 2010, some 11,900 Chinese were officially recorded as living in Prato, although the number of undocumented migrants was estimated to be as high as 20–43 percent of the Chinese immigrants (Zhang, 2015). With more than 4,000 firms, Chinese enterprises constituted 25 percent of the city's businesses (Zhang, 2015). The migrants worked and lived in the city's historical center, identified as "Macrolotto 0," and especially in neighborhoods on Via Pistoiese. Located behind medieval walls that separated the busy urban center from quieter suburban residential areas, this area was once occupied by migrants from southern Italy. The growth of Chinese population gave rise to an ethnic business community. In addition to small workshops off the main road on the side streets were shops, restaurants, and supermarkets spread out in several blocks of Via Pistoiese, where Chinese-language advertisements for employment opportunities, housing, language and driving lessons, and a variety of services and entertainments covered the walls, shop windows, lampposts, and telephone poles (Bressan and Cambini 2009, 149).

On the surface, the Chinese community in Prato does not seem to be different from contemporary ethnic clusters in urban America. In Flushing, New York, for example, new Chinese migrants who speak little English run hotels, restaurants, supermarkets, and service businesses of many varieties. The difference is that Chinese have lived in the United States for more than 160 years, and their ethnic community has become an integral part of American society. Although those congregated in Chinatowns may have limited contact with the general American population, they are closely connected to the large Chinese American population and can utilize existing ethnic networks for employment and business endeavors (Zhao 2010). The newcomers in Prato, however, did not have such ethnic recourses and had to figure out how to survive on their own. While public assistance did help the newcomers to get started, their integration into mainstream society started slowly without existing ethnic community networks.

As subcontractors, Prato's migrant entrepreneurs relied on the labor of family members, relatives, or fellow migrants and worked for long hours to make ends meet. Their factories were usually small; each focused on a specific task. Dividing the production process into small components enabled more migrants to enter the business, and, being small, these shops were flexible enough to switch to different production when needed. Closely connected to one another, these factories could deliver large volumes of products on a tight schedule.

Like their fellow natives in Beijing and elsewhere, the business clusters of the Wenzhou people expanded rapidly in Prato. A variety of service-oriented ethnic enterprises also appeared, including restaurants, bakeries, markets, beauty salons, telephone booths, and internet cafes, as well as Chinese-language schools and newspapers. Neither the self-employed shop owners nor the Chinese ethnic business clusters in Prato were problems for the local residents at first. The small- and medium-sized family-owned enterprises were actually similar to many of those once operated by the Italians. At a time when young local residents showed little interest in the garment industry, the newcomers made it possible for local companies to stay competitive by cutting down 50 percent of the labor cost. As the direct cost of assembling garments was reduced to as little as five percent of the retail price, these companies were able to stay afloat without outsourcing overseas (Ceccagno 2009, 51).

Things might have been different if the newcomers had done nothing else but take jobs that few Italians wanted. Subcontracting from Italian manufacturers might have worked out for the migrants because it allowed them to be their own bosses. But only a small number of the migrants managed to remain as subcontractors for long. Not being able to win contracts on a reasonable bid was the first problem, as one Chinese entrepreneur in Prato explained. To be competitive, companies tried to offer as little as possible. Additionally, there were also many contractors or subcontractors that stood between the fashion houses and the self-employed producers; each would take a share of the profit. An additional 30–40 percent discount was expected if Chinese entrepreneurs wanted to get the bid. A contractor who made a high-end designer suit, for example, would receive 200 euro in the past, but a Chinese contractor would receive just 40 to 50 euro per piece.[2] Entrepreneur Chen Wenlong, who later registered for a brand of his own, said that making a living as a subcontractor was "impossibly hard" because the manufacturers lowered the pay but would not compromise on the quality (Pan 2015). "The Italians are extremely picky," said another former subcontractor. "They could always find some problems with the finished products, problems that were entirely invisible." Asked why the Chinese couldn't respect the local artisan tradition and meet the quality standard, he shook his head and quipped, "How could that be possible when they pay us so little? No skilled worker would do it."[3] "The Italians didn't want to do the job, and when the pay was so low, no one could afford to slow down," said another entrepreneur.[4]

It was not uncommon for migrant subcontractors to go out of business because of the high risk of not getting paid. Antonella Ceccagno, who conducted fieldwork in Prato, noted that Italian companies paid Chinese subcontractors every two months, but their checks were not cashable until three or four months later. This practice meant that it was easy for companies not to pay for the work delivered, as long as they could claim that the quality was unsatisfactory. It was also common for migrant subcontractors to have to declare bankruptcy; some Italian business owners would shut down their companies to dodge payments and then restart under different names (Ceccagno 2009, 60–61). Without power in local business networks, the newcomers felt (often rightly) that they had no protection from business fraud.[5] As a result, most of the Wenzhou migrants who had once worked for Italian textile industries left for other jobs.

This situation ultimately facilitated the growth of ethnic-based economic networks, through which the migrants cooperated among themselves and developed rules to protect their business interests. "There were cases of frauds and scandals," said a prominent member of the Chinese community, "but trust is most important in our business circle. If you broke the rules, you would be denounced and not be able to find people to work with anymore. Dealing with the Italians is a different matter. They could take advantage of you and walk away."[6]

Unlike migrants to California in the late nineteenth century, the newcomers to Prato in the late twentieth century were worldly. Equipped with cellphones, internet, and television, they were well informed of developments around the world. They traveled across the continents, flying between Italy and China frequently; some had been in many parts of Europe and the United States. The migrants may not have known much about the city where they lived beyond their own neighborhood; they may not have recognized some of the most well-known Renaissance artwork; they may have had very limited contact with the local residents, but they did not see themselves as isolated. Quite the opposite: they were well informed through television, the internet, and Chinese-language newspapers published in Europe and China. As entrepreneurs they searched for opportunities constantly. Their previous association with the textile industry through subcontracting and their transnational business networks enabled some migrants, particularly the Wenzhou migrants, to regroup and develop their own textile products (Xiao 2015).

In Prato, Chinese entrepreneurs utilized their communal business complex, built upon small family-run factories. As early as 1992, Chinese migrants had already established 200 businesses; each would typically subcontract work from two or three Italian companies (Ceccagno and Omodeo 1995). Many of these factories had only a few employees. Clustering together, they formed collaborations of scale, allowing the migrants to carve out a niche making their own products. Their first fast fashion firms appeared in 1996. By 2005, there were as many as 2,414 Chinese-operated businesses in Prato, moving fabrics from one shop to another to be dyed, tailored, assembled, and distributed. All the work for the final products, from design to finish, was done in one setting (Denison et al. 2009, 6). Gabi dei Ottati, who studied Chinese entrepreneurship in Prato, applied the industrial district theory to describe the production system of Chinese migrants. Within the district were countless specialized and highly competitive small factories involved in every aspect of production. These shops, she discovered, formed a "reciprocal cooperation" enhanced by common economic interest, shared ethnic origin, and social values, operating like a gigantic assembly line (Ottati 2014, 1250). Keen competition in the district pushed many to work long hours and sometimes around the clock. With smooth logistics, the production process could be completed in the neighborhood within a few days. The migrants also cultivated their transnational networks for supplies, manufacturing, and retail, and moved toward industrial chain production. In 2010, some 3,364 Chinese-run factories were in the garment-making trade, occupying more than 70 percent of the downtown buildings (Ottati 2014, 1256). The migrants also created their own wholesale warehouses for their "Made in Italy" products as well as imported apparels, attracting wholesalers and retailers from elsewhere in Italy and countries in Europe, North America, and Asia. The growth of migrant entrepreneurship transformed Prato from a relatively small provincial town into a major European exporter of fast fashion (Zhang, 2015).

The rise of anti-Chinese hostility

Fast fashion, which manufactures goods quickly and offers the latest fashion trends to consumers at a low price, was not invented by Chinese migrants. Before the arrival of the Chinese, some Italian companies had already made huge fortunes by shifting to fast fashion. Like their European and American counterparts, some of Italy's most competitive companies had long benefited from globalization by adopting new production methods and developing new products (*The Economist*, June 9, 2011). By 1995, Benetton had opened some 8,000 stores in 110 countries. Led by Benetton, Zara, H&M, and Topshop, fast fashion revolutionized the fashion industry. By reducing production time and cost, it changed the manufacturing process and made mass-produced, trendy, affordable items accessible to consumers. While the industry appealed to young consumers, especially women, it has generated debates concerning globalization, migration, labor, and environmental issues (Sull and Turconi 2008; Kelly 2013; *The Economist*, Sept. 5, 2015). Fast fashion has been blamed for the decline of slow fashion, which features durable, quality products, and, to some, reflects a high quality of life.

The worldwide transition from slow fashion to fast fashion exerted tremendous pressures on the textile industry in Prato. Although this switch took place before the arrival of the Chinese, the concentration of the newcomers in fast fashion made them an easy target. The success of Chinese entrepreneurship brought significant economic benefits to the local economy, as their merchandise attracted large numbers of Italian and European wholesalers, retailers, and street vendors. Compared to the likes of Benetton, Zara, and H&M, the Chinese-run companies in Prato were small and less-known. There is no evidence that their factories caused the further decline of Prato's textile industry. After all, their products targeted very different groups of retailers and consumers. Regardless, local business owners seemed to be disturbed by the fact that the Chinese were successful with their own products instead of doing what they were expected to do: in other words, they moved from being factory workers to entrepreneurs too quickly. Soon, more buyers were going to the warehouses of Chinese manufacturers than to the usual Italian fashion houses. As Ottati noted, hostility toward the Chinese correlated with the Chinese factories developing their own fashion products (Ottati 2014, 1259).

This hostility became apparent in the media, which, as Giovanna Campani indicates, has close ties with powerful business groups (Campani 2001, 40). According to Kevin Latham's analysis, the media showed little interest in the development of the Chinese community in Prato when the migrants first arrived; local broadcast and television programs simply ignored them (Latham 2015, 143). By the late 1990s, however, negative reports on Chinese migrants were commonplace in regional newspapers. The Florence-based newspaper *La Nazione*, one of the oldest Italian newspapers and a major media outlet for the Tuscany region, for example, portrayed the migrants as a potential danger to society. It attributed the further decline of Prato's textile industry to the large presence of the Chinese and their flourishing businesses. The newspaper was particularly interested in incidents involving undocumented Chinese or Chinese violators of business regulations. Whereas illegal and criminal activities in general were reported without reference to the wrongdoers' nationalities, the Chinese "miscreants" were characterized with racial remarks. Renzo Rastrelli, who systematically examined two Italian regional newspapers, including *La Nazione*, found that the paper often used "*giallo*" (yellow) as a substitute word for "Chinese" (Chinese) and tended to use individual incidents to generalize characteristics of the Chinese in general. Calling them "yellow mafia," reports in the newspaper portrayed Chinese migrants as members of a morally inferior alien group and linked crime to the Chinese race (Rastrelli 1999). On January 29, 2011, the newspaper quoted the prosecutor of Florence, Giuseppe Quattrocchi, who argues that all Chinese community organizations were "Mafia-like associations" (*La Nazione* 2011). Without citing specific sources, the paper depicted Chinese-operated businesses as having laundered proceeds to evade taxation, generated hundreds of millions of euros from criminal activities, and transferred the money to China. It also broadly accused Chinese entrepreneurs of being people who received "stolen goods" or embezzled money (*La Nazione* 2010). Racializing and criminalizing the entire Chinese migrant community, the media worked to drum up fear of a Chinese invasion, paving the way for the rise of anti-immigration political forces in the region.

If the media portrayal of Chinese migrants as gang members, thieves, and lawless people reflected the hostility of the business community toward Chinese entrepreneurs, it also worked effectively to shape public opinion against the Chinese. Citing complaints about Chinese migrants, from the ways that they housed themselves and raised their children to the ways they spoke, interacted, and conducted their everyday lives, the media was able to reframe these problems in the context of Chinese culture (Williams 1995, 2004). Presenting violations of housing, business, and immigration regulations by individuals as representative of Chinese in general, the media was instrumental in developing stereotypes against the Chinese. It worked to instill the ideal that the Chinese way of life was fundamentally in conflict with that of the Italians, and that Chinese culture and traditions should be rejected by the Italians. Acts of hostility against Chinese people became widespread in Prato and beyond. In Milan, resentment of the locals toward the pushcarts that the migrants used to transport garment products led to an open conflict between the police and the Chinese migrant community, which, according to a report in *The New York Times*, signified "a battle of cultures, business and lifestyles" (Rosenthal and Povoledo 2007). To some Italians, the difference in culture was a serious matter: accepting Chinese migrants meant allowing the Chinese to change the Italian way of life.

The fear of a Chinese invasion was pervasive in Prato. Speaking to the camera of a news reporter, one Prato woman said, "The Chinese industry has sown dangerous seeds. It threatens the town's economic development. Because of the culture's illegality, it's like a virus spread through the healthy economy" (AFP 2010). Chinese communities in Italian urban centers, as frequently pointed out by the media, were evidence of territorial invasion (Rastrelli 1999). More threatening, as *La Nazione* warned its readers, was the economic invasion launched by the Chinese, for the migrant manufacturers had committed a "commercial fraud" by using the "Made in Italy" label (*La Nazione* 2010). Some stern media echoed the argument that depicted Italy as the victim of globalization. An essay in *The Wall Street Journal*, for example, attributed Italy's "loss of competitiveness" to competition from both China and "colonies of Chinese immigrants [in Italy]" and claimed that both in China and Italy the workers "toil on machines that were designed in Italy, sold to China, and then copied for use by the low-paid Chinese workers" (Stelzer 2010).

Beginning in the late 1990s, the Italian government sought ways to redefine the term "Made in Italy" through new regulations. Some laws restricted the "Made in Italy" label to products that were totally made in Italy, from planning to manufacturing and packaging. This alone was insufficient because the migrants manufactured their goods in Italy. One piece of legislation, known as the Reguzzoni-Versace Law, required manufacturers of textiles, shoes, and leather goods to meet regulations concerning labor, "hygiene and product safety," and "environmental matters" to be eligible for the "Made in Italy" label (Galli 2010). Although the "Made in Italy" label has been mostly recognized in four areas—fashion, food, furniture, and mechanical engineering—the Reguzzoni-Versace Law targeted fashion products, for most Chinese migrant manufacturers were in textile and leather goods production. Thus, by imposing other regulatory measures on Chinese-operated businesses, the law could prevent Chinese migrant enterprises from using the "Made in Italy" label without naming them. No restrictions were imposed on Chinese subcontractors, however. In other words, the Chinese migrants were not entirely excluded from the "Made in Italy" production process. They could participate as subcontractors or laborers, but not as manufacturers.

New regulations concerning the "Made in Italy" label generated an international debate. Many European business associations had long engaged in globalization of production, in which planning, designing, and manufacturing took place in multiple locations. Legal experts were quick to point out that some of the new regulations were not only practically impossible to enforce, but also contradicted EU laws and the Italian Constitution (Galli 2010). Perhaps because it targeted the Chinese, however, the "Made in Italy" controversy had an international appeal. Major European and US media outlets referred to the "Made in Italy" label as a glamorous and "prestigious" designation associated with world-class companies, whereas Chinese manufactured goods were cheaply made using fabric imported from China and illegal migrant workers. In these reports, Chinese migrant entrepreneurs in Italy were described as operators of sweatshop-like factories that violated health and safety regulations and labor laws, or as individuals who committed business fraud (*The Economist* 2013). A group of Italian manufacturers, led by Maurizio Bonas, organized the Consortium for the Protection of Made in Italy and campaigned to protect their reputation as quality producers (Ridgwell 2010; Vicziany, Fladrich, and DiCastro 2015).

The anti-Chinese narrative created a fear of an invasion by Chinese migrants, a fear that was fueled by the rise of China and its impact on Italy's economic growth. In "The Siege of China," Silvia Pieraccini, a reporter who wrote on Chinese businesses in Prato, situates the use of the "Made in Italy" label by migrant workers in the context of China's invasion of Italian manufacturing through globalization (Pieraccini 2011, Ridgwell 2010). Her arguments suggest that the newcomers had taken over the textile industry in the city by utilizing their transnational economic networks. Accordingly, the migrant business network "contains the entire supply chain—from buying the fabrics in China, importing them into Italy, cutting them, dyeing them, assembling the pieces and selling them directly to the retail outlets" (Pieraccini 2011). Her report was frequently quoted by Western newspapers and provoked a fear of China, where the migrants originated. A similar depiction of Chinese migration was found in a US-based online essay, "Chinese Conquer Prato." Portraying Prato as the victim of "yellow invasion," the essay featured a photograph of what looks like a bridal shop to illustrate its point. In the photograph, behind the window display of dresses, was a large framed wedding picture. Standing tall in a bright red dress, the Chinese bride smiled confidently at the camera. A red bouquet in one hand, she rested the other hand on the head of her partner. The groom, who appeared to be Caucasian, was positioned below the woman's shoulder at a lower corner of the picture. In a bright red shirt, he appeared "conquered" and wore a submissive look on his face (Ludwig, undated). The way in which the couple was staged in the photo, as well as their facial expressions and the color of their outfits, all seemed to suggest a helpless Prato fallen prey to a powerful invasion from a rising China.

Widespread anti-Chinese sentiment in Prato eventually gained momentum in local politics. Mayor Romagnoli, who had acknowledged the migrants as an economic "blessing," had tried to introduce Chinese culture to the community and develop policies and social programs to help the newcomers adjust. But his administration was under constant attack from political opponents from the right, especially those affiliated with the textile industry (Ehlers 2006). Assistance from the media was critical for the right-wing political groups to gain public support. In 2007, the city informed the Chinese migrants that they were not allowed to parade on the street during their New Year's celebration (Castro et al. 2009). As the business community, media, and politicians from the right joined forces to declare the Chinese to be the major problem facing the city, anti-Chinese sentiment began to dominate Prato's political debates. Romagnoli decided not to run for the 2009 election. The parties he represented, which had governed the city since the end of World War II, lost to parties that campaigned for tightening regulation of Chinese migration and entrepreneurship (Ottati 2014, 1259). This development was encouraged by politics in the national arena, as the conservative government led by Silvio Berlusconi had come to power in Italy during the parliamentary elections of 2008. Once in office, Berlusconi promised that he would create policies to imprison illegal migrants (Castro et al. 2009).

The election of Roberto Cenni as the city's mayor in 2009 indicated how anti-Chinese sentiment was played out in local politics. A wealthy businessman in the textile industry, Cenni won the election by scapegoating Chinese migrant entrepreneurships. His campaign was racially charged, depicting the newcomers as illegals, tax evaders, and labor law violators. He identified Chinese engagement in fast fashion as a threat to principles of Italian quality products (Vicziany et al. 2015, 218). He also urged the European Union to take action against a "Chinese invasion" (Kennedy 2010). Openly expressing his own distaste for cultural differences, he associated the Chinese migrants with "noise," "bad habits," and "prostitution," and said that they made people of European origin "sick" (Donadio 2010).

Once in office, Cenni kept his campaign promise and moved quickly to clean up Chinese-run businesses. He repeatedly authorized highly publicized raids of Chinese enterprises, as discussed at the beginning of this chapter. In the words of Linda Iervasi, the head of the Prato police's immigration division, these raids were "repressive in nature" (AFP 2010). The government claimed, however, that its actions were intended to crack down on unlawful business operations, end unsafe practices, and protect the workers from exploitation. Iervasi replied that her job was not to punish hardworking people, but rather to "try to educate those who work in the business. They have to respect the rules and the dignity of the workers" (AFP 2010). Ironically, when factories were shut down and business owners were fined, the workers were the ones who suffered the most. Those who had no work permits were arrested, and those who were set free were not allowed to return home (Dinmore 2010). The government showed no concern for the welfare of migrant workers, let alone their dignity.

The entire Chinese migrant community began to live in fear almost immediately after Cenni took office. Many entrepreneurs left the city; the influx of new migrants had declined by 46 percent a year later (Ottati and Cologna 2015). But the new municipal government stated that it had not done enough because its law enforcement units were understaffed. To crack down on the entire Chinese business community would require "an army of people," one official proclaimed (Donadio 2010).

To make the lives of the Chinese more difficult, the city government also initiated regulations against the cultural practices of the newcomers. In addition to prohibiting the Chinese from celebrating Chinese New Year in the streets, regulations prevented migrants from drying fish on balconies, and shopkeepers were required to speak Italian (Donadio 2010). Legal discrimination and police raids encouraged acts of racial hatred against the Chinese in Prato. In one incident, a wealthy Chinese businesswoman was forced to leave a nightclub because she entered the mezzanine level reserved for rich Italians (Duranti 2007a: iv).

Conclusion

The rise of anti-Chinese sentiment in Prato, featuring police raids, racially charged remarks in newspapers, restrictions on Chinese businesses and cultural practices, and public denunciation of Chinese migration, is reminiscent of the anti-Chinese movement in California more than one hundred years ago. In both cases, Chinese migrants were depicted as mysterious human beings with inferior cultural traditions and low morality, and they were blamed for creating unfair competition for workers and entrepreneurs of European origins. For Prato, a city that had had little contact with foreign migrants until recently, the lack of racial tolerance was sometimes seen as the result of its lack of ethnic diversity and interracial contact. But Prato was not alone: anti-Chinese raids and riots have taken place in other parts of Italy and around the world (Kington 2007; Suibian 2013). It is important to note that there was no apparent sign of racial hatred in Prato when the Chinese first arrived. Both the news media and the local citizens recognized the potential contributions that immigrants could bring to the society in times of economic difficulty. After the arrival of a large number of Albanians in March 1991, however, the mood changed, and the media began to portray immigrants in general as a threat to the nation (Campani 2001, 45).

Anti-Chinese hostility in Prato, although it seemed to address local conflicts (relatively few Albanian immigrants went to the region), was not an isolated incident, but rather a reflection of national politics at a particular historical time.

Whereas the situation in Prato concerning manufacturing processes is unique, it seems to be tapping into a wider, global-scale anti-Chinese narrative in the context of a rising China. This new anti-Chinese force has suggested that China's integration into the world economy has posed a serious challenge to a global order dominated by the West, turning places like Prato into victims of open borders. In this sense, the contemporary anti-Chinese sentiment is quite different from the one in late nineteenth-century California, for the latter was constructed around a deep conviction that China and Chinese civilization had reached an advanced state of decay. Whereas Chinese migrants of the late nineteenth century believed that the Qing government was too weak to support its people overseas, the new migrants in Italy sought help from the Chinese embassy and consulates and hoped their government could provide more trade and exchange benefits to Prato. Prato and Wenzhou, homes of the migrants at both ends, have since formed friendship cityhood status, which brings Chinese buyers to the Prato area for high-end textile products and wine (Hooper, 2010). The government of Tuscany also opened a trade office in Shanghai to promote tourism and commercial exchange (Dominici 2014). While it is still too early to assess the impact of these developments on the local economy, it is also unclear how connections with China would be played out in the context of anti-Chinese narratives that tend to associate Chinese migration with the threat of a rising China.

What is also important to note is that many of Prato's residents did not support racial discrimination and have been critical of their government (Castro et al. 2009). For example, some locals protested the ban of the Chinese New Year celebration in 2007. Led by a group of young Prato artists called Senza Dimora Fissa, the protesters ridiculed and denounced the "regime of fear" (Castro et al. 2009). A local survey showed that only 39.7 percent of Prato's residents sided with the city council decision, while 46.3 percent dissented. The latter argued that the Chinese festival could have been turned into an opportunity for the city's cultural enrichment (Castro et al. 2009). In addition, sharp criticism against xenophobia from scholars, writers, and ordinary citizens alike has raised racial consciousness among Italian citizens. In *The Horde: When We Were* the Albanians (*L'orda, quando gli albanesi eravamo noi*), Italian writer Gian Antonio Stella brought memories of the past alive by showing that foreign migrants in Italy are now experiencing what Italians experienced in northern Europe, Australia, and North America in the early and mid-twentieth century (Stella 2004). Both the book and its author have become immensely popular, indicating a growing pro-immigrant sentiment. Persistent economic difficulties, however, have made immigrant issues politically complicated. Because the Italian media is closely associated with political power and Italian journalists are largely free to use racial remarks, as the country's leaders continue to lean to the right, anti-Chinese and anti-immigration narratives and sentiment are almost certain to continue.

Notes

1 Interviews with the author, July 1–15, 2014. In Tuscany, Prato, Rome, Florence, and several other Italian cities, many Wenzhou migrants had once worked for Italian companies. Those who still contracted from Italian companies were proud. Others also valued the experiences.
2 Interview with Mr. Xu by the author, July 2, 2014, Prato.
3 Interview with Mr. Li by the author, July 2, 2014, Prato.
4 Interview with Mr. Xu by the author, July 2, 2014, Prato.
5 Interview with Mr. Zhang, Prato, July 2, 2014.
6 Interview with Mr. Dai, July 10, 2014, Rome.

References

AFP. 2010. AFP footage, "Police raid businesses in Italy's Little China,'" 19 Dec 2010. http://www.gettyimages.com/detail/video/it-is-one-of-the-biggest-chinese-communities-in-europe-news-footage/107770930. Retrieved Nov. 16, 2015.

Bo Yuan (博源). 2010. "普拉托华人社区到处布满了荷枪实弹的警员 (Armed police everywhere in Prato's Chinese Community)." www.chinanews.com, 21 Jan 2010, accessed on Nov. 15, 2015 at http://www.chinanews.com/hr/hr-ozhrxw/news/2010/01–21/2083895.shtml

Bressan, Massimo, and Sabrina Tosi Cambini. 2009. "The 'Macrolotto o' as a Zone of Transition: Cultural Diversity and Public Spaces." In *Living Outside the Walls: The Chinese in Prato*, eds. Graeme Johanson, Russell

Smyth, and Rebecca French. Newcastle upon Tyne, UK: Cambridge Scholars Publishing, 149–160.

Campani, Giovanna. 2001. "Migrants and Media: The Italian Case." In *Media and Migration: Constructions of Mobility and Difference*, eds. Russell King and Nancy Wood. London and New York: Routledge, 38–52.

Castro, Angelo Andrea Di, and Marika Vicziany. 2009. "Chinese Dragons in Prato: Italian-Chinese Relations in a Small European Town." In *Living Outside the Walls: The Chinese in Prato*, eds. Graeme Johanson, Russell Smyth, and Rebecca French. Newcastle upon Tyne, UK: Cambridge Scholars Publishing, 174–191.

Ceccagno, Antonella. 2009. "Chinese Migrants as Apparel Manufactures in an Era of Perishable Global Fashion: New Fashion Scenarios in Prato." In *Living Outside the Walls: The Chinese in Prato*, eds. Graeme Johanson, Russell Smyth, and Rebecca French. Newcastle upon Tyne, UK: Cambridge Scholars Publishing, 42–74.

Denison, Tom, Dharmalingam Arunachalam, Graeme Johanson, and Russell Smyth. 2009. "The Chinese Community in Prato." In *Living Outside the Walls: The Chinese in Prato*, eds. Graeme Johanson, Russell Smyth, and Rebecca French. Newcastle upon Tyne, UK: Cambridge Scholars Publishing, 2–25.

Dinmore, Guy. 2010. "Tuscan Town Turns Against Chinese Immigrants." *Financial Times*, February 8, 2010. http://www.ft.com/cms/s/0/e3ae8e02 –1519–11df-ad58–00144feab49a.html#axzz3sxWCfRjd

Dominici, Laura. 2014. "Italy targets Chinese tourists to catch a new, potentially enormous consumer market." *Il Sole 24 Ore*, Dec. 1, 2014. Accessed on Feb. 13, 2016, at http://www.italy24.ilsole24ore.com/art /markets/2014–12–01/italy-targets-chinese-tourists-to-catch-new-potentially-enormous—consumer-market-135924.php?uuid=AB5WzGKC

Donadio, Rachel. 2010. "Chinese Remake the 'Made in Italy' Fashion Label." *The New York Times*, Sept. 12, 2010. http://www.nytimes.com/2010/09/13 /world/europe/13prato.html?_r=0

Economist, The. 2011. "Benvenuto, up to a Point: The World Comes to Italy." June 9, 2011.

Economist, The. 2013. "Chinese in Italy: Seven deaths foretold." Dec. 2, 2013.

Economist, The. 2015. "Faster, cheaper fashion." Sept. 5, 2015.

Ehlers, Fiona. 2006. "The New Wave of Globalization: Made in Italy at Chinese Prices." *SPIEGEL ONLINE News—International*, 2006. http:// www.spiegel.de/international/spiegel/the-new-wave-of-globalization -made-in-italy-at-chinese-prices-a-435703-druck.html 5/6. Retrieved Nov. 15, 2015.

Fei Xiaotong (费孝通). 1999. (小商品, 大市场), in 费孝通文集, Vol. 10, 群言出版社, 455.

Galli, Cesare. 2010. "New rules on designations of origin and 'made in Italy' designations." International Law Office, June 1, 2010. http://www.internationallawoffice.com/Newsletters/Intellectual-Property/Italy/IP-Law-Galli/New-rules-on-designations-of-origin-and-made-in-Italy-designations. Retrieved Jan. 2, 2016.

Hooper, John. 2014. "Made in little Wenzhou, Italy: the latest label from Tuscany." *The Guardian*, 7 Oct. 2010. http://www.theguardian.com/world/2010/nov/17/made-in-little-wenzhou-italy. Retrieved Dec. 12, 2015.

Kelly, Cara. 2013. "Cheap, trendy 'fast fashion' in demand, despite factory dangers." *The Washington Post*, June 28, 2013. https://www.washingtonpost.com/lifestyle/style/cheap-trendy-fast-fashion-in-demand-despite-factory-dangers/2013/06/28/b10ceb74-d906-11e2-9df4-895344c13c30_story.html. Retrieved Dec. 20, 2015.

Kennedy, Duncan. 2010. "Coming into fashion: A Chinese mark on Italian clothes." *BBC News*, October 26, 2010. http://www.bbc.com/news/world-europe-11622809

Kington, Tom. 2007. "Italy's First Major Ethnic Riot Sparked by Parking Fine." *The Guardian*, April 13, 2007. http://www.theguardian.com/world/2007/apr/13/italy.tomkington

Kuhn, Philip A. 2008. *Chinese Among Others: Emigration in Modern Times.* New York: Rowman & Littlefield.

Latham, Kevin. 2015. "Media and Discourses of Chinese Integration in Prato, Italy: Some Preliminary Thoughts." In *Chinese Migration to Europe: Prato, Italy, and Beyond*, eds. Loretta Baldasar, Graeme Johanson, Narelle McAuliffe, and Massimo Bressan. New York: Palgrave Macmillan, 139–158.

Liu Xiao (小刘). 2010. "普拉托政府已从对华人企业罚款中收入 18 万欧元 (Prato government have received 180,000 euro worth of fines from Chinese enterprises)." 华人街新闻快递 (news.huarenjie.com), Nov. 10, 2010. http://www.huarenjie.com/article-100710-1.html. Retrieved Nov. 15, 2015.

Ludwig, Gerd. Undated. "Chinese Conquer Prato." Undated. Gerd Ludwig Photography. http://www.gerdludwig.com/stories/chinese-conquer-prato/#id=album-51&num=content-592. Retrieved Jan. 2, 2016.

Magrini, Graziano. Undated. "Museo Del Tessuto [Textile Museum]. http://brunelleschi.imss.fi.it/itineraries/place/MuseoTessuto.html. Retrieved Oct. 11, 2015.

Meichtry, Stacy. 2011. "Italian Police Raid Chinese Business." *The Wall Street*

Journal, June 22, 2011. http://www.wsj.com/articles/SB10001424052702304 88790457639990015803489o

Nazione, La. 2010. Mafia cinese, maxi blitz della GdF: 24 arresti. Feb. 28, 2010. http://www.lanazione.it/prato/cronaca/2010/06/28/350739-mafia_cinese _maxi_blitz.shtml. Retrieved Nov. 22, 2015

———. 2011. "Quattrocchi: In Toscana c'è allarme per mafia russa e cinese." Jan. 29, 2011. http://www.lanazione.it/firenze/cronaca/2011/01/29/450869 -quattrocchi_toscana_allarme_mafia_russa_cinese.shtml. Retrieved Nov. 22, 2015.

Ottati, Gabi Dei. 2014. "A transnational fast fashion industrial district: an analysis of the Chinese business in Prato." *Cambridge Journal of Economics* 38, 1247–1274.

Ottati, Gabi Dei, and Daniele Brigadoi Cologna. 2015. "The Chinese in Prato and the Current Outlook on the Chinese-Italian Experience." In *Chinese Migration to Europe: Prato, Italy, and Beyond*, eds. Loretta Baldasar, Graeme Johanson, Narelle McAuliffe, and Massimo Bressan. New York: Palgrave Macmillan, 29–48.

Pan Xianqun (潘贤群). 2015. "温商在普拉托创办 3000 家企业打造 快时尚之城" (温州网–温州都市报). June 26, 2015. http://news.66wz.com /system/2015/06/26/104492954.shtml. Retrieved Dec. 23, 2015.

Pieke, Frank N. 2004. "Chinese Globalization and Migration to Europe." Working paper No. 94, Center for Comparative Immigration Studies, University of California at San Diego, March 9, 2004.

Pieraccini, Silvia. 2011. L'assedio cinese. Il distretto senza regole degli abiti low cost di Prato. Gruppo 24 ore. https://silviapieraccini.wordpress.com /about/. Retrieved Nov. 12, 2015.

Qingtian huaqiaoshi bianxie zu (青田华侨史编写组). 2007. Qingtian huaqiaoshi (青田华侨史), 2007.

Rastrelli, Renzo. 1999. "Immigrazione cinese e criminalità: Analisi e riflessione metodologiche." *Mondo Cinese 105*. http://www.tuttocina.it /mondo_cinese/105/105_rast.htm

Rhoads, Christopher. 2003. "Threat from China starts to unravel Italy's cloth trade." *The Wall Street Journal*, Nov. 29, 2003. http://www.wsj.com/articles /SB107161541398247900. Retrieved Nov. 15, 2015.

Ridgwell, Henry. 2010. "Ancient Italian Town Turns against Chinese Migrants." *VOA*, Oct. 22, 2010. http://www.voanews.com/content/ancient -italian-town-turns-against-chinese-migrants-105597568/128777.html. Retrieved Dec. 24, 2015.

Rosenthal, Elisabeth, and Elisabetta Povoledo. 2007. "A Pushcart war in the streets of Milan's Chinatown." *The New York Times*, April 26, 2007. http://

www.nytimes.com/2007/04/26/world/europe/26iht-italy.1.5452099.html. Retrieved Jan. 6, 2016.

Stella, Gian Antonio. 2004. *L'Orda: Quando gli Albanesi eravamo noi*. Milan: Rizzoli.

Stelzer, Irwin. 2010. "Warning Signs Are There for Italy." *The Wall Street Journal*, Nov. 29, 2010. http://www.wsj.com/articles/SB10001424052748704700204575642970912894894. Retrieved Nov. 15, 2015.

Suibian (随辩). 2013. "西班牙政府在新年伊始就对华商进行大规模检查 (Spain Government Conducts Large-Scale Investigations toward Chinese Entrepreneurs at the Beginning of New Year)." 欧洲侨报 (China Press in Europe), Jan. 10, 2013.

Sull, Donald, and Stefano Turconi. 2008. "Fast Fashion Lessons." *Business Strategy Review*. 5–11.

Vicziany, Marika, Anja Michaele Fladrich, and A. Andrea Di Castro. 2015. "Religion and the Lives of the Overseas Chinese: What Explains the 'Great Silence' of Prato?" In *Chinese Migration to Europe, Prato, Italy, and Beyond*, eds. Loretta Baldasar, Graeme Johanson, Narelle McAuliffe, and Massimo Bressan. New York: Palgrave Macmillan.

Wang Hansheng, Liu Shiding, Sun Liping and Xiangbiao (王汉生, 刘世定, 孙立平, 项彪). 1997, "'浙江村': 中国农民进入城市的一种独特方式," (社会学研究) 1, 1997, 56–71.

Williams, Daniel. 1995. "No Welcome for Foreigners." *The Washington Post*, October 15, 1995. https://www.washingtonpost.com/archive/politics/1995/10/15/no-welcome-for-foreigners/ac588832-5c41-4304-86eb-1dcb367acd90/?utm_term=.004f90ce9592

Williams, Daniel. 2004. "Chinatown is a Hard Sell in Italy." *The Washington Post*, March 1, 2004. https://www.washingtonpost.com/archive/politics/2004/03/01/chinatown-is-a-hard-sell-in-italy/0af367e7-8193-411f-aedb-9680b7d24778/

Wen Shan (文山). 2010. "普拉托加倍对华人企业地毯式检查: 华商提抗议 (Pulatuo jiabei dui huaren qiye ditan shi jiancha; huashang ti kangyi)." 中国新闻网 china.com.cn, Jan. 22, 2010. http://www.chinanews.com/hr/hr-ozhrxw/news/2010/01-22/2086127.shtml. Retrieved Nov. 10, 2015.

Xiao Fei and Liu Yong (肖飞、刘勇). 2006. "意大利普拉托华人移民的喜与忧." 欧洲时报, Dec. 26, 2006, http://bbs.qyer.com/thread-65956-1.html. Retrieved Dec. 23, 2015.

Zhang Gaoheng. 2015. "'Made in Italy' by Chinese in Prato: The 'Carrot and Stick' Policy and Chinese Migrants in Italy, 2010–11." *China Policy Institute Blog*, The University of Nottingham, Oct. 22, 2015. http://blogs.nottingham.ac.uk/chinapolicyinstitute/2015/10/22/made-in-italy-by

-chinese-in-prato-the-carrot-and-stick-policy-and-chinese-migrants-in
-italy-2010–11/. Retrieved April 2, 2016.

Zhao Xiaojian. 2010. *The New Chinese America: Class, Economy, and Social Hierarchy.* New Jersey: Rutgers University Press.

Zhou Huanhuai (周欢怀). 2013. "从社会排斥角度解读海外华商遭受反华事件的原因 (Interpreting the Causes of Oversea Anti-Chinese Entrepreneurs Events from a Perspective of Social Exclusion)." 改革与开放 (Reform and Opening), April 2013.

CHAPTER 5

~

Yellow, Red, and Black

Fantasies about China and "the Chinese"
in Contemporary South Africa

ROMAIN DITTGEN AND ROSS ANTHONY

IN FEBRUARY 2014, the *Mail & Guardian*, one of South Africa's most influential newspapers, published two provocative cartoons[1] about the country's—and the continent's—growing and interlinked ties with China (see Figures 5.1 and 5.2). Raising the issue of foreign financing of political parties, the first cartoon mockingly hints at the Chinese government's strong (yet concealed) influence on domestic government policies. Of late, the impression that South Africa's ruling party is drawing closer to the Chinese government is increasingly evident. Media coverage of high-profile political exchanges and seminar tours, the hosting of the sixth edition of the Forum on China–Africa Cooperation (FOCAC) in Johannesburg in December 2015, the planned introduction of Mandarin into school curricula, and, more generally, a "looking East" rhetoric and enchantment about the so-called "China model," all seem to point toward the swift expansion of China's role in various parts of society. The second drawing (Figure 5.2) displays three large Chinese excavators temporarily—and somehow futilely—blocked by a single child-carrying black African woman. Invoking the image of the famous "unknown protester" from Tiananmen Square in 1989, this cartoon alludes to fears and anxieties that China, depicted as a dominant and unstoppable force, is embarking on an exploitative path of "industrial colonialism" with disastrous consequences for "Africa's environment" and its resources.[2]

FIGURE 5.1 "Foreign financing of political parties," Zapiro, published in the *Mail & Guardian* and the *Sunday Times*, February 9, 2014.

In the past two decades, South Africa's developing relationship with China has raised numerous concerns among various segments of the public. Unions, the media, political parties, and the business sector, among others, have been critical of Chinese engagements on a number of fronts. Their critiques include allegations of collusion with the government at both the political and commercial levels, with complaints over the influx of cheap (and fake) goods, concern about large numbers of illegal migrants outcompeting local businesses and, more recently, apprehensions about an imminent relocation of polluting and bottom-end Chinese industries to Africa. Some of these fears draw on earlier historical tropes of the "Yellow Peril," common at the turn of the twentieth century both within South Africa but also as part of a broader Western-based global imaginary of China. Then and now, China is depicted as threatening in a twofold manner: on one hand, it is associated with moral hazard and the fear of "the horde"; on the other hand, it is a source of anxiety in terms of its perceived ingenuity and connectedness to powerful sectors of society, including industry and government.

While there are similarities between these two notions, contemporary manifestations of the "Yellow Peril" are unfolding in a specific geopolitical context. Africa, for so long associated with Western powers, is increasingly engaging with an expanding number of "rising" economies, among which China features as the most prominent and visible. Admired for the swiftness of its development path, China is increasingly envisioned as an alternative or diversified form of modernity. Concomitantly, the decrepit and fragile condition associated with China's socialist era has gradually eroded, overtaken by the formidable success of the market-reform period. Yet, at the same time, the magnitude of China's vast economy and population, as well as the scale of its ballooning cities, creates demands for a substantial amount of resources, which can be seen as threatening to other nations. Thus, today's occurrence of the "Yellow Peril" draws on strands of its inception over a century ago, alongside fresh anxieties that require new forms of conceptualization.

South Africa, often portrayed as different or exceptional within the African context (in terms of its infrastructure and its financial and institutional landscape), is also host to a vast and multilayered Chinese presence. In the absence of rigorous statistics, it is roughly estimated that there are between 350,000 and 500,000 Chinese people[3] living in South Africa today[4] (Park 2012). If other countries across the continent, mostly confined to the Southern Africa region, have experienced earlier encounters with Chinese,[5] South Africa nonetheless offers the most diverse and extensive portrait. The overall scope stretches from the tens of thousands of indentured laborers (eventually repatriated to China) joined by smaller ranks of "free" migrants lured by the gold rush toward the end of the nineteenth century (the latter making up the historical bedrock of the Chinese presence in South Africa), followed by the Taiwanese industrialists and wholesalers of the apartheid era, attracted by favorable government incentives, to the more recent and significant numbers of mainland Chinese arriving from the mid-nineties onwards.

Despite the diversity of actors, interests, temporalities, and spatial translations, "the Chinese"[6] are often lumped together and seen as connected pieces of one monolithic bloc. Alongside this more generic view, perceptions of "everything Chinese" are nested in a distinctive South African reality that includes the legacy of apartheid, high rates of crime, serious levels of unemployment, and a highly unequal society, which takes into account the socioeconomic breadth of Chinese people present in the country. Even more than 20 years after apartheid, South Africa remains very divided, along both racial and socioeconomic lines.[7] Indirectly, this is also mirrored in the differentiated ways in which segments of the society formulate or engage with the idea of "Yellow Perils": while the poor (and predominantly black) working class are mostly concerned about economic competition and job losses, the middle and upper classes (primarily white and including fewer members of other racial groups) are worried about forms of political collusion and high-level cronyism. In examining how variations of stereotyped representations of "the Chinese" as both "docile pets and nefarious invaders; potential citizens and inassimilable aliens" (Cheung 2007, 293) have travelled from nineteenth-century Western societies to twenty-first-century South Africa, we get a better understanding of the way "fragments of a seemingly distant past" "continue to echo into the present" (Tchen and Yeats 2014, 17, 23).

Besides separating myth from reality, this chapter aims to make sense of the ways the "multitude of expressions to denote different aspects of China and Chinese-ness" (Chun 1996, 111) feed into the socioeconomic and political landscape as well as the everyday life of South Africa. Although the term "Yellow Peril" now feels somewhat out of date, "having emerged at a specific moment of crisis and consolidation" (Tchen and Yeats 2014, 14), it remains useful for raising questions about the ways in which different perceptions of Chinese threats are deployed within a multiracial and multiclass society. A crucial thread that links nineteenth- and early twentieth-century notions of the "Yellow Peril," with the persistence of anxieties around Chinese-ness, is the role of capitalism on an international scale. Both then and now, issues of international markets, labor, and commodities, as well as questions of colonialism and "neocolonialism," are pertinent, although in very different contexts. While at the turn of the century, Chinese in South Africa were largely subjects of an international labor regime focused on mining, within the present context of multinational capitalism, the Chinese presence is highly multivalent, ranging from the role of petty traders to capitalist titans of industry, often backed by the state. The amalgamation of past and present, then, has contributed toward a highly varied understanding of the current Chinese presence in South Africa. Fredric Jameson has referred to the overwhelming complexity of contemporary global capitalism as *cognitive dissonance* (1991), reflected in the disjointed, fractured, and fragmented cultural expressions in contemporary experience and reflected in art, electronic media, and literature. As a dimension of this process, the Chinese presence within South Africa, driven largely by market forces at a variety of scales, is reflected locally in a general condition of dissonance in which South Africans battle to grasp this new condition from a number of different angles.

The colors from the title of this article—"Yellow, Red, and Black"—speak directly to this plethora of fears, from the general ones—such as "red (communist) China," "red money," and "Yellow Peril"—to more contextualized ones, namely "the Chinese" benefiting from the status of being considered "black." Through drawing on a range of local phenomena, including media outputs, the circulation of commodities, the development and expansion of visible urban landmarks, and the figure of the migrant, an ambivalent and evolving notion of anxiety is portrayed. Torn between desire and fear, fantasies about "China" and "the Chinese" therefore not only provide insights about predominant Chinese features and dynamics in South Africa, but also help to shed light on the host society itself.

Sick and encroaching yellowness

Although emerging from different economic conditions, today's "Yellow Peril" anxieties resonate with the conception of "the Chinese" at the turn of the twentieth century. A significant part of Asian migration during this earlier period can be situated within the context of nineteenth-century European capitalism (Bayly 2004). Independent former colonies (such as the United States, Australia, and South Africa) as well as Russia and the American West all drew on Asian labor pools to supplement their workforces, particularly in the agriculture and extractive sectors. With regard to the latter, new metallurgical technologies developed at the turn of the twentieth century led to massive capital investments on a global scale (Cass and Van Helten 1991, 177). This included Indian indentured laborers brought into regions of East and Southern Africa as well as Japanese and Chinese to Australia, South Africa, the West Indies, and North America. Indigenous labor was considered erratic. In the South African mining industry in the early 1900s, for instance, labor supply dwindled during times of drought and disease, increasing the need for imported labor (Chen 1923, 128).

The expansion of European influence occurred globally in tandem with dire domestic conditions in late nineteenth-century China (Spence 1991). The Qing Empire was in a state of rapid decline, with the result that China acquired the unfortunate moniker in the West of "The Sick Man of Asia." China had been subject to territorial annexation by several European states and Japan, two successive Opium Wars (British and Franco-British), as well as the humiliating conditions of the Treaty of Versailles. Population density and land scarcity put immense pressure on communities;[8] ultimately the population outstripped the food supply and forced a large-scale exodus of Chinese during this period.

In the first decade of the twentieth century, over 60,000 Chinese were brought in to work as unskilled laborers on the Witwatersrand gold fields of South Africa, the largest in a series of labor importation schemes (Bright 2013). In 1903, colonial administrator Lord Alfred Milner wrote that the white population required to carry out the labor could not be provided in the "immediate future," and black labor, despite all attempts to increase its numbers, could "not be sufficient to supply our wants in the early future" (Harris 2002, 69). This led to the decision to "call in the aid of the Asiatics" (ibid., 69), and the above-mentioned Chinese population were recruited in 1904 to the Transvaal and repatriated in 1910. It was during this period that laws were implemented that sought to restrict Chinese ownership, trade, land rights, and citizenship, such as the Cape Chinese Exclusion Act of 1904, which was a direct response by the Cape Colony to the Chinese indentured labor scheme in the Transvaal. At the same time, mining magnates, the Chamber of Mines, and labor brokers mobilized a pro-China labor campaign in order to smooth over local tensions. Anxiety was, in part, driven by fears that many local laborers' livelihoods would be threatened by the Chinese who were vying for these same jobs.

The move to bring in overseas labor was resisted mainly by "overseas trade unionists and politicians, members of the Transvaal commercial sector, clergy, prominent Boer leaders and their followers, as well as white colonists of the other local and overseas British territories" (Harris 1998, 121). Harris also mentions some "rare" instances of black African responses to the Chinese migrant situation, which portray their presence as a threat to the Western civilizing mission and to black native laborers (ibid., 127). During one parliamentary debate, a Progressive Party member claimed that "the Colony had been swamped by Chinamen," that they were "at our doors," and involved "in every kind of business" (ibid., 239). Another criticized the Afrikaner Bond, which had been in power for the previous 15 years, for their role in welcoming the over 1,000 "Chinamen" already trading in the country under licenses, and declared that every one of them was "driving out a white man and his family" (ibid., 239).

In addition to white settlers' concerns of being swamped, there were anxieties around Chinese collusion with the bosses of South Africa's mining magnates. A cartoon from the *South African News* (January 14, 1904) features the caption, "Forecast of 1906—From a Chinese point of view," depicting a gentrified Chinese man with a white boy bowing before him. In the background, a "Chinese Only Barrier," with hordes of Chinese fading into the background, is shared with a sign stating "Capital," referring to the exploitative mine owners bringing labor from abroad. In the Transvaal, whites and Indians frequently protested that the Chinese took "Whites Only" rickshaws, and that they "did not know their place" (Bright 2013, 102). We can see this anxiety surfacing around perceptions of Chinese entrepreneurship and the Chinese work ethic. One commentator noted "their narrow, tireless industry, pushed beyond a virtue to the level of a defect, coupled with their excessively low standard of living" (Harris 1998, 123). In a British periodical published in March 1903, the author, writing on the Chinese labor question in South Africa, noted the following:

> The natural condition of the white man appears to be a state of rest. Not so the Chinaman; his natural condition is one of ceaseless activity; it requires no effort on his part to commence work, and when once started, he goes on forever like a steam machine . . . [they] would go on forever if they were not stopped. (ibid., 123)

Chinese immigrants in South Africa were additionally dehumanized through stereotypical Orientalist depictions (Harris 1998, 2004; Huynh 2008; Bright 2013). The portrayal of the Chinese as a faceless mass who could "take over" from Westerners, in addition to their enclavization, was often made in terms of moral depravity through "unnatural crime"— that is to say, homosexuality—(Harris 2004), opium, prostitution, sickness, disease, and gangsterism. Referred to as "celestial vices," this was compounded with a quasi-mysticized othering, personified in the likes of Dr. Fu Manchu (Frayling 2014), and coupled with the reification of exoticized customs (Chinese opera, pole dancing, dragons, etc.) that fit into the broader "Chinoiserie" craze, particularly in Europe at the turn of the twentieth century. This ambivalent notion of the Chinese Other, portrayed simultaneously in both positive and negative terms, has been noted both within the South African context (Huynh 2008; Park 2013) and more broadly in relation to attitudes from Europeans toward the Orient (Bhabha 1994).

Times have changed, and so have the characteristics of the Chinese presence in South Africa. Forms of capital accumulation have evolved or, according to Jameson, "mutated" from monopoly capital (or imperialism) to a new regime of multinational capital (Jameson 1991). For Harvey, the transformative and speculative logic of capital has produced new regional trade and political alignments, new flows of information, and new patterns of mobility and settlement (Harvey 1989). Yet, despite this radical transformation, "the Chinese" are still (if not increasingly) seen as "coming" and threatening the sovereignty of postcolonial societies in Africa. If, in South Africa, the fear of "everything yellow" has become at once subtler and more obvious, it has simultaneously taken up new forms, ranging from the power of the Chinese state to the figure of the "nefarious" migrant.

The politics of image versus the image of high politics

In recent years, the relationship between the People's Republic of China and South Africa has deepened significantly, evidenced by a raft of economic and political proclamations. These range from the lofty upgrading of South Africa to "Strategic Comprehensive Partner" of China in 2010 to the celebrations of the "Year of South Africa in China" in 2014 and the "Year of China in South Africa" the following year. For many ordinary South Africans, however, these events mean little to nothing, existing in a stratosphere of a "public" diplomacy that in fact is not at all public. Rather, most South Africans' views of China are shaped by interactions on a very different level: with Chinese traders (both men and women), Chinese goods, and Chinese-run malls, frequently associated with an illegitimacy that alludes to the "knock off," "the copy," and "the fake" (Huang 2015), which has led to a scrutiny of the rights of Chinese citizens to live in South Africa. None of this is helped by occasional overtly Sinophobic South African media pieces, whose allegations include Chinese Communist Party plans to flood South Africa with Chinese petty traders and dictate to South African politicians policies favorable to China.[9]

Notwithstanding, a growing number of statements and actions expressed by the South African government in recent years have displayed growing support for China. For instance, the ruling ANC's (African National Congress) 2015 National General Council (NGC) discussion document identifies a new "Cold War" in which "the exemplary role of the collective leadership of the Communist Party of China in this regard should be a guiding lodestar of our own struggle." President Jacob Zuma has stated that his respect for China is based on how they treat South Africans as "brothers and sisters," rather than "second- and third-class citizens"—alluding to South Africa's historical treatment by the West (*Republic of South Africa* 2014). In addition to the deepening of state ties, party-to-party relations have also strengthened in recent years; for example, in 2014, the ANC sent members of its National Executive Committee to Beijing for three weeks of management and organizational training (Alden and Wu 2014, 9). The South African government has in turn sent several delegations to China to study their state-owned enterprise model so as to aid South Africa in expanding and reforming its industrialization program.[10] Conversely, bureaucratic obfuscation preventing the Dalai Lama from visiting South Africa on three different occasions[11] and the Chinese government's funding of an ANC Party school[12] have led to suggestions that the ANC-led government is making a geopolitical turn toward China (see Figure 5.1). Some fear that China's political model, in which the party has ultimate power over the state, offers a worrying precedent to ANC leaders, who have become increasingly hostile toward civil society, the media, and government oversight bodies. The South African media (accused by the ruling party and other critics as a vocal, liberal class of largely white South Africans who disproportionately dominate the South African media landscape), as well as civil society groups and others, have expressed a weariness regarding state-to-state and party-to-party relations between the two countries.[13]

Such relations have fed into the perception that, by strengthening South Africa's relationship with China, the South African government is compromising on its post-apartheid mission of commitment to human rights and democracy. The largest opposition party, the Democratic Alliance, is particularly critical of these developments. Members have expressed concerns about certain agreements between the two countries; in the case of the recent cyber security pact with China, for example, the Democratic Alliance Party has raised the issue of China's Internet censorship and how this may compromise the agreement.[14] In 2015, the announcement that Mandarin will be offered as an option in South African primary schools led to a major outcry. The general secretary of one of South Africa's main teaching unions, the South African Democratic Teachers Union, issued a statement declaring that "as during colonialism [. . .], we see it as the worst form of imperialism that is going to happen in Africa."[15]

China's economic relationship with South Africa offers further concern. Beyond the fact that China has been South Africa's largest trading partner since 2010, with a total trade volume of USD $24 billion in 2014 (the balance being largely in China's favor, by more than USD $6.5 billion[16]), the announcement on December 3, 2015, that China will be committing an additional USD $6 billion to South Africa only confirms skeptics' fears of growing economic subordination (see Figure 5.2). Nonetheless, reactions to China's engagement tend to overlook the fact that while, at least ideologically, the South African government is aiming for multiple international engagements to develop its economy, Europe and the United States continue to be significant trading partners, with Foreign Direct Investment (FDI) from these regions far surpassing that of China. India, for instance, is the only BRICS (Brazil, Russia, China, and South Africa) country in the top five sources of FDI in South Africa.[17] As in many other resource-rich African countries, while the bulk of exports to China are mineral reserves, South Africa's developed infrastructure, the fact that local companies compete with Chinese companies, and the political clout of the domestic labor unions have kept Chinese FDI at the periphery.[18] Thus, China's engagement with South Africa needs to be situated within the broader international political economy. The former's integration into the global market system, its growth of a consumer-oriented middle class, and its outward-bound commodity forays to support both domestic and international consumption make it a dominant player in the arena of global capitalism while still espousing theoretical commitment to Marxist-Leninism. China's engagement in Africa appears to be an extension of this process.

FIGURE 5.2 "China's industrial colonialism in Africa," Zapiro, published in the *Mail & Guardian* and the *Times*, February 20, 2014.

Localized imaginaries, discourses, and impressions

If China's macroeconomics and its official relations with the outside world (in particular with the African continent) are high on the news agenda, it often seems difficult to grasp the immediate and tangible effects on the ground. Today's anxieties have become more complex, are voiced in a different regime of capitalism, and their resulting visual representations exist in the realm of "the faceless," "the unknown," or "the mystical." Locally, i.e., in Johannesburg, however, it is rather the figure of the small migrant-entrepreneur, the prevalence of goods, and a range of urban markers that emerge as the most visible projections of transnational Chinese capital. Related media coverage might be limited and is often based on anecdotes; yet, simultaneously, it offers a glimpse of existing views of the "common Chinese"[19] and related features embedded in the urban landscape. A few years back, a well-known South African fast food restaurant chain produced a TV commercial aimed at promoting its varied menu by comparing it to the diversity of the country's population. Deliberately provocative, the ad critically engages with the place foreigners occupy in South Africa and featured Chinese migrants alongside Cameroonians, Somalis, Zimbabweans, Nigerians, Pakistanis, Indians, Zulu, Xhosa, Tswana, Afrikaners, and others.[20] Their incorporation can be seen as a sign that, for the general public in South Africa, "the Chinese," at least in Johannesburg, have progressively become an integral (yet somewhat anomalous) part of the urban imaginary. At the same time, being depicted as traders operating in the shady informal sphere indicates that representations of Chinese people in the South African press and public opinion are often associated with this type of activity. Apart from indirectly referring to notions of visibility and invisibility, as well as characteristics of Chinese urban dynamics (Harrison et al. 2012), it also raises the question of the predominant nature of "Chinese-ness" in urban South Africa (Dittgen 2017).

The massive internal changes that China has undergone in the past few decades have led to large-scale migration both internally, from the countryside to the cities, and abroad. The arrival of new Chinese migrants to South Africa—legal and illegal—picked up significantly toward the end of the 1990s and again at the turn of the century (Park 2008, 159), adding an additional layer on top of an already complex and multiform Chinese presence[21] (Hyunh et al. 2010). If it became much easier for mainlanders to enter the country following South Africa's recognition of the PRC, links between the official representation from Beijing (in the form of an embassy as well as a consulate-general) and immigrants have, at least in the early stages, remained either non-existent or very limited.

Concurrently, imaginaries of "the Chinese" as traders are often closely tied to anxieties about the ubiquity of "Made in China." The continuous decline of the South African textile and clothing industry since 1994, both in terms of GDP and in numbers, has largely been attributed to the rising competition from imports, mainly coming out of Asia— China in particular. The sector, having lost half of its workforce since 2003 (or more than 350,000 jobs), was severely affected by domestic shifts (currency appreciation between 2003 and 2010 as well as rising labor costs) and, internationally, by China's dominant position as the leading producer of affordable textiles and clothing, especially after joining the WTO in 2001 and following the expiry of the multifiber arrangement[22] in 2005 (Nattrass and Seekings 2012). The level of market penetration is felt most strongly in labor-intensive sectors such as clothing and textile, making Chinese products a serious source of concern for the sustainability of the industry. In response to pressure from the Confederation of

South African Trade Unions, a close ally of the ruling party at the time, the South African government decided to impose a two-year import quota of some 200 clothing items, with the agreement of China. However, these temporary measures (effective between 2006 and 2008) had little impact and also failed to reform an outdated domestic textile industry (Alden and Large 2011, 31). In the absence of a comprehensive restructuring, it was simplistic to blame (only) China for all the ills of the industry, which are in fact related to a lack of adaptation to globally interconnected commercial circuits (Draper and Alves 2006, 4–5).

Accusations of a Chinese-led imperialism and direct government orchestration of the Chinese migrant influx have also popped up on the South African media landscape. One of the most blatant examples was featured in a cover article for the October 2012 edition of the widely read monthly magazine *Noseweek*, South Africa's only investigative publication.[23] The author compared the rapid mushrooming of Chinese shops to "the country's biggest-ever chain store," "a largely unlawful enterprise threaten[ing] to destroy local commerce," marked by an "increase in fraud," and a "well researched, well-planned, well-organized and well-financed project." The author not only insinuates that Chinese migrant-entrepreneurs are behind the massive surge of "Made in China" in South Africa, but also asserts that a highly organized and centralized network collaboration exists between these shopkeepers.[24] Such allegations of a stereotyped monolith mark the constitution of a "spectacular Chinese othering" (Sylvanus 2009, 68), obscuring much of the more complex and differentiated economic realities.

If rumors and the invocation of a scapegoat are classic responses in the context of deprivation and change (Sylvanus 2009, 66), these narratives are also associated with the ways Chinese products are marketed. While making up the bulk of the commercial offer in South Africa, attitudes toward "Made in China" evolve depending on the type and location of the point of sale. Within South Africa, Chinese products sold in the numerous "China stores" are often referred to as "Fong Kong." The term, while referring to goods manufactured in China, mostly resonates with the image of cheap, poor quality, and fake material. Ultimately, if local chain stores are associated with social modernity and increasing purchasing power (despite a highly unequal society), Chinese malls are often correlated with low-end globalization and commercial dumping.

However, due to decreasing profit margins in clothing, more and more Chinese traders—admittedly still limited in numbers—have started selling electronic equipment such as hi-fi systems, televisions, CCTV cameras, and LCD lights. Most are Chinese brands and are marketed as high-quality products, while still cheaper than similar counterparts produced by internationally renowned brands. If textiles, clothing, and other small commodity goods from China suffer from bad reputations, perceptions of Chinese technological items (for example, *Hisense* TVs or *Huawei* cellphones) are less unfavorable and increasingly convey the idea of a modernity alternative to the West.

Apart from images linked to the movement of people and to the commercialization of consumer goods, perceptions of things "Chinese" are also associated with the built environment. In Johannesburg, existing Chinese footprints are diverse, ranging from spaces concentrated in specific areas such as the corporate presence in the financial heart of Sandton in the Northern suburbs, the large number of Chinese-run malls in the Southern outskirts of the agglomeration, and two Chinatowns (one historic and limited in size, the other more recent and expanding), to scattered instances of residential or economic presence. Out of all the aforementioned, it is the second Chinatown in Cyrildene, located in the Eastern parts of Johannesburg, around which most of the negative perceptions are concentrated. Due to its late development at the beginning of the early 1990s, the Chinese neighborhood breaks out of the archetypal configuration of a Chinatown, often characterized by a central location and historic embeddedness. A noodle bar owner, who relocated to Derrick Avenue, was the first visible Chinese marker in the main strip alongside Portuguese greengrocers, delis, and kosher butcheries. All of the latter gradually closed down and made way for swelling numbers of Chinese-run restaurants and supermarkets (Accone 2008). During the mid-nineties, Taiwanese ran the bulk of businesses, but little by little they were taken over by mainlanders (mostly from Fujian province) following the exodus of most of the former migrants in light of increasing crime rates and concerns about the political future during that time. The swift proliferation of Chinese-run businesses, from around 40 in 2004 to 167 units by mid-2011 (Harrison et al. 2012, 918), has had an impact not only on the real estate value, with high demand pushing up the prices, but also on the overall dynamic of the area.

In the absence of an overall coordination,[25] Derrick Avenue resembles a disorderly band made up of different businesses and activities. The arrival of the Chinese in the neighborhood has—either implicitly or explicitly—been seen as responsible for a surge in crime, to the extent that, in local newspapers, Cyrildene has (until recently) regularly been mentioned in connection with shady dealings, from triad activities, a mafia network, illegal prostitution, cases of kidnapping, and racketeering to various kinds of trafficking.[26] This stereotyped and simplified portrait of filth, depravity, violence, and immorality resonates very strongly with historic pictures of "whorehouses, gambling joints and opium dens" in major American Chinatowns at the turn of the twentieth century (Light 1974, 367–368; Shah 2001). At the same time, Derrick Avenue and surrounding streets are mainly an entry point for Chinese migrant workers with limited means in search of a relatively familiar environment and a place of ethnic belonging (however transient) in light of limited (or non-existent) English proficiency as well as ambivalence about integrating into South African society. If, for non-Chinese, the area appears at once exotic, mysterious, and unknown, for the Chinese, perceptions about Cyrildene are primarily informed by class and precedence in the country. For many local Chinese (or South African–born Chinese), Taiwanese, and the mainlanders who have been in South Africa for much longer, Cyrildene is often derogatorily referred to as dirty, dodgy, and dangerous,[27] pointing toward a disconnection not only between different waves of immigration but also increasingly between ethnic and socioeconomic categories (Shih 2007).

Similar to Chinatowns in large Western or Asian cities, which evolved from vice districts to tourist attractions (Light 1974), the perception of Derrick Avenue is slowly changing in the minds of the average Johannesburg inhabitant. While most of the businesses along the strip are primarily directed at Chinese migrants who either live there or pass through, the area is also attracting an increasing number of South Africans and tourists (both local and from abroad) who are eager to gain some exposure to an "oriental" atmosphere. The inauguration of one of the two entrance gates[28] by former South African president, Jacob Zuma, in October 2013 is a reflection of this dualism; on the one hand, it symbolizes the official acknowledgment of the Chinese presence in the country; on the other hand, there is a growing interest on the part of the City of Johannesburg in shaping Chinatown into a commercial and (desired) cultural landmark, seen as part of the city's push for an increased globalized identity. While focused on Chinatown, this localized example also raises broader questions about where exactly in society the Chinese fit.

In the new South Africa, the so-called rainbow nation, color and race still matter. As stated in her book *Paper Sons and Daughters: Growing up Chinese in South Africa*, Ufrieda Ho, herself a Johannesburg-based South African–born Chinese, talks about how, at the dawn of democracy, "the Chinese still felt too black for some, too white for others and economically, socially and politically they were still pushed up against the margins" (Ho 2011, 215). In another passage of the memoir dealing with identity and belonging, she recalls the feeling of "[waking] up black—legally black, that is" (ibid., 222) one morning in June 2008. As victims and previously disadvantaged under the apartheid regime, some of the local Chinese applied, as early as 1999, to "be included in the definition of 'black people' in terms of the broad-based Black Economic Empowerment Act and the Employment Equity Act" (Park 2008, 147) alongside black Africans, Indians, and Coloreds. While applicable to less than 10,000 people,[29] in most media outlets this ruling was presented as if all Chinese in South Africa would, henceforth, benefit from affirmative action, triggering initial concerns that the influx of new Chinese migrants would steal away the limited number of available jobs. Although none of these fears have materialized, they nonetheless show how heterogeneous categories of migrants are often conflated into one group and that historic fears of invading hordes of Chinese continue to surface. Further confusion arises from the fact that, on the one hand, among those who can legally claim "black" status, most are well integrated, pursue liberal professions, and tend to adopt a suburban way of life, generally correlated with the idea of "whiteness."[30] On the other hand, the bulk of the new Chinese migrants, trying to make a (meager) living as traders (or employees) and, at least in theory, socioeconomically closer to the black African–dominated working class, are largely living in isolation from the host society. Although it is difficult to establish a direct causal link, a higher socioeconomic status and level of integration seems to have a partial influence on reducing racial and cultural differences. In practice, it is also among these categories of Chinese people in Johannesburg that interracial marriages (if numerically still limited and mostly between Chinese and whites), relationships, and social mixing are the most common.

The Yellow Peril and late capitalism in the twenty-first century

One of the most notable differences between China's current relationship with South Africa and its previous connection is that China has now become a formidable global economic and political power. This contrasts significantly with the late nineteenth century, when the Chinese state was weak and when Europe controlled vast swathes of the globe. Now South Africa, and the world more broadly, operates in an increasingly multipolar world in which countries such as those in the BRICS alliance claim to offer their own form of market capitalism with a significant degree of state intervention. This is expressed in ways that would not have been intelligible a century ago—as representations of China in Africa today reflect a very distinct reality—and reflects a very different form of engagement within the broader global political economy. South Africa, in this regard, is but one fragment of a much larger process internal to China's shift from a command economy toward a neoliberal one, in which state actors now play a crucial role in fostering economic growth at the level of the populace (Anagnost 2004; Greenhalgh and Winckler 2005).

A key feature of this is China's self-conscious staging of itself as modern within the context of its increasing integration into the global economy—and how that is playing itself out in the Global South. Domestically, China's economic transition has resulted in a massive urbanization process that has been accompanied by numerous expressions of this modernity, from both above and below (Ren 2013). Nationally, the Chinese state is eager to display and promote this modernity or postmodernity, encapsulated in images of hyper-sophisticated urbanization, as well as in the rise of a desiring consumer class (Rofel 2007; Zhang and Ong 2008) and a state ideology that encourages urbanization and middle-class prosperity (Wang 2015). Abroad, particularly in the Global South, China has made an impression as a robust development partner, with the lion's share of infrastructure development in Africa now implemented by Chinese firms. Financially backed by powerful policy banks, such as China's Exim Bank, state and private companies offer assistance predominantly to developing world countries in the form of infrastructure development, technology transfer, trading zones, and medical and educational assistance (Brautigam 2009). A Chinese bank, the Industrial and Commercial Bank of China (ICBC), now owns significant shares in one of South Africa's major banks, Standard Bank.[31]

Within South Africa, coming to terms with China as a form of neoliberal or late capitalist actor is increasingly embedded in South Africa's own neoliberal economy. China's presence as a major international competitor can be seen in places like Johannesburg's financial center, Sandton, where buildings such as the Sinosteel Plaza and the China Construction Bank punctuate the landscape of other local and multinational high-rises (Harrison et al. 2012). In 2013, the Shanghai Zendai company, a private Chinese property developer, announced plans to build the "New York of Africa"[32] in the form of a massive USD $6.4-billion urban development project, projected to house 100,000 people and include a financial center, schools, and light industry facilities. For the Economic Freedom Fighters, a leftist and very vocal opposition party,[33] the sale of 1,600 hectares of land to Chinese hands amounts to "putting South Africans on sale in the world's markets for the benefits of global ruthless capital."[34] Notwithstanding some of the local reactions, these shifts contribute toward at least one portrayal of contemporary China as a formidable figure of capitalist economic development.

Another highly symbolic element is China's political relationship with South Africa, and Africa more broadly. This has occurred in tandem with a concerted effort by Chinese institutions to engage in a global soft-power initiative (Nye 2004), of which Africa is a significant recipient. Within South Africa five Confucius Institutes have been introduced—centers that partner with local universities and promote Chinese language and culture. China stages spectacles of gift-giving, embodied in the tri-annual Forum on China–Africa Cooperation event[35] and in the funding and construction of the new African Union headquarters and a connected permanent mission in Addis Ababa. Additionally, China is one of Africa's largest UN peacekeeping contributors in Africa. Certain African politicians have even spoken of emulating the "China model."[36] This form of representation, a far cry from the "Sick Man of Asia," promotes a sense of formidable economic and geopolitical clout.

While containing vestiges of the old "Yellow Peril" mentality, engagements with China today are based on a very new reality. In the current China–South Africa relationship, there are certainly allusions to the old fears of collusion between Chinese laborers and local power brokers at the turn of the twentieth century. Yet, in the present context, such anxiety functions largely at the level of state-to-state relations, rather than in a relationship between mining companies, labor brokers, laborers, and the like. Such anxiety also spills over into concerns around how politics is linked to financial engagements. The often non-transparent relationships between the political elites in the country and powerful foreign actors such as Chinese corporations and the Chinese government state extends further into the notion of "the Chinese" more generally, referring to everything from the local small shop owner to members of the highest echelons of state. Within such conceptualization exists the implicit assumption that "the Chinese" are a single, coordinated actor from top to bottom. In Johannesburg, where numerous Chinese traders operate inside Chinese-run malls, this assumption is false. The mushrooming of these malls during the first ten years of the 2000s and the concurrent influx of increasing numbers of Chinese migrants, all trying to succeed in business, generated high levels of competition. In the present context of slow economic growth and a quasi-saturated market (given the more general expansion and availability of affordable goods), business opportunities and profit margins have dropped significantly. This has resulted in direct rivalry, mistrust, and the absence of close business cooperation between Chinese traders, leading to increasingly differentiated and individualized entrepreneurial trajectories.[37]

Nonetheless, the notion of a monolithic presence and its collusion with government persists, as can be seen in the *Noseweek* article (2012) when it asks of the South African government, "Why has the South African government gone soft on Chinese immigration—or, rather, turned a blind eye to the mass of illegal immigrants from China who have quietly settled in as if nothing was the matter?" While there are overlays in this paranoiac association, and that of the inception of the Yellow Peril threat, the current perception is reflective of China's "rise" in the twenty-first century, and thus feeds into a narrative in which South Africa, the weaker state, has succumbed to China's powerful economic and political influence.

The "horde" anxiety, expressed in the nineteenth century, has resonance within South African discourses today (although the majority of Chinese in South Africa are involved in trade, as opposed to labor). What is significantly different is how anxiety now extends to the "flood" or "tsunami" of "cheap" goods into the country[38]—a phenomenon that did not yet exist at the turn of the twentieth century. The notion of cheap or fake goods inundating local markets functions almost as an extension of the anxiety around Chinese people themselves, that is to say, the notion of being swamped by a force of dubious character. Nevertheless, this stereotype does not portray the entirety of the Chinese goods market in South Africa today. Goods at large franchises—also for the most part imported from China—are stripped of their origins and identity and marketed as fashionable and upscale products. Consequently, in an increasingly consumer- and commodity-driven society, the image and sociocultural value attributed to products [in this case Chinese] appear to play a particularly important role (Sack 1988, 643–644, cited by Goss 1993, 20). Contrary to common beliefs attributing the "invasion" of cheap products to Chinese traders, the latter's share is rather limited in comparison to other major economic players. The South African retail sector remains largely dominated by a handful of local franchises (such as *Woolworths*, *Edgars*, *Foschini*, and *Mr Price*), accounting for about 60 to 70 percent of all sales nationwide (Robbins et al. 2004, 15), that are by far the main importers of Chinese ready-to-wear fashion.[39]

While having repeatedly been labeled as responsible for job losses in the South African manufacturing sector, Chinese wholesalers (mainly operating from within malls) are, although unintentionally, playing an important role in the informal economy. As suppliers of flexible quantities of goods, Chinese wholesalers and more specifically the Chinese-run malls have become significant resource spaces for a wide collection of economic operators, ranging from intermediate wholesalers and shopkeepers to hawkers, each adopting different strategies to resell the purchased commodities (Dittgen 2015, 59–60).

At an individual level, the "successful" and "unlawful" Chinese migrant-entrepreneur, perceived by some as an economic threat, is also increasingly singled out by criminals. Positioned at the edge of the formal and informal economy, Chinese traders almost exclusively resort to cash to handle commercial transactions (both bulk and retail). While appealing in terms of profit maximization due to (partial or complete) tax avoidance, this market strategy also comes with dangerous side effects. In a city such as Johannesburg, where physical violence and other risks are an integral part of everyday life—aspects that strongly influence business conduct—"the Chinese" are increasingly shaped into soft targets.

Being Chinese in South Africa is often correlated not only with economic success and cash accumulation, but also with illegal immigration, lack of language proficiency, and operating at the margins of society. While simplistic and incomplete, these imaginaries are interpreted as weaknesses and have a direct effect on the lives of all Asian people (whether Chinese or mistaken for Chinese) in Johannesburg. Believed to carry large amounts of cash, their racialized "yellow" bodies fall increasingly victim to armed heists and attacks.[40] In this regard, the clustering of Chinese wholesalers within enclosed and secured mall environments has not eradicated criminal risks, but rather transplanted them outside the premises in the form of car hijackings and violent house robberies (ibid., 53–56).

At the same time, racial profiling is not only limited to criminal activities but also emerges as a recurrent theme when Chinese people engage with police forces. The aforementioned stereotypes of alienation form the basis for harassments and bribery requests by corrupt metro cops. While "the Chinese" are not the only ones to be affected by this widespread misconduct, they are generally seen as an easy prey. Due to poor English, newer migrants are more easily inclined to pay bribes "because they have little means of either expressing their grievances or interrogating the reasons for a demand for payment" (McNamee et al. 2012, 22). Their willingness to resolve problems with money, without any major complaints, helps to perpetuate this practice. Several Chinese traders in Johannesburg mentioned attempts to circumvent this problem by avoiding certain routes known for traffic blocks or, at least in one case, by hiring a white informal taxi driver to avoid police controls.[41]

The complex and diversified pattern of present Chinese engagements is not easily encapsulated by these earlier models. The most inadequate of these, of course, is grappling with China as a sophisticated market economy that is interlinked globally and competes with actors in South Africa and beyond. This is coupled with new global groupings, such as BRICS, which point toward an increasingly multipolar world. In terms of economic power, South Africa today is, despite Chinese rhetoric of "win-win" and "harmonious cooperation," both politically and economically the junior partner in this relationship. At present, ambivalence around the notion of Chinese superiority lingers, not as a force for good, but rather as a malevolent presence at both the state and individual levels. This is further complicated by the fact that the opening up of China has led to an increase in migrants, many of whom earn only a meager living in South Africa; this leads to a contradictory image of China as, at once, a "developing economy" and a "global superpower."

Conclusion

The early twentieth century phenomenon of the Yellow Peril has been revived in the twenty-first century, serving as a trope to account for the contemporary rise of the Chinese presence in South Africa. As with the earlier Yellow Peril phenomenon, a similar subtext of anxiety permeates contemporary discourses on the Chinese in South Africa—including the persistence of viewing Chinese as physically, morally, and spiritually bankrupt. Nevertheless, this trope has, at the same time, proved to be an inadequate social model within the context of twenty-first-century global capitalism and the role China plays in it. Within this contemporary context, it is not only a Chinese underclass, such as petty traders, that continues to be viewed as a threat; the latter now also extends to an entirely different class of Chinese—large state and private corporate actors, often with strong backing from the Chinese government. In many respects, the fears articulated within mainstream media continue to draw on earlier representations of Chinese—particularly insofar as they are untrustworthy and collude with powerful actors in business and government.

However, within the contemporary world of global capitalism and China's increasing integration within this system, the singling-out of this global actor (i.e., China) as negative tends to detract criticism from the broader spectrum of foreign investors in Africa (including the European Union, the United States, Australia, India, Brazil etc.), of which China is merely one player. Additionally, while the Yellow Peril discourse persists within mainstream South African discourses, sporadic violence against foreigners has been directed mainly at migrants from sub-Saharan countries such as Zimbabwe, the Democratic Republic of Congo, Somalia, and Mozambique. This is not to say that Chinese people do not face forms of everyday violence including demands for bribes, robbery, kidnapping, and even murder, but rather to point out that sporadic xenophobic outbursts in the past have not directly targeted Chinese people. It suggests that the anxiety over the Chinese presence within South Africa expresses itself in unique ways, which are different to how certain other foreign communities are perceived. Unlike the Chinese laborers at the turn of the century, who directly challenged the employment security of black and white mine laborers alike, today's Chinese actors, from the level of the trader to the executive, inhabit a series of economic niches that appear not to directly threaten the most impoverished in society. Rather, contemporary forms of anxiety around the Chinese frequently stem from their perceived threat to the elite, liberal, and largely white establishment, whose interests are perceived as threatened by Chinese capital and its integration with local state actors. In this vein, the anxiety around the Chinese presence poses—or at least is perceived as—an existential threat to this establishment.

Overall, neither the image of a "dreamworld," in which China—through the advent of "industrial modernity—could and would provide happiness for the masses," nor of a "catastrophe" or "nightmare," where the influx of Chinese capital and people, "indifferent to the well-being of the masses and unfettered by political constraints" (Buck-Morss 2000, xiv), crushes the local economy, fully applies in the South African case. Aside from the ubiquity of Chinese-made goods as well as rather isolated examples of business competition and opportunities, today's relevance (as well as fear) of China and "the Chinese" has, thus far, remained limited in light of more pressing issues related to socioeconomic inequalities, crime, and various challenges regarding service delivery in a post-apartheid setting.

This being said, the persistence of Yellow Peril tropes signifies a general failure to grasp the contemporary presence of China in South Africa and more globally. It is partly informed by the referential context of education, still largely dominated by the West. Many African countries, often due to earlier colonial influence, lack educational capacity (or interest) in terms of engaging with Asia.[42] Furthermore, outside of occasional (official) embassy communiqués, Chinese people in South Africa tend to keep a low profile. Perhaps, as Jameson has argued in terms of the bewilderment of late capitalism, a new kind of "cognitive mapping" is required, one that can help reorient societal thinking so as to better grasp this overwhelming context. In certain quarters, this issue is increasingly explored in new forms such as the visual arts, cinema, and literature, within both Africa and China, which is presently hosting sizable numbers of African migrants (Haugen 2011; Li et al. 2013; Castillo 2014). Given the historicity and complexity of the Chinese presence in South Africa, some of the more established Chinese have started to become more vocal and, subsequently, more visible to other segments of society. These subtle changes unfold in various forms, such as the existence of a few (partly) autobiographical memoirs on identity, hardship, and belonging (Accone 2004; Chen 2009; Ho 2011),[43] occasional outcries and marches organized by Chinese communities following incidents of crime specifically directed at them, the celebration of the Chinese New Year in Johannesburg, and the growing appetite for Chinese food and flavors, as well as a growing number of individuals of Asian descent who speak with local accents. While encounters between the host society and the Chinese remain fragile and tentative, the emergence of new trends and daily interactions is creating alternatives that could lead to more substantial engagement.

Notes

1   "Foreign financing of political parties" (http://mg.co.za/cartoon/2014–02–10-anc-agang-foreign-funding), "China's industrial colonialism" (http://mg.co.za/cartoon/2014–02–20-chinas-industrial-colonialism; both accessed September 19, 2015).

2   Eight years earlier, the same cartoonist (Jonathan Shapiro, known as Zapiro) produced a sketch of a product-shaped Asian tsunami (with the products being mostly from China) flooding and crushing the remainder of an ailing industrial landscape in Africa, showing that fears, far from being static, evolve as well ("Another Asian tsunami," https://zapiro.org/cartoons/060601mg, accessed September 15, 2015). A few days after the conclusion of the 6th FOCAC meeting, Zapiro produced another cartoon showing President Xi pushing a price-tagged African continent in a shopping trolley, alluding to anxieties about Africa being sold to China and becoming a "Chinese takeaway" (http://mg.co.za/cartoon/2015–12–08-africa-becomes-a-chinese-takeaway, accessed December 10, 2015). Apart from work by Zapiro, a number of other cartoonists have produced similar drawings. For instance, one by Dr. Jack & Curtis shows President Xi on a Chinese junk filled with labeled boxes of purchased "goods" ranging from politics, power, business, and transport to property loans pulling away from the South African coast, leaving behind a waving Zuma, the South African president, and a "sold" sign on a billboard with the inscription "Junk status country for sale." (Published by *City Press* on December 7, 2015, accessible on John Curtis's Twitter feed, https://twitter.com/digitaljungle, accessed February 15, 2016). On the same day

(December 7, 2015) *Business Day* published a cartoon by Brandan Reynolds showcasing Xi Jinping waving outside his presidential plane while holding two bags containing miniature figures of Presidents Zuma and Mugabe in his other hand. Available at http://brandanreynolds. com/2015/12/07/business-day-monday-7-december-2015, accessed February 15, 2016. The thinking bubble "Such generous people" hovering over Xi Jinping's head in the cartoon alludes to the same idea that China is gaining favorable deals at the expense of South Africa and the entire continent.

3   Although these numbers are significant, out of a total population of almost 55 million people in South Africa, the Chinese make up less than one percent. While the bulk of Chinese migrants arrived towards the end of the 1990s, it is nonetheless difficult (if not impossible) to provide exact numbers of Chinese who lived in South Africa during apartheid, given their inclusion in the "Asian" racial group (alongside Indians) following the Population Registration Act of 1950.

4   More recently, some of the Chinese migrant-entrepreneurs importing commodities from China have decided to leave due to the declining value of the South African currency (resulting in an unfavorable convertibility with the US dollar) and a difficult economic outlook.

5   The gradual abolition of slavery towards the middle of the nineteenth century catalyzed an increased demand for cheap labor forces used for the development of new colonies in Southeast Asia and Africa. With the launch of the coolie trade, thousands of indentured laborers from Asia were hired to work on sugar plantations (on Reunion Island, in Mauritius, in the Seychelles, and in Madagascar), on large infrastructure projects (such as the construction of the railway line connecting Mombasa with Kisumu), and in South Africa's gold mines.

6   Throughout this chapter, whenever the term "the Chinese" is used with quotation marks, it refers to the stereotyped and perceived version.

7   While the overall picture has become more complex and layered, race and economic power in South Africa are still strongly correlated.

8   Two of the Southern provinces in China—Fujian and Guangdong—have been particularly impacted as major suppliers of Chinese coolies.

9   See, for instance, *Noseweek* (2012), "Howzit China," November 1. Available at http://www.noseweek.co.za/article/2836/Howzit-China?, accessed October 2, 2015.

10 In July 2015, Deputy President Cyril Ramaphosa traveled to China accompanied by the Minister of Public Enterprises and Higher Education, as well as other deputy ministers, senior government officials, and an entourage of business leaders and SOE executives. Admittedly the same

delegation also travelled to Japan and South Korea to assess which "model" would be most suitable for emulation in South Africa.

11 The Dalai Lama visited South Africa in 1996, 1999, and 2004. However, from 2009 onward, he was refused permission to visit on three occasions. While the official reasons given by the Department of International Relations and Cooperation (DIRCO) were procedural in nature, it was widely interpreted that South Africa had acquiesced to Chinese wishes. The opposition parties, Archbishop and Nobel Prize laureate Desmond Tutu and his foundation appealed to the government to grant a visa to the Dalai Lama, but to no avail. A representative of the Chinese Foreign Ministry thanked South Africa for its "correct position." *Mail and Guardian* (2014), "China thanks SA for 'support' over the Dalai Lama," September 5. Available at http://mg.co.za/article/2014–09–05-china-thanks-sa-for-correct-position-on-dalai-lama, accessed October 4, 2015.

12 It was announced in 2014 that the ANC will be building a Party institute, funded by China and modeled on the China Executive Leadership Academy in Pudong (Shanghai), where Party members will be trained (Findlay 2014).

13 More recently, though, South Africa's Independent Media group, bought out by a conglomerate that includes both South African and Chinese government investment arms, has offered fawning reports on China–Africa relations in its coverage of the 6th FOCAC meeting. See, for instance, "Chinese God of Prosperity Smiles on Africa," *African Independent*, December 4–10, 2015; "Independent Media Hails Friendly Relations with China," *DFA*, December 2, 2015, p. 11.

14 *Democratic Alliance* (2015), "Alarm over Cyber Security Pact with China," June 10. Available at http://www.da.org.za/2015/06/alarm-over-cyber-security-pact-with-china, accessed July 29, 2015.

15 Historically, the issue of language of instruction in South African schools has been associated with political struggle—epitomized in the 1976 Soweto Uprising in which scores of black students, protesting against Afrikaans as the primary language of instruction, were shot by police forces. *Mail and Guardian* (2015), "Like it or not, SA schools set to teach Mandarin," August 12. Available at http://mg.co.za/article/2015-08–12-like-it-or-not-sa-schools-set-to-teach-mandarin, accessed August 11, 2015.

16 Source: Trade Statistics for International Business Development, Trade Map. Available at http://www.trademap.org/Bilateral.aspx, accessed February 2, 2016.

17 "FDI plays a large role in developing South Africa's economy," *Cape Business News*, October 5, 2015, https://www.cbn.co.za/news/services

/money-matters-in-business/fdi-plays-a-large-role-in-developing-south
-africa-s-economy-dti, accessed January 12, 2016.

18 Chinese companies are mostly active in telecoms (*Telkom* and *Huawei*),
finance (*Standard Bank/ICBC*), mining as well as renewable energy.
In terms of Foreign Direct Investment (FDI), a handful of large South
African companies have invested significantly in the Chinese economy,
including SABS-Miller and Naspers' share in *Tencent*.

19 While perceptions of Chinese traders are mostly associated with men,
Chinese migrant-entrepreneurs in Johannesburg encompass a much
larger picture, ranging from men or women (of various age categories)
travelling on their own or in couples to larger families or kinship-
related groups.

20 The commercial intended to raise public awareness in relation to
xenophobia and intolerance, especially after the violence in 2008. The full
clip can be viewed at the following link on *Nando's Diversity*: https://www
.youtube.com/watch?v=cBIDkW2_FnQ, accessed December 1, 2015.

21 These various waves of migrants arrived at different periods, thus leaving
and entering different "Chinas" and "South Africas" (Huynh et al. 2010,
288–289).

22 Active between 1974 and 2004, the multifiber arrangement referred to an
international trade agreement on textile and clothing that imposed quotas
on the amount of yarn, fabric, and clothing developing countries could
export to developed countries.

23 The Audit Bureau of Circulations of South Africa lists *Noseweek* as
the third most widely circulated business publication in the country.
Available at http://www.marklives.com/2016/05/abc-analysis-q1–2016-the
-biggest-circulating-consumer-mags-in-sa/, accessed December 21, 2016.

24 *Noseweek* (2012), "Howzit China," November 1. Available at http://www.
noseweek.co.za/article/2836/Howzit-China?, accessed October 2, 2015.
The same piece triggered a number of reactions, both in the local media
and among a group of scholars examining the Chinese presence in
South Africa.

25 A few years ago, influential Chinese businessmen, interested in expanding
the economic component of Chinatown, filed an application for a business
precinct plan with the City of Johannesburg. Eventually developed by the
City and approved in May 2015, the plan provides development guidelines
for differential land use, zoning, spatial structure, and built form, with a
focus on business and higher densities (due to the pressure of the steady
influx of migrants) around the core section of Chinatown.

26 The following news headlines are just a few examples: *The Star* (2010),
"Businessman gunned down in Chinatown" (August 5); *Saturday Star*

(2010), "Terror stalks Cyrildene streets" (August 7); *The Star* (2008), "Cyrildene residents decry hookers, drugs and bribes" (August 6); *Saturday Star* (2010), "It's the Wild East as bullets, punches fly in Chinatown" (August 7).

27 This became particularly evident when one of the authors, after relocating to Johannesburg, wanted to find accommodation in Cyrildene and asked several of his Chinese contacts and friends (admittedly all financially stable and living in suburbia) for advice.

28 While both extremities of Derrick Avenue were supposed to boast an entrance gate marking the limits of Chinatown, only the one intersecting with Friedland Avenue has been finalized. The one adjacent to Marcia Street, expected to be smaller, has not been finalized due to insufficient funding.

29 While Taiwanese industrialists were physically present in South Africa before 1994, they benefited from special incentives under the apartheid regime, being qualified as "honorary whites," thus not qualifying for affirmative action policies. As for the mainlanders, the vast majority of them arrived after the advent of democracy.

30 During an interview about identity with an influential South African-born Chinese businessman, he jokingly referred to himself as a "banana," being "yellow" on the outside (i.e., Chinese), but "white" on the inside, in reference to his urban practices and way of living (series of conversations conducted in Johannesburg in December 2009).

31 In 2006, the Industrial and Commercial Bank of China (ICBC) bought a 20 percent share (USD $5.6 billion) in South Africa's largest bank, Standard Bank. *Mail and Guardian* (2007), "ICBC to buy 20% of Standard Bank for 5.6 billion," October 25. Available at http://mg.co.za/article /2007–10–25-icbc-to-buy-20-of-standard-bank-for-56billion, accessed October 20, 2015.

32 The company's chairman used this phrase in 2013. See *Biznews.com* (2015), "Construction begins at Chinese-owned 'African Manhattan' in Modderfontein," January 8. Available at http://www.biznews.com/briefs /2015/01/08/construction-begins-chinese-owned-african-manhattan -modderfontein, accessed October 3, 2015.

33 Established in 2013 by expelled former ANC Youth League President Julius Malema, EFF describes itself as a revolutionary socialist party (in the Marxist-Leninist tradition), aiming to defend (often by referring to populism) the rights of the working class.

34 Economic Freedom Fighters (2013), "EFF calls on the competition commission to decline the selling of 1,600 hectares of Gauteng land by AECI to Shanghai Zendai," November 6, available at https://www

.facebook.com/economicfreedomstruggle/posts/331602293647576,
accessed December 25, 2015.

35 During FOCAC V in 2012, China pledged USD $20 billion to
African development.

36 See, for example, comments made by Togo's foreign minister, Robert
Dussey. *CCTV* (2013), "Togo urges Africa to emulate Chinese development
model," September 29. Available at http://english.cntv.cn/20130929/103798
.shtml, accessed September 29, 2015.

37 This has been one of the key takeaways from a survey of over 70 Chinese
shopkeepers (conducted by one of the authors in 2011) in addition to
a series of in-depth interviews between 2009 and 2013 in a selection
of Chinese-run malls in Johannesburg (see Dittgen 2015). A research
report by the Brenthurst Foundation on Chinese traders within several
countries in Southern Africa (Zambia, South Africa, Lesotho, Botswana,
and Angola) similarly highlighted that 68 percent of the Chinese
entrepreneurs interviewed responded that they compete mainly against
each other (McNamee 2012, 28).

38 See, for instance, COSATU alliance's statement lambasting the "Chinese
tsunami." *Business Day Live* (2009), "Chinese tsunami," August 24,
available at http://allafrica.com/stories/200908240059.html, accessed July
27, 2015.

39 Interview with a Chinese intermediary sales manager, Johannesburg,
September 2012.

40 Among the most recent and gruesome examples is the brutal murder of
a 63-year-old Chinese shopkeeper and the rape of his 85-year-old mother
in December 2015. Enraged and shocked, members of various Chinese
communities organized a protest march in order to stand up against
crime in this eastern part of Johannesburg. *Saturday Star* (2015), "Letter to
a killer" (December 12); *News24* (2015), "Joburg march planned after man
killed, elderly woman raped," December 13, http://www.news24.com
/SouthAfrica/News/joburg-march-planned-after-man-killed-elderly
-woman-raped-20151213, accessed December 15, 2015.

41 Joint interview (together with Xu Liang) in Cyrildene, Johannesburg,
October 2012.

42 The countries that had ties with China during the Cold War (due to
Soviet influence, the ANC in exile was not one of them) symbolically
base their historical memory on, amongst other things, the overthrow
of capitalism—a far cry from the large commodity engagements of these
states today.

43 While these three existent books were written either by local Chinese (South African–born Chinese) or Taiwanese, to date there are no English publications by newer migrants from mainland China. At the time of writing, there is, however, a plan to screen a finalized documentary on the Chinese presence in South Africa, produced by a mainland Chinese citizen, on one of the main local television broadcasting channels.

References

Accone, Darryl. 2004. *All Under Heaven. The Story of a Chinese Family in South Africa*. Claremont: Africa Books Ltd.

———. 2008. "Chinatown Chronicles." In *The Joburg Book*, edited by Nechama Brodie, pp. 118–120. Johannesburg: Pan Macmillan, Sharp Sharp Media.

Alden, Christopher, and Dan Large. 2011. "China's exceptionalism and the challenges of delivering difference in Africa." *Journal of Contemporary China* 20, no. 68: 21–38.

Alden, Christopher, and Yu-Shan Wu. 2014. "South Africa and China: The making of a partnership," Occasional Paper 199, Johannesburg, South African Institute of International Affairs.

Anagnost, Ann. 2004. "The Corporeal Politics of Quality (Suzhi)." *Public Culture* 16, no. 2: 189–208.

Bayly, Christopher. 2004. *The Birth of the Modern World, 1780–1914*. Oxford: Blackwell.

Bhabha, Homi K. 1994. *The Location of Culture*. New York: Routledge.

Biznews.com. 2015. "Construction begins at Chinese-owned 'African Manhattan' in Modderfontein." January 8. https://www.biznews.com /briefs/2015/01/08/construction-begins-chinese-owned-african -manhattan-modderfontein/

Bloom, Kevin, and Richard Poplak. 2012. "Nosedive: Chinese shopkeeper cover story a new low for South African journalism." *Daily Maverick*, October 30. http://www.dailymaverick.co.za/article/2012–10–30 -nosedive-chinese-shopkeeper-cover-story-a-new-low-for-south-african -journalism#.VjyMyNIrLcs

Brautigam, Deborah. 2009. *The Dragon's Gift: The Real Story of China in Africa*. Oxford: Oxford University Press.

Bright, Rachel. 2013. *Chinese Labour in South Africa, 1902–10: Race, Violence, and Global Spectacle*. New York: Palgrave Macmillan.

Buck-Morss, Susan. 2000. *Dreamworld and Catastrophe: The Passing of Mass Utopia in East and West*. Cambridge, MA: MIT Press.

Business Day Live. 2009. "Chinese tsunami." August 24. http://allafrica.com
/stories/200908240059.html

———. 2013. "What South Africa's citizens think of foreign policy." July 19.
https://www.businesslive.co.za/bd/opinion/2013-07-19-what-south-africas
-citizens-think-of-foreign-policy/

Castillo, Roberto. 2014. "Feeling at home in the 'Chocolate City': An
exploration of place-making practices and structures of belonging
amongst Africans in Guangzhou." *Inter-Asia Cultural Studies* 15, no. 2:
235–257.

CCTV. 2013. "Togo urges Africa to emulate Chinese development model."
September 29. http://english.cntv.cn/20130929/103798.shtml

Chen, Da. 1923. "Chinese Migrations, with Special Reference to Labor
Conditions." *United States Bureau of Labor Statistics*, 340, Washington,
D.C., Government Printing Office.

Chen, Emma. 2009. *Emperor Can Wait. Memories and Recipes from Taiwan.*
Johannesburg: Picador Africa.

Cheung, Floyd. 2007. "Anxious and ambivalent representations: Nineteenth-
century images of Chinese American men." *The Journal of American
Culture* 30, no. 3: 293–309.

Chun, Allen. 1996. "Fuck Chineseness: On the ambiguities of ethnicity as
culture as identity." *Boundary 2* 23, no. 2: 111–138.

Cosatu Today. 2011. "COSATU statement on the BRICS Summit in China."
April 15. http://www.cosatu.org.za/show.php?ID=4795#sthash.MstR3ywy
.dpuf

Democratic Alliance. 2015. "Alarm over Cyber Security Pact with China." June
10. http://www.da.org.za/2015/06/alarm-over-cyber-security-pact-with
-china/

Dittgen, Romain. 2015. "Of other spaces? Hybrid forms of Chinese
engagement in Sub-Saharan Africa." *Journal of Current Chinese Affairs*
44, no. 1: 43–73.

———. 2017. "Features of modernity, development and 'orientalism': Reading
Johannesburg through its 'Chinese' urban spaces." *Journal of Southern
African Studies* 43, no. 5: 979–996.

Drainville, André C. 2013. *A History of World Order and Resistance: The
Making and Unmaking of Global Subjects.* New York: Routledge.

Draper, Peter, and Phil Alves. 2006. "South Africa, China and clothing
conundrums: a briefing," Evian Group Policy Brief.

Findlay, Stephanie. 2014. "South Africa's Ruling ANC Looks to Learn from
Chinese Communist Party." November 24. http://time.com/3601968
/anc-south-africa-china-communist-party/

Frayling, Christopher. 2014. *The Yellow Peril: Dr. Fu Manchu and the Rise of Chinaphobia*. London: Thames and Hudson.

Goss, Jon. 1993. "The 'magic of the mall': An analysis of form, function and meaning in the contemporary retail built environment." *Annals of the Association of American Geographers* 83, no. 1: 18–47.

Greenhalgh, Susan, and Edwin A. Winckler. 2005. *Governing China's Population: From Leninist to Neoliberal Biopolitics*. Stanford, CA: Stanford University Press.

Grimm, Sven, Yejoo Kim, and Ross Anthony. 2014. *South Africa's relations with China and Taiwan: Economic realism and the "One China" doctrine*, Centre for Chinese Studies, Stellenbosch University.

Harris, K. 1998. "A History of the Chinese in South Africa to 1912." Unpublished doctoral dissertation, Pretoria, University of South Africa.

———. 2004. "Private and Confidential: The Chinese Mine Labourers and 'Unnatural Crime'," *South African Historical Journal* 50, no. 1: 115–133.

Harrison, Philip, Moyo Khangelani, and Yan Yang. 2012. "Strategy and tactics: Chinese immigrants and diasporic spaces in Johannesburg, South Africa." *Journal of Southern African Studies* 38, no. 4: 899–925.

Haugen, Heidi. 2011. "Chinese exports to Africa: Competition, complementarity and cooperation between micro-level actors." *Forum for Development Studies* 38: 157–176.

Ho, Ufrieda. 2011. *Paper sons and daughters: Growing up Chinese in South Africa*. Johannesburg: Picador Africa.

Huang, Mingwei. 2015. "Hidden in plain sight: Everyday aesthetics and capital in Chinese Johannesburg." Paper presented at a Wits Interdisciplinary Seminar in the Humanities (WISH), University of the Witwatersrand, Johannesburg, October 5.

Huynh, Tu T. 2008. "Loathing and Love: Postcard Representations of Indentured Chinese Laborers in South Africa's Reconstruction, 1904–10." *The Journal of South African and American Studies* 9, no. 4: 395–425.

Huynh, Tu T., Park Yoon Jung, and Anna Ying Chen. 2010. "Faces of China: New Chinese migrants in South Africa, 1980s to present." *African and Asian Studies* 9, no. 3: 286–306.

Jameson, Frederic. 1991. *Postmodernism, or, The Cultural Logic of Late Capitalism*. Durham: Duke University Press.

Li, Zhigang, Laurence J. C. Ma, and Desheng Xue. 2013. "An African enclave in China: The making of a new transnational urban space." *Eurasian Geography and Economics* 50, no. 6: 699–719.

Light, Ivan. 1974. "From vice district to tourist attraction: The moral career of American Chinatowns, 1880–1940." *Pacific Historical Review* 43, no. 3: 367–394.

Mail and Guardian. 2015. "Like it or not, SA schools set to teach Mandarin." August 12. http://mg.co.za/article/2015–08–12-like-it-or-not-sa-schools -set-to-teach-mandarin.

———. 2014. "China thanks SA for 'support' over the Dalai Lama." September 5. https://mg.co.za/article/2014–09–05-china-thanks-sa-for-correct -position-on-dalai-lama

———. 2007. "ICBC to buy 20% of Standard Bank for 5.6 billion." October 25. http://mg.co.za/article/2007–10–25-icbc-to-buy-20-of-standard-bank -for-56billion

McNamee, Terence, Greg Mills, Sebabatso Manoeli, Masana Mulaudzi, Stuart Doran, and Emma Chen. 2012. "Africa in their words. A study of Chinese traders in South Africa, Lesotho, Botswana, Zambia and Angola," Discussion Paper 2012/03, *Strengthening Africa's economic performance*, Johannesburg, Brenthurst Foundation, p. 47.

Natrass, Nicoli, and Jeremy Seekings. 2012, "Differentiation within the South African clothing industry: Implications for wage setting and employment," Working Paper 307, Centre for Social Science Research, University of Cape Town, p. 34

Noseweek. 2012. "Howzit China?" November 1. http://www.noseweek.co.za /article/2836/Howzit-China

Nye, Joseph S. 2004. *Soft Power: The Means to Success in World Politics.* New York: Public Affairs.

Park, Yoon J. 2008. *A Matter of Honor: Being Chinese in South Africa.* Johannesburg: Jacana Media.

———. 2012. "Living in between: The Chinese in South Africa." January 4. *The Online Journal of the Migration Policy Institute.* http://www .migrationpolicy.org/article/living-between-chinese-south-africa

———. 2013. "Perceptions of Chinese in Southern Africa: Constructions of the 'Other' and the role of memory." *African Studies Review* 56, no. 1: 131–153.

Republic of South Africa. 2014. "Lecture by President Zuma at Tsinghua University on the occasion of the state visit to the People's Republic of China, Beijing." December 5. http://www.thepresidency.gov.za/pebble .asp?relid=18596

Robbins, Glen, Alison Todes, and Myriam Velia. 2004. "Firms at the crossroads: The Newcastle-Madadeni clothing sector and recommendations on policy responses." Report prepared for the Project Steering Committee, KZN DEDT and Newcastle Municipality, p. 59.

Rofel, Lisa. 2007. *Desiring China: Experiments in Neoliberalism, Sexuality, and Public Culture.* Durham: Duke University Press.

Shah, Nayan. 2001. *Contagious Divides: Epidemics and Race in San Francisco's Chinatown*. Berkeley: University of California Press.

Shih, Shu-mei. 2007. *Visuality and Identity: Sinophone Articulations Across the Pacific*. Berkeley, CA: University of California Press.

Smith, Iain R. "Capitalism and the War," in David Omissi and Andrew S, Thompson (eds.), *The Impact of the South African War*. Basingstoke: Palgrave.

Spence, Jonathan. 1991. *The Search for Modern China*. New York: W.W. Norton & Company.

Tchen, John Kuo Wei, and Dylan Yeats. 2014. *Yellow Peril! An archive of anti-Asian fear*. London: Verso.

Van Helten, Jean Jacques, and Youssef Cassis (eds.). 1990. *Capitalism in a Mature Economy: Financial Institutions, Capital Exports and British Industry, 1870–1939*. Aldershot: Edward Elgar Publishing.

Wang, Meiqin. 2015. "Advertising the Chinese dream: Urban billboards and Ni Weihua's documentary photography." *China Information* 29, no. 2: 176–201.

Zhang, Li, and Aihwa Ong (eds.). 2008. *Privatizing China, Socialism from Afar*. Ithaca, NY: Cornell University.

CHAPTER 6

⤳

"The Chinese are Coming"

Social Dependence and Entrepreneurial Ethics in Postcolonial Nigeria

YU QIU

China: A friend or a neo-colonizer of Africa?

In 1971, a bilateral diplomatic relationship between China and Nigeria was established, under the ideological roof of "Sino–Africa friendship." This diplomatic tie with Nigeria is part of China's strategy of alliance with many African countries, promoting solidarity among those developing countries that share struggles against imperialism and colonialism. It was a diplomatic strategy deployed at a time when an internationally isolated China strove for international recognition from Africa, against the objections of the West (led by the US) and the Soviet Union.[1] In the 2000s, after a period of absence, the Sino-African friendship discourse reappeared in official diplomacy and media in China. While the old friendship discourse was aimed mainly at mobilizing revolutionary sentimentality, this new form is essentially about collaboration based on shared interests.[2] Indeed, as China's second largest trading partner in Africa, Nigeria has a longstanding position in China's international trade. In past decades, the volume of China–Nigeria trade increased drastically, from $10 million in 1971 to $13 billion in 2015. The majority of trade exchange consisted of China's import of oil and natural gas, along with export of telecommunications and textile production.[3]

The Chinese state's efforts to befriend Africa have provoked critiques and doubts. Many scholars point out sharply that China's renewed engagement with Africa, which is portrayed as different from its relationship with the West, remains rather rhetorical and hard to fulfill (Alden and Large 2011), and that at its core, the engagement is an economically driven turn to the global South (Strauss 2013). In a simplistic sense, the more China projects a seemingly profound love of Africa based on equality and mutual trust, the less convincing it is that this love can consist of solely one-directional affection, with no request for a reciprocal return of "love."

Moreover, China's increasingly prevalent presence in Africa is seen as a threat to the West's once-secure influence on the African continent and to its access to natural and geopolitical resources in Africa (Sautman and Yan 2006).[4] In this particular form of "Yellow Peril" discourse, China is portrayed as a "neo-colonizer," and the essential fear hidden in such an accusation is of China becoming such an exploitative superpower that its economic cooperation–centered policies will override Africa's economic and political autonomy and independence. The economic and commercial proximity that China has established with many African states also becomes a moral anchor for a larger story about Euro-America's hardcore economic and political interests and "proper" transnational collaboration in postcolonial Africa, as it is blatantly defined by the Western countries. Yet, in spite of the fierce debate about China's role in Africa, ironically Africa itself is reduced to a concept, an idea, and a muted "Other" to be loved, assisted, and exploited. This neglect of the African voice in global politics, however, does not mean that Africa remains marginalized, playing minimal roles in the global political economy. On the contrary, just as Jean-François Bayart (2000) provocatively argues, Africa has always been an active agent in its process of colonial and postcolonial struggles, deploying strategies of "extraversion" to interact with the rest of the world. External resources, in this way, have been actively absorbed and translated into forces to be used in national and regional politics in Africa. In a similar vein, with regard to the China–Africa engagement, we shall ask, What about Africa (the Africas), in terms of its/their collective voice and diverse reifications? Which side do the African people take? Do they regard China as a symbol of danger, as a neo-colonizer, as a dear friend, or as something else?

In this regard, this chapter calls attention to the distinctive African voices in China–Africa interactions, and insists on the significant impact that African agents exert on China's changing cultural and social representations in Africa. So far, some valuable yet limited scholarship has touched on various aspects of the local perception of the Chinese in Africa, and indicates a complex spectrum of opinions and feelings regarding China's role in Africa. China's involvement in Africa has been laden with disputes over labor rights and employment, exploitation of natural resources, lack of transparency, and economic activities of an illicit nature.[5] However, reactions of African locals to China's impact in Africa also suggest that China's interaction with Africa fosters new collaborative patterns and new means of innovation and adaptation.[6] In particular, there is a clear orientation that has been implicitly mentioned but not comprehensively explored, that indicates public recognition of the entrepreneurial ethics of the Chinese population, especially its traders and entrepreneurs, in Africa. For example, the Chinese are seen as "hardworking" in South Africa and Lesotho (Park 2013: 138), while "Chineseness," as seen by the Togolese people, lies in its double nature: a kind of savvy flexibility in business and a force within the new global neoliberal competition (Sylvanus 2013). A Chinese version of capitalist calculation and reasoning is manifested in the Chinese-owned factories of Ghana, through the Chinese employers' emphasis on material exchange, rather than the social exchange that includes voluntary gift exchange and long-term sponsorship going beyond mere labor payment. This instrumental exchange practice differs from the local expectation of non-material reciprocity (Giese 2013).

While these studies have merit, curiously little work has been done to further examine the manifestations and implications of these moral stereotypes in relation to colonial historicity, cultural mimesis, and social dependence and inequality, aspects that have so far been largely overlooked and only implicitly mentioned in the burgeoning scholarship on China in Africa. This chapter intends to fill this gap by offering a range of complex expectations of and opinions about the roles of China and the Chinese people, all of which appeared in my interactions with different Nigerian and Chinese individuals in Lagos, and by showing how certain "old" terms were deployed to justify certain "old" interactive patterns as well as to signify "new" social dynamics and power relations between the Chinese and the Nigerians.

The Chinese *oyibo* and the living colonial past

Since the early Chinese migration to Nigeria in the 1950s, the number of Chinese people in Nigeria has increased steadily, exceeding 100,000 in 2007 (Mohan and Tan-Mullins 2009).[7] The majority of these Chinese migrants are the officials, workers, and experts of state-owned companies, who remain relatively low-key and tend to live in communities of their own. By contrast, a rising number of Chinese businessmen and entrepreneurs have begun gradually to interact with the local society. They reside mainly in the Ikeja area, a suburb containing many small-scale traders and businessmen, where they do business in clothing, shoes, mining, and many other lines of production, besides running hotels, restaurants, and supermarkets.

In recent decades in urban Nigeria there has been an increasingly visible presence of "China" as a social and commercial label. In spite of the people's relatively slight knowledge of China, the imprint of "China" has appeared everywhere: the Chinese-made cellphones, the influx of cheap and low-quality fabrics and shoes and other products in the local markets, media portraits, and reports of Chinese collaborative construction projects, such as the Abuja-Kaduna railway, the Lagos Rail Mass Transit System, and other projects spread widely throughout Nigeria.

On January 2, 2013, a few days after my first arrival in Lagos, I was taking a stroll with two colleagues, one from China and the other from a local Nigerian university, at a dam on the outskirts of Lagos. As it was the beginning of the New Year, the dam was full of festive joy. Kids were running up and down on the pathway with colorful balloons on their hands, followed by their parents, who were chatting with others. Vendors were selling sweets, snacks, and drinks, among other things, in small shops lined up at the dam, while plastic bottles and waste papers were carelessly thrown on the ground. As we stood, I felt someone touching me. When I turned around, a little Nigerian girl wearing a shiny skirt murmured, "*Oyibo, oyibo, oyibo!*" Having no idea what she was talking about, I meant to walk away but was stopped by the girl's mother, a woman in her late twenties who was dressed up in a bright suit and held a little baby boy in her arms. Without any explanation, she pointed to a cameraman, who was standing not far from us. Holding a little digital camera in his hand and bending one of his knees, he seemed about to take a photo of the three of us. "Smile!" he said. My attention was directed to the flash of the camera, and the man pressed the shutter button to capture the moment. A photo of the young woman, her little baby, and me was soon printed out in his nearby boutique, and the woman happily walked away with the photo in her hands. Right after that, another Nigerian woman with her little child came to me and pointed to the same cameraman. No words were exchanged at the scene and I had no excuse for not accepting her invitation. Soon quite a few Nigerians with their children were standing in line for a photo with this *oyibo*.

This vernacular expression, *oyibo*, stemming from diverse variations in the Yoruba and Igbo ethnic languages, refers essentially to "white men," or people of mixed parentage (Achebe 2011:43).[8] Dating back to colonial Nigeria, historical accounts suggest that the British people were among the first groups of foreign people to be perceived as *oyibo*. The term *oyibo* could also be used to refer to something foreign, Western, and superior.[9] For example, Western education was identified as *oyibo*, English was called the "*oyibo* tongue," and salaried work was also called "*oyibo* work." In the postcolonial period, the word has been used in more flexible and neutral ways, and has penetrated so deeply into the fabric of Nigerians' everyday life that its original political and cultural significance has largely faded. But the connotation of "whiteness" of skin remains. Even though nowadays the term *oyibo* can be used to refer to Western experts and bureaucratic officials, foreign migrants, children of mixed Nigerian–foreign parents, and a small number of Nigerian locals whose skin color is lighter due to disease, it is not clear what the word connotes regarding the racial and social characteristics of a Chinese *oyibo* in contrast with those of other people. A more fundamental question is the relation between the old *oyibo* in the colonial era and the new one at present; whether the persistence of racialized categories implies a continuity of social hierarchy and power relations operating in Nigerian society; and whether the Chinese *oyibo* signifies a different kind of "whiteness" in the eyes of the Nigerian public.

Indeed, this personal experience of being looked up to as an *oyibo* at the dam came as a cultural shock at the beginning of my fieldwork, a shock that was later shared by many Chinese migrants in Lagos. Part of that shock comes from the fact that, even in a heartfelt gesture of photo taking, it became apparent that there was an element of "white supremacy" associated with the Chinese. At the moment the photo was taken, I was not just seen as a "nobody" by the Nigerian locals; rather, their eagerness to be photographed with an *oyibo* suggests that I had become an auspicious figure to be approached on special occasions, to whom the locals extend admiration and respect. To a certain extent, I realized with discomfort that at that very moment I was connected to the locals' colonial past, on the basis of which the locals established some sort of familiarity with the newcomer who might otherwise have expected to be treated as a stranger of little significance. The cheerfulness and admiration of the Nigerian locals at the dam were genuine; yet at the same time they were profoundly historical, shaped by cultural and social processes of imperialism and colonialism, in which the Nigerians were subjugated to fundamental exploitation and condemnation by the superior Westerners. At the dam, however, the locals' historical inertia imposed on me a seemingly illusory complicity with the colonial past, and my presence thus became a highly politicized arena for the performance of certain historic and cultural sentiments.

However, in an awkward way, the white supremacy associated with the Chinese in Lagos contradicts the mainstream historical construction of the "yellow race," a label that has long been applied to the Chinese, with various connotations and positioning in different racial hierarchies. For example, students of race and ethnicity have long documented the shifting racial hierarchy in China since the late nineteenth century, a process that could not be discussed separately from the shifting connotations attached to the yellow race, with which the Chinese self-identified. Frank Dikötter (1992) notes that if the "yellowness" associated with the Chinese nation before the Opium War was about the construction of a hierarchical racial structure in which the Chinese were positioned at the top, the significance of "yellow race" changed to facilitate the formation of cultural nationalism aimed at enhancing physical and cultural strengths. In today's China, the meanings of "yellowness" have very much become a tool for people to pay what Cheng (2011) calls "patriot tribute," and for the essentialized construction of Chinese cultural identity.[10]

By contrast, in the West in the late nineteenth and early twentieth centuries, the yellow race appeared as a deadly, soulless menace to peace and civilization. The historical background to this perception was the radical transformation of the image of "China" from a civilized entity with a Confucian tradition to a symbol of historic stasis and "backwardness," disdained by the West. At that time, the influx of "yellow hordes," consisting mainly of cheap labor migrating to Europe and the US, was largely received with fury and fear (e.g., Blue 1999; Keevak 2011; Okihiro 1994). In the US, the "hemisphere orientalism" (Lee 2007) associated with Asians largely shaped the ways the Chinese were perceived by the locals. While the "Yellow Peril" discourse in the early twentieth century focused mainly on the Chinese as symbols of immorality and incivility, gradually, with the development of hygienic science and public health, the Chinese were associated with disease and dirt (Miller 1969). Despite the changing meaning of "Yellow Peril" in different social periods, none of the cases instanced above suggests that the "yellowness" associated with the Chinese population implied a sense of superiority.

In different social and historical contexts, the Chinese population in Africa has held ambiguous and sometimes contradictory racial positions in local identity politics, and the discussion of race here associated with Chinese population has gone beyond the idea of "yellowness." For example, in South Africa, where socio-racial classification is largely related to the access to jobs, social benefits, and resources, the Chinese community strengthened their desire to be properly recognized in South Africa's official categorization and identification (Park 2011). Their appeal to be associated with the black population in the affirmative action legislation for the disadvantaged group (the Broad-based Black Economic Empowerment Act 2003 and the Employment Equity Act 1998) has been met with fierce debates among the black South African locals, which reveal a deep unsettling in-betweenness of the Chinese in South Africa. Indeed, as Dittgen and Anthony (Chapter 5 of this volume) explore, with the diversified ways that the Chinese population penetrates into the local social life and ambiguously engage with the local and global economy, notions of "China" and "Chineseness" in South Africa have been undergoing tremendous changes.

It is precisely against the larger context of changing racial connotations associated with the Chinese population that I conducted my fieldwork with Nigerian and Chinese people in Lagos. Among them, Rase, a Chinese woman working in a Chinese-owned company as an English translator and later as the public relations manager, introduced me to her work network at the company, which served as a starting point of this research. Later my research radar extended to the Chinese residential community in Ikeja and many other social spaces where Nigerians and Chinese had the chance to meet and work with each other. Semi-structured interviews were conducted with Nigerian workers in Chinese-owned companies, Nigerian small-scale entrepreneurs involved in international business with Chinese business partners, college graduates, and many other people who had had direct and indirect contact with Chinese entrepreneurs and traders. For these Chinese I associated with, being *oyibo* appeared to be a double-edged experience. Apart from appearing as an auspicious sign of hope to the locals, they were viewed as foreigners possessing accumulated wealth. When I was in Lagos in early 2014, I was constantly affected by the sense of fear and insecurity described by the Chinese, who often mentioned the increase in cases of kidnapping of Chinese managers and workers on construction projects in exchange for large ransoms.[11] To prevent unwanted interracial contact, the Chinese would not take the risk of going out and moving about alone; when an outing was necessary, especially to go to the marketplace in central Lagos, they would go in a car driven by a Nigerian local, in which black curtains were used to cover the windows next to the passengers in order to avoid direct contact with the people outside. Several times during my own travels, someone, who might have been either a local policeman or a local gangster, stopped the car upon noticing some Chinese people inside. Usually, in situations like this, the Nigerian driver, acting as the agent of the Chinese managers in the back seat of the car, would deal with the situation, fending off harassment by police and locals through face-to-face confrontation and, sometimes, by paying bribes. In other words, against the social background that made the racial divide a cruel reality of the Chinese life experience in Lagos, the relationship between the Chinese and the locals, entangled with racial and cultural ideologies, seemed to be deeply embedded in a complex tension between mutual dependence and segregation in everyday life. Given this, three simple yet paramount questions appear: What distinctive social and racial roles were the Chinese *oyibo* perceived as playing in Lagos? How were these roles constructed and altered in everyday interactions between the Chinese migrants and the Nigerian locals? How did the Chinese react and respond to these roles?

The Chinese "master" and reliable dependence

The Vopa Company is one of the first Chinese-owned companies I visited. It is a medium-sized company based in Lagos, producing dairy products, mineral water, and other beverages. Apart from the Vopa headquarters and the main factory, which are located in the Ikeja area of Lagos, there are three other Vopa factories scattered around Lagos and the state of Ogun. I spent most of my time in the company's headquarters and the main factory site.

A brief overview of the Vopa Company is necessary. As one of the most successful Chinese-owned companies in Lagos, Vopa has a wide sales network across Nigeria, and hires a considerably higher number of Nigerian local workers than other Chinese-owned factories in adjacent areas. Vopa has an administrative structure in the shape of a pyramid. The Chinese managers remain at the top of the pyramid, while the majority of Nigerian workers are organized in different work units at the bottom. The number of workers hired from Lagos and other neighboring areas far exceeds that of workers from China. In total, at the time of my study, there were approximately 110 Chinese employers, and the number of Nigerian workers was more than ten times that of the Chinese, reaching 1,300 in 2014. Most of the Nigerians in the factory are manual workers whose life world is confined to factory work units and construction sites. Each work unit is led by a unit head, usually a Nigerian local; this unit head reports the daily production to the Chinese manager who supervises several work units. Apart from that, there are Nigerian sales managers, whose job is to promote Vopa products at local markets. All the supporting staff members (drivers, cleaners, etc.) at Vopa are Nigerian nationals, while the cook at the Chinese staff canteen is Chinese. A clear, race-based divide at work is also reflected in the striking differences in income between the Chinese and the Nigerians. Even though the income of a Nigerian sales manager can be greatly increased by commission fees earned from sales, the monthly salary of a low-skilled Nigerian manual worker can be as low as 12,000 naira (approximately 66 dollars). Even that is not guaranteed. There is a high degree of mobility among the workers since not all the Nigerian manual workers are full-time employees; most of them are non-contractual workers who receive a daily wage and shift between different small jobs at different factories. In comparison, the starting salary of a Chinese employer is 8,000 yuan (approximately 1,150 dollars), excluding maintenance, housing, and transportation subsidies.

Similarly, a clear spatial segregation exists between the Chinese and the Nigerians. The Chinese all live in a residential area, the "Chinese zone," which has high walls and is well protected by armed security guards. This "Chinese zone" contains a multi-floor dormitory building with furnished single and double rooms, a 24/7 supply of water and electricity, and a spacious Chinese canteen for Chinese employees only. Food served in the canteen, either imported from China or purchased at Chinese supermarkets and stores in town, is freshly prepared every day. The "Chinese zone" is a forbidden area to which all Nigerian workers are denied access, except by special permission. During the lunch break, while all the Chinese employees enter the "Chinese zone" to have lunch and take a nap, the Nigerian workers usually lie on the ground or take a rest against the wall of the hallway within the factory site. Many even skip lunch and have their first meal only after returning home from the factory.

The lack of basic English-language skills on the part of most Chinese employees also creates an invisible barrier between them and the locals. More often than not, issues related to communication are passed on to English translators recruited on short-term contracts from China. Only the top managers are able to speak some English, consisting of sentences used at work and in everyday communication. To sum up, with the indirect administrative structure and strict social segregation between the Nigerians and the Chinese, the Chinese managers endeavor to follow what they believe are professional modern management principles, in order to avoid unnecessary contact and to overcome difficulties with communication and other cultural differences.

During my time at Vopa, I found that these administrative and spatial arrangements at Vopa greatly shaped Nigerian workers' ambiguous and sometimes even contradictory attitudes toward their Chinese associates. On the one hand, they criticized the Chinese people's lack of basic interaction with the locals. The majority of Chinese were regarded as rude, indifferent, and lacking in civility. As one Nigerian worker complained to me, "Most Chinese would not know our names. All they do is to shout at you, '*wei, wei, wei*'!"[12] However, during my time spent with them, I often heard the Nigerians calling the Chinese "master." For example, when summoned for a task by a Chinese employee, a Nigerian would reply, "Yes, master." This term was widely used by Nigerian workers, especially those low-skilled workers at production workshops, to refer to all the Chinese at Vopa, regardless of a particular Chinese person's rank in the factory. During my conversations with some Chinese workers, they also mentioned their surprise when first hearing this term. Patently, the use of the term "master" by the Nigerian workers was more than a simple matter of naming. Articulated in tandem with certain expectations, this term seemed to be used to express a particular kind of relationship that could not be expressed otherwise.

But what exactly did "master" mean to the Nigerian workers? Some workers later described to me "how a good master looks like" in their eyes: he should be the one from whom his subalterns could obtain benefits, and who inspired loyalty. Moreover, the master should provide comprehensive care and protection to the subalterns. A good master was a benefactor who provided moral guidance, necessary financial support, and non-material assistance for the workers and their extended families, reflecting an intimate bond between the master and his subaltern that could not be created by a mere transactional exchange of labor and cash. A key issue in this master–subaltern relationship was the idea of "benefits." For Nigerian workers, "benefits" were not simply based on an exchange of labor for money; rather, they were also unilateral gifts from the "master" that required nothing in return. Well immersed in the art of talk, some of them did succeed in borrowing small amounts of money and asking for food and clothes from the Chinese. Yet gradually the Chinese began to refuse their demands, and many of the Nigerians complained that the Chinese managers had failed to live up to their image of "a good master."

The Chinese managers' attitude toward the Nigerian workers' demands for financial and emotional support was marked by surprise and dissatisfaction. They refused to agree to the mastership within which the Nigerians tried to frame them. On the contrary, they regarded Nigerian workers' habit of asking for money as a "shameless" (buyaolian in Chinese) act. After lending them money a few times, most Chinese gradually realized that none of them would seriously consider paying it back in any form. Lack of gratitude was another subject of complaints commonly expressed by the Chinese managers. For example, Rase, one of the English translators at Vopa, complained during a conversation that after a few attempts to buy lunch for the cleaning staff, she realized that none of them ever expressed any appreciation for what she voluntarily did for them; rather, her kind gesture was taken for granted. As the translator, she had more opportunities to communicate with the workers, and so asked for assistance. Hoping to establish a good relationship with her subalterns at the beginning, she confessed that she eventually lost her temper and refused to offer the Nigerians any financial or non-financial assistance. Instead, like other Chinese managers, she firmly insisted on a purely labor-for-cash work relationship.

Not everyone agreed to call the Chinese "master." Tony, for example, worked as a local consultant, a driver, and a guide for the Chinese managers at Vopa who were now allowed to go out by themselves alone, according to the company's safety policy. In a casual chat in his office, he talked about his opinion of the Chinese managers he worked with, that is, the high-ranking Chinese officials and factory heads. He said,

> I do not call anyone master, even the Chinese. I prefer to address
> them by their family names. For example, if I see a Chinese man
> here, I call him, for example, Mr. Tong. Or if I want to address
> him, I call him "Sir". People have their own level of understand-
> ing. If I call him master, it is not appropriate . . . As they see any
> white person, they see this person as someone superior. It is a
> *white thing.* (February 2, 2015; Lagos; italics mine)

Tony's comment reveals a different kind of sociality perceived by some Nigerian workers. He described the master–subaltern work relationship as a "white thing," which, according to him, should be abandoned. Instead, he used a more neutral title to refer to the Chinese and called for a more equal work relationship with his Chinese associates. Yet, Tony's voice remained largely marginal. It seemed that the majority of Nigerian workers felt compelled to recognize the Chinese as the "master." So what exactly was the "white thing" that Tony refused to comply with? Why did the Nigerians feel obliged to place themselves in a seemingly unequal position?

The conflict centered on "how to behave like a good master" at Vopa is associated with issues of social dependence and hierarchy that are common to postcolonial societies extending far beyond Nigeria. James Ferguson (2013), in his discussion of cases in Southern Africa, points out incisively that social dependence is not inherently a passive state of bondage, as many liberal thinkers maintain; rather, it creates the possibility of establishing a sense of belonging and kinship-like interaction (2013: 236–238). Here persons are perceived primarily not as liberal individuals, but as people who are inextricably connected to others. In other words, the issue of independence cannot be socially meaningful unless persons well embedded in social networks have the autonomy and freedom to choose from among multiple and diverse forms of dependence (2013: 227). Otherwise, persons who try to achieve an absolute state of independence will be reduced to liberal individuals, locked out of the labor market and consequently deprived of the means of day-to-day survival. It is in this sense that dependence is "a mode of action" (Ferguson 2013: 226; cf. Bayart 2000: 218), and a way of actively realizing full personhood. Here in this Chinese-owned company, social dependence operates similarly to that in Southern Africa, in the sense that the Nigerians expect their membership in the workforce to be the means of expanding their social relations in a person-centric Nigerian society (Smith 2004, 2011, 2014), rather than a cold exchange based on the values of capitalist professionalism. In Ferguson's Southern African case, there is a form of agency that "seeks its own submission" (2013: 237). However, what remains underexamined is the issue that dependence must be, to a certain extent, reciprocally agreed on by the side to which one offers submission. What if one's attempt does not receive a reciprocal response from the other? This is exactly the case for the Nigerians when the Chinese, the "stranger-king" in Marshall Sahlins' (2008) sense, with his external sources of wealth and power, explicitly refuses to participate in the culture of mastership that Nigerian laborers are used to.

Let me return to the ethnographic case. While the Chinese, to a great extent, failed to act as good masters on whom Nigerian workers could be dependent, a form of interdependence among the Nigerians became highly desirable. In stark contrast to the Chinese masters with whom the Nigerians grew discontented, there were local leaders, usually called *oga*, with whom the Nigerian laborers in turn cemented a relationship of social dependence. These local *oga* gradually obtained a growing power of control over day-to-day maintenance at Vopa. *Oga*, or "big man," was originally a Yoruba term. At Vopa, it commonly referred to a local Nigerian who held direct power over a number of Nigerian laborers. The *oga* politics between a local boss and his clients is a continuation of the traditional chiefdom system and has been widely used at every level of society in all Nigerian regions today. The power of the *oga* was much more concrete, direct, and intimate than that of a "master." I was told that when a Chinese manager visited a production line and made a specific request, hardly any local workers would obey; instead, they would usually say, "Let me ask my *oga*," despite the fact that the Chinese manager's role was certainly more senior than that of the head of the work unit. What is noteworthy about this response is the lack of control over the Nigerian laborers by the Chinese at the top of the administrative hierarchy that it reveals. Without the intermediary function of the local *oga*, the Chinese managers indeed became superior yet abstract leaders to be feared and kept at a distance, but whose words could hardly be translated into concrete orders and actions. As a result, this seemingly ineffective communication would provide grounds for the Chinese managers to impose economic punishment, usually a deduction of a certain amount of money from a laborer's salary.

This Nigerian–Chinese conflict reached its climax in the spring of 2014 when hundreds of Nigerian workers tried to initiate strikes against unfair labor practices at Vopa. This first came to the notice of the Chinese managers through an election for labor union leader at one of the Vopa factories in March 2014. In response, concerned that the local oligarchs might interfere with the structuralized administrative management of the factory, the Chinese managers cultivated some accomplices from among the workers through bribery, and thus secured the election of their desired leader, who was less "rebellious" than the other candidates. However, disappointed by this failure, some *oga* later threatened to strike in order to press demands for higher wages and a reduction in working time from ten hours to eight. What was the reaction from the Chinese side? The Chinese regarded these local leaders as "bandits" (*tufei* in Chinese), meaning members of a gang typically engaged in illicit activities and demanding benefits at any cost. According to the Chinese managers, the requests were unreasonable, as the Nigerian workers had been extremely "lazy and dumb," and had not met the minimal workload requirements. Besides, they insisted, everything the factory did was perfectly legal and the extra two hours of work had been well remunerated. According to the Chinese managers, the local labor union intended to recruit more members in the factory and plot a strike that would be extremely damaging to any entrepreneur, especially the Chinese, in order to receive more membership fees, which were proportionally deducted from the wages of union members. After some key members who had planned the June 2014 strike were discharged for various reasons, the production line returned to normal.[13]

A more fundamental conflict appeared between different conceptions of work-based sociality at Vopa. The Nigerian workers felt that the person they worked for should assume a corresponding obligation to provide certain welfare provisions and benefits. However, the Chinese entrepreneurs thought that the amount of money given to the worker should reflect just the value of the labor, with no extra social connection involved. Moreover, they believed that hard work today meant better enjoyment tomorrow. In an early study exploring why the Chinese work so hard, Stevan Harrell (1985) points to three elements defining the Chinese version of entrepreneurial ethics: being future-oriented, group-oriented, and security-minded. These same elements were mentioned by the Chinese entrepreneurs and employers at Vopa. "Nigerian workers are too lazy. You cannot treat them equally," said Mr. Shen, a Chinese man in his early 30s who was the head of one dairy factory at Vopa. He sought his fast-growing fortune by working closely with his Chinese boss, the founder and head of the Vopa Company, who, according to Mr. Shen, built from scratch a strong business network that extended throughout Nigeria. Similar opinions were found among other Chinese entrepreneurs. Mr. Liang, head of the Chinese Commercial Union in Lagos, told me that, unlike other Chinese people who migrated to Western Europe, Chinese migrants to Africa valued the "Law of the Jungle" (namely, whoever has power and money wins); they regarded industriousness and shrewdness in business as the best qualities for embarking on entrepreneurship in the distinctive conditions of Africa, where there was often a lack of social order and political transparency. Shen and Liang's views widely represent those held by Chinese businessmen and independent entrepreneurs. They have very pragmatic and individualist attitudes toward their roles and missions in Nigeria. To them, interpersonal relationships with Nigerians are not necessarily oriented by financial interests, but are still, more often than not, unrelated to emotion and care. Being migrants themselves, they tend to protect their individual rights and manage their businesses by complying with what they see as "the Law of the Jungle," a simple yet crude principle that is held as the key to business success in countries like Nigeria, known for their largely malfunctioning public services and corrupt bureaucracy.

It is too simple to ascribe the conflicts at Vopa to a matter of social inequality. Rather, there were asymmetrical expectations on the part of the Nigerians and the Chinese about the distribution of care and interests attributed to work relations. To the Chinese, a work relationship based on pre-agreed contracts was perceived as a manifestation of professionalism, and the endless demands for small favors were perceived as indicating a lack of self-esteem and were thus strongly disparaged. For this reason, the Chinese felt that they were far superior to the Nigerians, who were simply "lazy." This moral justification stemmed from a constructed contrast between their legitimately earned wealth in return for hard work, and illegitimately earned gifts in return for the seemingly effortless action of asking. By contrast, to the Nigerian workers, social interdependence was a prerequisite of livelihood, wealth, and opportunity. The strong views entertained by these Nigerians on the similarities between the roles the Chinese played and those played by British colonizers suggests a sort of colonial nostalgia. Curiously, instead of resenting the predominantly negative impact of colonialism, these people established an implicit complicity with the colonial past, regarding the master–subaltern relation as an ideal social arrangement in order to justify their demand for a work relation involving more than a labor-for-cash exchange. Only by this means could social equality be realized. Here, nostalgia could be seen in the willingness to become subaltern and dependent, transforming a reciprocal yet unbalanced social exchange into one of emotionally charged attention, care, and material support—the free gift—from the superior.

"China gives, China takes," a widely circulated discourse among traders, brokers, and businessmen involved in China–Nigeria transnational trade, follows the same logic. The underlying meaning is a market-based transactional logic applied to China's investment in Africa. It expresses the popular view that when giving something to Africa, China never thinks of it as a free gift, but as a loan to be reciprocally returned; capital comes, capital returns, and nothing is left for others. Yet what is the "surplus" asymmetrically diverted to the Nigerian side—that of the clients—that they expect from these Chinese *oyibo*?

By way of illustration, I cite comments by Aku, a Nigerian Igbo trader in his late 40s who has been in the garment and motor accessories business and has traveled frequently between Guangzhou and Lagos since the early 2000s. When asked his opinion of the Chinese in Nigeria, he bitterly condemned the Chinese for being a less qualified "colonizer." He argued that a fundamental difference between the Chinese and the "British masters" lay in the contrasting nature of their involvement with Africa, i.e., the difference between "investment" and "contract-based business":

> The Chinese are really wicked. All the Chinese care about is money. They don't want to pay the extra money . . . You know,

we are thankful to our previous colonizer, the British people. They *invested* in Africa. You see, how do the Chinese do? They do according to the contract. Even the workers, they bring them from China! They don't want anyone else to earn the money. When the Chinese leave, they will even remove the temporary tents there. The British people, they built nice buildings there. When they left, the houses still remained there. But for Chinese, they only build plastic houses . . . This is not an investment. This is a contract. People pay the Chinese to do so. (June 7, 2013; Guangzhou)

Christopher, a college graduate working in a startup music firm in Lagos, who felt impelled to participate in China's growing impact on Nigeria and its emerging cultural industry, hesitated as to whether he should become closer to the Chinese. In explaining his hesitation, he naturally brought up a comparison between the Chinese and the Europeans. While the European colonizers arrived in Nigeria with standards, regulations, and legal frameworks that have been implemented in Nigeria to this day, in his eyes, the Chinese were rule-breakers. "Even though they want to please the local economy, they break the law and try to take shortcuts to get the business they want," he summarized.

Both comments present highly essentialized stereotypes of "European colonizers" and "the Chinese." Yet the disappointment expressed by Aku and Christopher is telling. It represents two forms of "surplus" that the Chinese fail to bring to the locals. One is the hardcore benefit brought to the public; in Aku's understanding, it is the houses left by the colonizers. The other is the cultural, legal, and social imprint. In Christopher's case, it is the standardized social and legal norms that cannot be taken away by the Europeans. With China's construction projects and shops springing up throughout Nigeria, following the logic of global capitalism, both of them reach the same conclusion that the presence of China is suspiciously "non-colonial."

Ferguson (2015) argues that the question of the means of production should be replaced by the question of how the means of and access to production are allocated. The essential issue is not about teaching people how to fish, as the saying goes, if those people have no opportunity to join the labor market in the foreseeable future. Cash payments, on the other hand, give little long-term security to the individual in the job market and offer only a minimum of the social dependence that Nigerian workers expect and rely on. From this point of view, the locals' urge to participate in master–subaltern politics with the Chinese is no less striking. Here, the significance of "colonial" has changed, pointing to an aspect that seems rather intimate, close, and mundane, and that is ambiguously linked to a historic legacy that can be democratically shared and remembered in the most quotidian areas of life. To a certain extent, the colonial master, in a strange form, becomes a phantom-like figure used to defend one's struggle for a more just and equal allocation of resources. The only possible "surplus," in this sense, consists of the public goods that are free from the logic of capitalist transactional exchange, and that may be accessible to ordinary individuals who cannot be equal negotiators in any game of power.

The alternative Chinese "master" and the art of fishing

Let us turn to another idea of "mastership" appearing among college graduates, small-scale entrepreneurs, and other ambitious young unemployed Nigerian urbanites who gradually see the need to break from the conventional association with the Chinese. Among these groups of people, there is an increasingly popular view that sees China not necessarily as a "threat," but as a new global force representing new modalities of trade and business, and new entrepreneurial values and practices in the global market. People who hold this view tend to treat the Chinese as equal friends and business partners, who may help them to acquire advanced knowledge and so to meet the demands of the global economy. They speak highly of what they call "Chinese entrepreneurial ethics," characterized by an emphasis on independence and self-empowerment, and on the merits of hard work and entrepreneurial shrewdness.

"He is my master," said James, an ethnic Hausa with a bachelor's degree in finance, who worked for Mr. Yan, a well-established Chinese entrepreneur conducting business mainly in the production of iron barrier walls, with a trading network spreading beyond Nigeria. James' declaration suggests a different meaning of the term "master" from that used by the Nigerian laborers at Vopa. Indeed, although he was employed as a driver, he ran almost all the daily errands for Mr. Yan, ranging from hotel reservations and negotiations with Nigerian clients to shipping arrangements. In return, Mr. Yan allowed him to take part in every stage of his business plans, a master–apprentice relationship from which James benefited greatly. To James and others, instead of personal reliance on a secured social/work relationship, the close contact established by working for Chinese people provides an opportunity to learn from Chinese businessmen in order to further their own entrepreneurial plans. One of the biggest lessons he learned was about business shrewdness, as James told me. He described how he gained some tips on business calculation from Mr. Yan, who calculated commercial gains and losses not in terms of the net profit he gained from a single transaction, but in line with the interpersonal lending and borrowing network popular in the Yiwu area of China Mr. Yan came from. In other words, if the interest rate gained from an investment was around five percent, while the rate in an interpersonal lending and borrowing network in which Mr. Yan took part was around ten percent, then Mr. Yan would usually not participate in the investment, as the gain from it would be minus five percent, which was a comparative loss for Mr. Yan. However, many Nigerians, like James, saw a total gain of five percent in this type of transaction. This comprehensive calculation of costs provided James with new insight into relative benefits and net gains in a business transaction.

The Chinese way of making the most from payment by installment also revolutionized many Nigerians' ideas of time. For example, a Nigerian businessman, Ugo, who worked as a business consultant in telecommunication in Lagos, told me that he was amazed at the way his Chinese business partners maneuvered differences in time. He explicitly compared the Chinese way to the typical understanding of "African time," which nearly always referred to delay.

> Let me give you an example. While the European customers charge for a full payment of one dollar per piece at the time of purchase, the good thing about the Chinese is that they will allow you to do this without so much money. When you do business with the Europeans, they will need the money right away. But you do business with a Chinese man, they will say, OK, if you do not have the money to pay me now, then pay me tomorrow. But when you pay me tomorrow, you are not going to pay me one dollar, you are due to pay me 1.1 dollar. When the man is good at business, he will calculate, if my profit is enough for me to pay the extra tomorrow, so if the Chinese man wants to have the 0.1

dollar from my pocket, I will give him . . . so that is the key thing
I have learnt from the Chinese. (February 1, 2015; Lagos)

How to insert added value into goods appears to be another Chinese
lesson. An example was given by a local Chinese businessman who had
witnessed the changes taking place in the Morocco Market of Ikeja in
Lagos, one of the biggest food markets frequented weekly by the Chinese.
He told me that a few years ago, if he wanted to cook chicken meat he had
to buy a whole chicken and pull out all the feathers by himself, which was
tiresome work. Therefore, he started paying the Nigerian vendor extra in
exchange for the service of plucking the chicken, and gradually plucked
chicken became a widely available service in the market.

  These three lessons exemplified here—business shrewdness, management of time, and labor as added value—are just a small fraction of the
business techniques and knowledge that the Nigerians are eager to participate in. If we examine these positive voices carefully, it is not difficult
to find that "learning from China" is, first of all, perceived as an effort to
make the most of the presence of the Chinese in Nigeria, as well as to look
for an alternative solution to long-lasting social issues such as poverty,
inequality, and corruption at a time when China is debatably seen as an
alternative framework of development in Nigeria. Like other members of
the young generation in Africa, the youth in Lagos put great emphasis on
material wealth and individual prosperity.[14] This point is well articulated
in Daniel Jordan Smith's (2007) work. In his study of the fast-growing
e-mail scams notoriously practiced among Nigerian youth, Smith argues
that the content of e-mail letters, often in the name of the principal managers of the state, with extra millions of dollars to be transferred to foreign accounts, reflects the deeply worrying situation of increased poverty
and corruption among the privileged, and young people's ambivalently
expressed aspirations for personal enrichment and the means of achiev-
ing it. Lacking access to goods and materials, many young Nigerians tend
to establish work/business relations with the Chinese, believing that an
association with Chinese people and the local business strategies learned
in the process can ultimately benefit them. This kind of "master," associated with the Chinese, emphasizes the significance of the pedagogical
skill and personal autonomy that the master can bring to local Nigerians.
Here, social inequality may not be simply an explanation for poverty, a
different point from Daniel Jordan Smith's (2011) assertion; rather, social

inequality becomes a well-accepted reality and the enabling condition of people's alternative pursuit of a prosperous future.

A grassroots permeation of "soft power," in which Chinese individuals have consciously and unconsciously participated through everyday interactions with their Nigerian workers, employees, and colleagues, has become evident in tandem with the Chinese state–led penetration of the official "soft power" into Nigerian society. Progress in the areas of cultural and social exchange suggests a distinctive feature of China–Nigeria collaboration that differs from the conventional impression of the capital-for-natural-resources strategies that China has deployed in its relations with many African countries. In 2007 and 2009, Confucius Institutes were established in Nnamdi Azikiwe University (Akwa) and the University of Lagos (Lagos) to teach Chinese language and culture to Nigerian students. Cultural linkage was forged through the newly established Chinese Cultural Research Center in Akwa, and further collaboration on Igbo language teaching in China's Xiamen University was on the way. Under the umbrella of a strong Beijing–Abuja diplomatic liaison, knowledge transfer, skills training, and cultural exchange have become essential parts of China's involvement with Nigerian society.

Certainly, the equally prevalent doubts about China's "invasion" of Nigeria, and public suspicion surrounding the unequal distribution of benefits and techniques received from China, cannot be concealed and replaced by positive voices. This chapter does not intend to paint a rosy picture of the presence of the Chinese. Yet, it calls attention to the telling fact that the growing discourse of "learning from China" in the business and commercial sector echoes Nigeria's "look to the East" take on foreign policy and public opinion. For example, in his personal blog published on November 30, 2015, Uzoma Dozie, a Nigerian writer, after his trip to China, listed the lessons that Nigeria should learn from China, a country that in his eyes had undergone a great transformation from a developing country to one able to compete with the developed world. The lessons listed in his blog concern China's infrastructure, its innovation in commerce and food markets, governance, and the transparency of its policies.[15] Others mention that China can also be a good model with which to help Nigeria solve the problem of gender violence and family dysfunction.[16] In an interview with China's Xinhua News Agency on March 4, 2016, Eric Osagie, the Managing Director of Sun Publishing Limited, one of Nigeria's most popular newspapers, stated that the Chinese experience of economic development can provide a useful lesson for Nigeria: "Because we have not been able to manage our oil wealth properly, sadly we have had people who have stolen our oil wealth, mismanaged the economy in the past years, so what we can learn from China is how to be a great country without oil, so we can learn from China."[17] Those new discourses are profoundly significant and compelling, suggesting new modes of interaction and new aspirations that seem to be largely shared by some young Nigerian urbanites, intellectuals, and political elites, even though the effects and implications of the emerging hope placed on China and the Chinese people remain to be seen. However, we should also be reminded that discourses on "learning from and collaborating with the Chinese" can be conveniently used to win the hearts of the public, concealing complicit relationships forged among the Nigerian business and political elites and their Chinese counterparts, and resulting in increasing social inequality between rich and poor. As this chapter suggests, the grassroots engagement between the Nigerians and the Chinese is deeply filled with both the hope and anxiety associated with colonial sociality and the rational and individualist pursuit of prosperity in Nigerian society. To what extent the new aspiration expressed by the young Nigerians can be fulfilled and the new business techniques and ethics learned from the Chinese can be put into practice are questions largely remaining to be explored.

Conclusion

For the Nigerians, who bear historic memories of the colonial past, the Chinese represent a new kind of "master," and deeply embedded in this representation is an "interlocking of pasts, presents and futures" (Mbembe 2001, 16). First, it confirms the point that the practice and discourse of colonialism, once an unbearable moral burden that the West is painstakingly seeking to wash away, still leaves a strong imprint on the African continent (Bloch 1998; Comaroff and Comaroff 1999), and that memory of the past can be a moral and social phenomenon shared by the collective (Werbner 1998). Local knowledge of the Chinese people brims with nostalgic colonial sentiments derived from an imagined racial and social inferiority, which has been exported from a historically constructed segregation within British colonial governance, and which still plays an important role in today's Nigerian society. It was found that, based on this historic memory, many Nigerian workers with low levels of education expected a kind of mastership characterized by the subaltern's claim for social dependence, a mastership that the Chinese, debatably, had not performed well. However, at the same time, Chinese entrepreneurs and businessmen consciously and unconsciously engaged in the teaching of entrepreneurial ethics and related business skills, bringing hope for the future to those Nigerians who were not satisfied to ask for dependence in the diversifying contact zones between the two parties.

In addition, the complex spectrum of different expectations, dismay, and hope on the part of Nigerians of different social backgrounds, as presented in this chapter, indicates that the China–Nigeria interaction is neither a one-directional "friendship" extended by an affectionate China to a resistant Nigeria, nor a replica of the old colonial social relations in the contemporary context. There is a more profound triangulation that manifests itself through the Nigerians' contradictory attempts to reapply colonial nostalgia to the Chinese newcomers, and at the same time to accommodate their hope of independence, economic prosperity, and self-empowerment to the practice of "learning from the Chinese."

This preliminary conclusion seems to entail several questions to be answered in future research. In the face of Nigeria's excitement about "learning from China," does China actually want to fulfill these expectations, and can it become the kind of master the Nigerians expect? Clearly it is far too early to draw firm conclusions. Yet, consideration of the Chinese presence in Nigeria as neither a friend nor an enemy, but as a new actor to be questioned, experienced, judged, or learned from at individual, collective, and state levels, implies a need to go beyond a binary analytical framework. It poses the challenge of taking seriously the shadow of the country's colonial heritage, which comes not only in forms of economic exploitation, but also in forms of cultural hegemony and domination of values and morality, a shadow by which China is inevitably influenced and against which China is moving toward the central stage of cultural and economic competition in and beyond Africa. Only by paying attention to the changing cultural and social mechanisms of mimesis and exclusion can we begin to appreciate the nuances and overtones of the often oversimplified and misleading phrase, "the Chinese are coming."[18]

Notes

I am grateful to the Chiang Ching-kuo Foundation for providing me with support during the writing-up process. My thanks to Franck Billé, Sören Urbansky, and Lianghao Dai for their invaluable comments on many early drafts of this chapter.

1 See Jan Julius Lodewijk Duyvendak's (1949) work for an early history of China–Africa relations, and Sun Yun's (2014) overview of China's Africa policy.

2 The new friendship is best manifested in the political announcement of Xi Jingping, the current President of China, which stresses that the nature of China–Africa interaction lies in *zhen, shi, qin, cheng* (sincerity, real results, affinity, and good faith).

3 "Nigeria–China trade volume exceeds \$13 billion in 2015," *Premium Times*, February 5, 2016, available at http://www.premiumtimesng.com /business/198008-nigeria-china-trade-volume-exceeds-13-billion-2015 -envoy.html, extracted on March 6, 2016.

4 See Barry Sautman and Hairong Yan's (2006: 44–64) discussion of the Western media's portrait of China's "colonialism" in Africa and its problems.

5 See, for example, the Collum Coal Mine shooting event in Zambia, documented by Barry Sautman and Hairong Yan (2014); see further the racial politics of China in South Africa, discussed in Yoon Jung Park's work (2013). See also Daniel Large's (2007) work.

6 See Jamie Monson and Stephanie Rupp's review (2013) of studies of China–Africa engagement.

7 Mainly driven by aspirations for entrepreneurial adventure, the early Chinese migrants to Nigeria were best represented by the Dong, Li, Wang, and Zhai Groups, the well-known Four Bangs of Lagos, who have contributed to the development of Nigeria's basic infrastructure of Lagos since the 1950s.

8 In the 1850s, Rev. J. C. Taylor, a Western missionary, was called *oyibo* in Onitsha of the southeast Igbo land, one of the earliest documentations (cf Chambers 2000: 60).

9 See Osonye Tess Onwueme's (1994: 24–48) novel for an interesting description of the anxiety and cultural burdens that Nigerian rural women had to bear when articulating the *oyibo* tongue (the English language).

10 Admittedly, racial identities, such as yellow and black, have been strategically deployed to demarcate boundaries of ethnicity and gender,

and of rural and urban households (e.g., Han 2010; Schein 1994; Solinger 1999).

11   Several cases of Chinese workers and managers being kidnapped in central Nigeria's Kogi state in 2015 were reported in local and international media. See, for example, "3 Chinese Kidnapped In Kogi State Again," Channels Television, March 13, 2015, available at https://www.channelstv.com/2015/03/13/3-chinese-kidnapped-in-kogi-state-again/, extracted on December 20, 2016. Apart from that, in 2016, two Chinese people were reported as having been kidnapped in Nasarawa State. See "Two Chinese kidnapped in Nasarawa," *Punch*, August 6, 2016, available at http://punchng.com/two-chinese-nationals-kidnapped-nasarawa/, extracted on December 20, 2016.

12   A Chinese greeting that is generally considered rude.

13   The whole event is an ethnographic reconstruction based on interviews.

14   Also see Marshal's (1995), Marshall-Fratani's (1998), and Smith's (2011) work for the relation between the pursuit of material prosperity and the popularity of Pentecostal churches among young Nigerians.

15   "What can Nigeria learn from China?" Personal Blog of Uzoma Dozie, November 30, 2015, available at http://www.uzomadozie.com/blog/what-can-nigeria-learn-from-china/, extracted on March 6, 2016.

16   See "Domestic Violence: What Nigeria Should Learn from China," *City People*, December 29, 2015, available at http://citypeopleng.com/domestic-violence-what-nigeria-sould-learn-from-china/, extracted on March 6, 2016. Also see "10 lessons from China that can transform Africa," *New African*, November 11, 2014, available at http://newafricanmagazine.com/ten-lessons-china-can-transform-africa/, extracted on March 6, 2016.

17   See "Interview: Nigeria can learn from China's experience: media chief," *Xinhua Net*, March 4, 2016, available at http://news.xinhuanet.com/english/2016-03/04/c_135156506.htm, extracted on March 6, 2016.

18   This phrase, "the Chinese are coming," is borrowed from the title of a TV series about China's role in Africa, produced by the British Broadcasting Corporation (BBC) in 2011. Available at http://www.bbc.co.uk/programmes/b00ykxfh/episodes/guide, extracted on May 15, 2016.

References

Achebe, Nwando. 2011. *The Female King of Colonial Nigeria*. Bloomington: Indiana University Press.

Alden, Chris, and Daniel Large. 2011. "China's Exceptionalism and the Challenges of Delivering Difference in Africa." *Journal of Contemporary China* 20 (68): 21–38.

Bayart, Jean-François. 2000. "Africa in the World: a History of Extraversion." *African Affairs* 99 (395): 217–267.

Bloch, Maurice. 1998. "Why Do Malagasy Cows Speak French?" In *How We Think They Think: Anthropological Approaches to Cognition, Memory, and Literacy*, 193–196. Oxford: Westview Press.

Chambers, Douglas B. 2000. "Tracing Igbo Into the Diaspora." In *Identity in the Shadow of Slavery*, edited by Paul E. Lovejoy, 55–71. New York: Continuum.

Comaroff, John L., and Jean Comaroff. 1999. *Civil Society and the Political Imagination in Africa*. Chicago: University of Chicago Press.

Dikötter, Frank. 1992. *The Discourse of Race in Modern China*. London: C. Hurst & Co. Publishers.

Dikötter, Frank. 1997. *The Construction of Racial Identities in China and Japan*. London: C. Hurst & Co. Publishers.

Duyvendak, Jan Julius Lodewijk. 1949. *China's Discovery of Africa*. London: Arthur Probsthain.

Ferguson, James. 2013. "Declarations of Dependence: Labour, Personhood, and Welfare in Southern Africa." *Journal of the Royal Anthropological Institute* 19: 223–242.

Ferguson, James. 2015. *Give a Man a Fish*. Durham and London: Duke University Press.

Giese, Karsten. 2013. "Same-Same but Different: Chinese Traders' Perspectives on African Labor." *The China Journal* 69: 134–153.

Han, Dong. 2010. "Policing and Racialization of Rural Migrant Workers in Chinese Cities." *Ethnic and Racial Studies* 33 (4): 593–610.

Hanser, Amy. 2012. "Yellow Peril Consumerism: China, North America, and an Era of Global Trade." *Ethnic and Racial Studies*, 1–19.

Harrell, Stevan. 1985. "Why Do the Chinese Work So Hard? Reflections on an Entrepreneurial Ethic." *Modern China* 11 (2): 203–226.

Keevak, Michael. 2011. *Becoming Yellow: A Short History of Racial Thinking*. Princeton: Princeton University Press.

Large, Daniel. 2007. "Beyond 'Dragon in the Bush': The Study of China–Africa Relations." *African Affairs* 107 (426): 45–61.

Lee, Erika. 2007. "The 'Yellow Peril' and Asian Exclusion in the Americas." *Pacific Historical Review* 76 (4): 537–562.

Marshall, Ruth. 1995. "God Is Not a Democrat: Pentecostalism and Democratisation in Nigeria." In *The Christian Churches and the Democratisation of Africa*, edited by Paul Gifford, 239–260. Leiden: Brill.

Marshall, Ruth. 1998. "Mediating the Global and Local in Nigerian Pentecostalism." *Journal of Religion in Africa* 28 (3): 278–315.

Mbembe, A. 2001. *On the Postcolony*. Berkeley, Los Angeles and London: University of California Press.

Miller, Stuart Creighton. 1969. *The Unwelcome Immigrant: The American Image of the Chinese, 1785–1882*. Berkeley: University of California Press.

Mohan, Giles, and May Tan-Mullins. 2009. "Chinese Migrants in Africa as New Agents of Development? An Analytical Framework." *European Journal of Development Research* 21 (4): 588–605.

Monson, Jamie, and Stephanie Rupp. 2013. "Africa and China: New Engagements, New Research." *African Studies Review* 56 (1): 21–44.

Onwueme, Osonye Tess. 1994. *Tell It to Women: An Epic Drama for Women*. Detroit: Wayne State University Press.

Okihiro, Gary Y. 1994. *Margins and Mainstreams*. Seattle: University of Washington Press.

Park, Yoon Jung. 2011. "Black, Yellow (Honorary), White or Just Plain South African? Chinese South Africans, Identity and Affirmative Action." *Transformation: Critical Perspectives on Southern Africa* 77 (1): 107–121.

Park, Yoon Jung. 2013. "Perceptions of Chinese in Southern Africa: Constructions of the 'Other' and the Role of Memory." *African Studies Review* 56 (01): 131–153.

Sahlins, Marshall. 2008. "The stranger-king or, elementary forms of the politics of life." *Indonesia and the Malay World* 36 (105): 177–199.

Sautman, Barry, and Hairong Yan. 2006. *East Mountain Tiger, West Mountain Tiger*. School of Law, University of Maryland.

Sautman, Barry, and Hairong Yan. 2014. "Bashing 'the Chinese': Contextualizing Zambia's Collum Coal Mine Shooting." *Journal of Contemporary China*: 1–20.

Schein, Louisa. 1994. "The Consumption of Color and the Politics of White Skin in Post-Mao China." *Social Text* 41: 141–164.

Schmitt, Carl. [1927] 2008. *The Concept of the Political*. Chicago: University of Chicago Press.

Smith, Daniel Jordan. 2007. *A Culture of Corruption*. Princeton: Princeton University Press.

Smith, Daniel Jordan. 2011. "The Arrow of God: Pentecostalism, Inequality, and the Supernatural in South-Eastern Nigeria." *Africa* 71 (04): 587–613.

Smith, Daniel Jordan. 2014. "Okada Men, Money and the Moral Hazards of Urban Inequality." In *AIDS Doesn't Show Its Face*, 31–50. Chicago: University of Chicago Press.

Solinger, Dorothy J. 1999. *Contesting Citizenship in Urban China*. Berkeley: University of California Press.

Strauss, Julia C. 2013. "China and Africa Rebooted: Globalization(S), Simplification(S), and Cross-Cutting Dynamics in 'South–South' Relations." *African Studies Review* 56 (01): 155–170.

Sun, Yun. 2014. *Africa in China's Foreign Policy.* Washington: Brookings Institution Press.

Sylvanus, Nina. 2013. "Chinese Devils, the Global Market, and the Declining Power of Togo's Nana-Benzes." *African Studies Review* 56 (01): 65–80.

Werbner, Richard P., ed. 1998. *Memory and the Postcolony.* London: Zed Books.

CHAPTER 7

~

Sinophobic Tales

Imaginations of China from the Northern Border

FRANCK BILLÉ

I N EARLY APRIL 2015, a story broke on several of China's main news Web sites such as Sina, Weibo, and Apple Daily, generating angry comments from Chinese netizens. While hiking up the Burkhan Khaldun mountain in Khentii province in eastern Mongolia, a group of Chinese tourists suddenly encountered several Mongolian members of the nationalist group Dayaar Mongol. One of the tourists found himself surrounded by seven or eight of the Mongolian men, who pushed him to the ground and forced him to kneel in the snow. A video, filmed by one of the Mongolian men and later uploaded online, shows the assailants shouting ethnic slurs such as "hujaa"[1] and asking repeatedly in Mongolian whether or not he is Mongolian (Apple Daily 2015). Finally satisfied that he is an ethnic Mongol from China (*Övör Mongol*, or Inner Mongolian), they let him go. In response to the incident, the mayor of Mongolia's capital, Ulaanbaatar, quickly offered an official apology and pledged to hold the perpetrators accountable. Mongolian President Tsakhiagiin Elbegdorj also criticized the actions of the nationalist group, insisting that Mongolia should remain a "responsible, friendly and open country" (China Daily 2015).

While the incident was shocking to many Chinese and Mongolian viewers alike, the underlying issue of the fraught relations between the two countries—and notably the strong anti-Chinese sentiments currently prevalent in Mongolia—was not particularly newsworthy. Articles previously published[2] in the Chinese press had already made Chinese readers aware of rising nationalism in Mongolia, while in Mongolia itself anti-Chinese messages have long been ubiquitous in the public sphere (Billé 2015). Over the last few years, Dayaar Mongol's vocal xenophobic claims have also been examined in the Western media, often accompanied by pictures of the group's members wearing swastikas and other Nazi-themed insignia (Branigan 2010; Genté 2013; Hamilton 2010; Moxley 2009).

Assessments of such xenophobic outbursts by Western and Mongolian analysts as well as by lay people have been surprisingly similar.[3] There is the fundamental assumption, on the one hand, that Dayaar Mongol and other nationalist factions are fringe groups and as such are not representative of Mongolian society overall. On the other hand, anti-Chinese sentiments are rationalized as the last-ditch response of a small ethnic community facing gradual but ineluctable incorporation into its giant southern neighbor. While both explanations are partly correct, they are nonetheless inadequate. As I will illustrate in this chapter, Mongolian anti-Chinese sentiments, though of course not in such violent and extreme form, are in fact found deeply embedded within Mongolian society. Similarly, the rationalization that these sentiments are powered by a fear of being engulfed is only partly accurate. Mongolian Sinophobia in fact precedes by several decades China's economic rise and is a phenomenon far more multilayered and complex than simply a response to economic pressure. As a landlocked country wedged between two giant neighbors, Mongolia has had to navigate, and position itself politically and culturally, in reference to both of these giants. Statements disparaging China are therefore tied to unspoken assumptions about Russia, and are entangled in pledges of allegiance to particular geopolitical formations. While the bulk of my argument in this chapter will focus on Mongolia, examples will also be drawn from recent fieldwork carried out on the Russia–China border, notably in the frontier city of Blagoveshchensk, between 2011 and 2014. Russian attitudes toward China—and indeed toward Asia more generally—will further underscore the unspoken allegiance to Russia packed within Mongolian Sinophobic statements and their attendant claims to cultural alignments.

Astride a geopolitical fault line

One of the first statements a foreign visitor to Mongolia is likely to hear and read is that "Mongols hate the Chinese." From graffiti on the capital's walls to popular music, from newspaper articles to casual off-hand remarks, Sinophobia has been rampant in the country from the end of the socialist period if not earlier.[4] While ambivalence about China and its meteoric economic rise is shared by many of China's smaller neighbors, narratives in Mongolia are far more strident.[5] The violent brand of xenophobia put forth by the extremist group Dayaar Mongol finds no counterpart in former Soviet republics. Although it may well be a fringe discourse—its prominent treatment in the Western press is due, in part, to the seemingly incongruous image of a group of Asian men wearing Nazi insignia—it constitutes nonetheless the end of a spectrum that ranges from a mild dislike to very violent utterances. As I have discussed at length elsewhere, the silent collusion with, and acceptance of, artistic forms such as songs or music videos[6] calling for the violent removal, and occasionally murder, of Chinese citizens underpins the strategic and central role played by Sinophobic discourse in contemporary Mongolia (Billé 2015: 151–163).

The strong anxiety indexed by these narratives is also palpable through the substantial body of rumors that circulate in the country, both through the media and through word of mouth. From the well-entrenched and resistant suspicion that China exports poisonous vegetables to Mongolia to annihilate the population, or the belief that the Chinese government offers subsidies to Chinese men to travel to Mongolia and reproduce with local women in order to dilute the genetic pool, China has long been squarely positioned as the main enemy. The overwhelming majority of my interlocutors affirmed in our conversations that the Chinese saw Mongolia as theirs, that they had never truly accepted the country's independence, and that their ultimate goal was to take it back and reintegrate it into the fold (Billé 2015).

Mongolia gained formal autonomy and independence from China at the end of the Qing dynastic era (1644–1911). The newly established Republic of China considered itself the successor of the Qing and therefore deemed Mongolia to be part of its territory. The Mongolian view, by contrast, was that both Mongolia and China had been administered by the Manchu during the Qing, and that the fall of the Qing signified that the contract of Mongolian submission to the Manchu had become invalid. After a brief turbulent period during which it established a temporary government only to find itself occupied once again by troops under the leadership of Chinese warlord Xu Shuzheng, Mongolia declared its independence in 1921 and sent a delegation to Russia to request assistance. Three years later, a communist government was established with the help of Soviet troops.

The year 1921 marks an important caesura for Mongolia's geopolitical alignment. Having become the second socialist nation in the world, Mongolia entered the Soviet sphere of influence, initially to the exclusion of much of the rest of the world. For a long time, the only diplomatic tie Mongolia had with any foreign country was with the Soviet Union. Moscow was keen to hold Mongolia as a protectorate, and to disentangle it from Asia, and from China in particular. Commercial connections to China were thus inhibited and then gradually suspended altogether. From a near monopoly before the revolution,[7] Chinese imports fell to a few percentage points a decade later (Murphy 1966). While Mongolia shares little in terms of culture, language, or traditions with China, it had until then been firmly located within the Chinese cultural sphere. Virtually all of the manufactured goods found in the country hailed from China, against which were traded animal husbandry products, and it was also from China that the most popular beverage, tea, originated.[8] From the 1920s onwards, and especially following the Sino–Soviet split[9] in the mid-1960s, China increasingly became an unknown, even alien, presence on the edge of the polity. By 1989, when the Soviet Union imploded, few Mongols were able to speak Chinese or had visited China. The populous nation to the south had also morphed—in part due to the overt policy of a Soviet Union eager to keep Mongolia within its cultural orbit—into the principal, if not sole, threat to watch out for.[10] This cultural positioning has in fact become so prevalent and entrenched that Mongols continue to this day to define themselves in opposition to China. To be a "real Mongol" (*jinhene Mongol*) is to be *not-Chinese* (Billé 2015).

The crucial role played by China in the construction of contemporary Mongolian identity is paralleled—and in fact directly sustained—by a virtual absence of cultural influence. Mongolia, and particularly its capital city Ulaanbaatar, is both cosmopolitan and multilingual, but this cosmopolitanism is not evenly distributed. In spite of China's physical nearness and growing economic clout, Chinese artistic forms are not part of the Mongolian cultural landscape.[11] The music played on radios is either homegrown or Western (including Russian, and occasionally Korean[12]) but Chinese music is virtually absent.[13] The selection of films at movie theaters or on TV channels shows a similar international distribution.

By contrast, the place of Russia is almost a complete reversal of China's in that it is both ubiquitous and unproblematic. While its capability in shaping Mongolia's political and economic life is much attenuated now in comparison with the socialist era, Russia remains a very potent cultural force. The present Mongolian political elite was trained nearly exclusively in the Soviet Union (Ginsburg 1999), and most educated individuals over the age of forty-five usually speak excellent Russian. Mongols who are too young to have studied Russian at school are nonetheless culturally proficient about Russia. Even when linguistic competence is limited, younger Mongols frequently hold an emotional connection to Russian through the many children's cartoons and TV programs from Russia that are broadcast in the original language. And although Russian and Mongolian belong to two different language groups and are unrelated, the symbiotic relationship the two nations have enjoyed for over eighty years has brought them closer together. Many Russian loanwords have entered Mongolian, thereby fusing the Russian language with emerging trends and with the notion of modernity itself.[14] The phonology of Mongolian, written in the Cyrillic alphabet since 1941, has even shifted to accommodate new sounds imported by way of Russian loanwords.[15] For example, the introduction of the letters "f" and "p" through the adoption of the Cyrillic alphabet turned these foreign sounds into Mongolian phonemes, making their correct pronunciation critical to fluency and literacy in Mongolian (Billé 2010).

Rarely posed as problematic or even as a source of cultural dilution, the role played by Russia in framing Mongolian culture has been far more extensive and sustained than China's. Contemporary Mongolia is in fact comparable to many postcolonial societies in that its views of the world, and especially of China and the rest of Asia, have been deeply colored by Russia's political, economic, and cultural involvement in Mongolia throughout the course of the twentieth century. Thus, despite China's meteoric rise, the country tends to remain associated in the eyes of Mongols with the poor and shabbily dressed Chinese that populated Soviet propaganda. The photographs of Chinese individuals appearing in the Mongolian press are overwhelmingly of Chinese migrant workers, in positions emphasizing their low social status: either huddled together at the train station about to be deported back to China, or contained within fenced construction sites.[16]

Conversely, erstwhile protector and a model to emulate, Russia continues to be regarded as a big brother even if it has lost much of its former international standing. The dramatic cultural transformation that Mongolia experienced in the course of the twentieth century was intimately tied to Russia's own path and beliefs. Following the Mongolian revolution of 1921, extensive propaganda campaigns were carried out against religious practices, particularly the Buddhist establishment, and they were accompanied by a great deal of violence, including mass killings of Buddhist lamas and the destruction of most Buddhist temples. While it would be reductive to argue that the Mongolian government slavishly followed instructions from Moscow (see Kaplonski 2014), the Soviet example loomed large.

The decades following the Mongolian revolution, up until the end of the socialist era in 1990, saw a complete cultural reframing against Mongolian practices perceived as "feudal," backward, uncivilized, and fundamentally at odds with modernity. In particular, European notions of health and hygiene were imparted to Mongols with the view to transform them into "proper socialist citizens." These efforts were intensive and very broad, ranging from biomedical practices and cleanliness, to mothering and domesticity.

These transformations affected non-European practices most of all. If capitalism was seen as a deeply flawed system that should eventually give way to a socially more progressive socialism, the "feudal societies" of Asia ranked even lower, just above the most primitive stages of society.[17] Asian aspects of Mongolian culture were thus perceived with considerable ambivalence, and much effort was expended to eradicate them. At the same time, ideas of modernity and progress inculcated through propaganda campaigns and formal education were lastingly fused to Russian, i.e., European, high culture.[18]

Testament to the success with which this cultural hierarchy has become embedded in the Mongolian psyche is the persistence of negative associations with Asia, and China in particular, and the enduring reluctance to identify with this part of the world. The word "Asian" (*Aziin*) tends in fact to be used to refer to Asia to the exclusion of Mongolia. Mongols may not be Europeans, but they are certainly not fully Asians either.[19] This cultural positioning reflects a wider postsocialist situation whereby former parts of the Soviet Union, notably parts of Central Asia, continue to a large extent to identify culturally with Russia and the rest of the Soviet bloc. This cultural enmeshment was also further reinforced by educational and work exchange programs that saw many Mongols frequently spend years working or studying in the Soviet Union or in Eastern Europe. In the course of my research in Ulaanbaatar (2006–2007), for instance, I met several individuals who spoke fluent Bulgarian, Serbian, or Hungarian and who had created lifelong ties in those countries, after having spent several years there.

This extended discussion on the relation Mongolia entertains with Russia (and by extension with the "West") may seem a digression from the topic of this chapter but is in fact at the core of the issue. As a landlocked nation wedged between two giants, Mongolia's international relations are never conducted with just one of its two neighbors but always involved both. Just as it has learned to expertly play off one neighbor against the other to retain its autonomy, in the cultural realm Mongolia has also long looked to both Russia and China as exemplars of "the West" and "Asia" respectively. Its identity as a modern nation was thus not simply established in opposition to its southern neighbor; rather, it was triangulated in reference to both China and Russia. More importantly, Mongolia's views of one neighbor have been colored by its relations with the other. As discussed above, the Soviet Union actively painted China as a threat to keep Mongolia in its political orbit. Conversely, the anxiety attached to China has excused many of the Soviet Union's policies, some of which caused a great deal of destruction as well as human suffering (see Kaplonski 2014).

During the socialist period, the Soviet Union was one of the two poles of the spectrum, standing for "the West," while China was shorthand for "Asia." Now that Mongolia enjoys a more direct access to Western nations—insofar as Mongolia's diplomatic relations no longer have to be mediated by Moscow—Russia has become a liminal model, somewhat Western but incompletely so. In fact, since the collapse of the Soviet Union, Western Europe and the United States have gradually replaced Russia in this equation. This shift is visible in the way English has eclipsed Russian as the vector of cosmopolitanism and "cool," and in the dominance of American artistic forms such as hip-hop. Yet the disappearance of the Soviet Union has not led to a more complex and multipolar cultural landscape, but to a possibly even more ossified binary opposition in that the two contrasting models are now found at the extreme ends of the East–West spectrum.

I have argued elsewhere that Mongolia's Sinophobic statements are less a symptom of genuine hatred than a speech-act of disengagement and uncoupling (Billé 2015). And while it can be considered a form of "hate speech," it is not a discourse addressed to the Chinese but to fellow Mongols. As utterances seeking to underscore differences between Mongols and Chinese—and indirectly Mongolian alignment on Western culture—these statements are also directed at a putative Western audience. It is therefore not coincidental that anti-Chinese speech is readily audible to Western visitors to Mongolia, and that it is also communicated in English, notably through popular music.[20] For much of the twentieth century, being a modern nation was contingent on separation from China, and despite China's rapid development in the last couple of decades, cultural benchmarks have remained largely unchanged. Being confused for a Chinese, or to be perceived as Chinese-like, is something that must be avoided at all costs.[21]

Oriental imaginings

The word "imaginings" in this subtitle, just like "tale" in the title of the chapter, seeks to draw attention to the imaginary aspect that structures and sustains geopolitical and cultural alignments. The term "imaginary" here does not mean intangible or illusory. If stereotypes rely on imagery that is not rooted in past experience, they are nonetheless extremely potent in shaping and interpreting new encounters. One of the most enduring images of the Chinese in Mongolia is that of a devious and cunning people holding long-term designs over the country. During my fieldwork in Ulaanbaatar in 2006–2007 this belief was ubiquitous and well entrenched, and no amount of positive experience seemed able to unseat it. An informant who had just returned from her first ever trip to Beijing told me that she had a great time, and that a Chinese person had helped her find her way in the subway. But rather than make her confront her bias, it led her instead to question the real motives of that kind stranger. Why had he been so friendly? Had he tried to scam her in some way?

In spite of its importance, the imaginary is rarely given analytical attention. The assumption remains that xenophobic sentiments are primarily a response to societal stress. Particularly strong irritants in the context of contemporary Mongolia are China's demographic size, its growing economic power, and its involvement in the mining industry and other extractive activities. While these are all anxiogenic in their own right for a sparsely populated country such as Mongolia, one should not lose sight of the fact that anti-Chinese discourse was already well-established in Mongolia before the emergence of China as a global power. Rather than assume parity between threats and societal responses, then, it is crucial to look at the context and interpretative frame of these threats, the global discourse in which they are embedded, and the ways in which Mongolia transects these narratives. In the 1960s, anti-Chinese narratives hinged on concerns linked to socialist morality such as mercantilism or hygiene, whereas current ones have genetic dilution or environmental degradation as their dominant theme. Resisting the temptation to provide a contemporary interpretation to a narrative that has been woven into Mongolian political views for decades can help us disentangle apparent causes from underlying cultural premises.

The alternative (and often supplementary) analysis that current Sinophobic sentiments in Mongolia are grounded in thousands of years of hostility is also problematic. Traumatic events such as battles and massacres clearly have an impact on international relations, even when those events have not taken place in living memory; transmission of history thus plays a crucial role. In the Mongolian context historical accounts have been narrated so as to ensure allegiance to the Soviet Union and separation from China. The potency of reframing historical events is clear when one considers that anti-Mongolian antipathy is virtually absent in China, even though China has been the recipient of much of this "millennia-old" violence.

Speaking of "thousands of years" of warfare also presumes that enmity can accrue with time and that, the longer it goes back, the deeper it becomes encoded. Unsurprisingly, Mongols frequently claim that they have evolved a natural and innate antipathy for the Chinese, and this is an essentialism that many scholars, both Mongolian and Western (Bulag 1998; Hyer 1978; Lattimore 1962), have largely failed to critique. The idea that anti-Chinese narratives go back several millennia also offers a view of Mongolian history that is linear and constant, whereas Mongolia's relation to China has fluctuated enormously. Traumatic historical events do provide a context, texture, and strength to these narratives, but they gain their force only through the use that is made of them. It is through formal education, media narratives, and popular tales that these events are reanimated, repackaged, and reinterpreted, filtered through the modern notions of ethnicity, nationalism, and borders.

Similarly, the personages that populate these narratives are stock figures smuggled into historical accounts colored through, and framed by, the political imperatives of the day. The figure of the cunning Chinese merchant who exploited the Mongols in the prerevolutionary period thus emerged through Soviet propaganda. He wasn't "invented" in the sense that a Chinese merchant class did trade in Mongolia, but Soviet literature turned him into a one-dimensional "baddie" who fleeced naïve and illiterate Mongolian herders. The situation was in reality far more complex. The trade that Chinese merchants carried out with the local Mongolian population required trust and thus extended well beyond a simple commercial and exploitative relationship. Mongols typically bought Chinese goods when they needed them and paid for them in animal products such as wool and meat later in the year when those became available. This staggered commercial exchange was therefore contingent on solid personal ties. Chinese traders and their Mongolian customers knew each other well and their relationships frequently spanned several years. Many Chinese residents took a local wife, and illegitimate children were neither rare nor frowned upon. Historical sources suggest Chinese traders made handsome profits, but the well-established belief that the Chinese merchant class was hated is probably an oversimplification. In fact, when Russian merchants began trading in Mongolia in the early twentieth century, they were unable to compete with their Chinese counterparts who were the Mongols' preferred partners (Tang 1959; Rupen 1964).

The second dominant stereotype of the Chinese as poor and shabbily dressed migrants also originates in the socialist period, specifically in the 1950s when contingents of Chinese workers were invited by the Mongolian government in the context of development aid projects to help build bridges, roads, and housing developments. Dressed in Mao suits and housed in isolated living quarters, these "blue ants" (Bitsch 1962) were visible throughout the city. These construction brigades provided the Mongols with a visual confirmation that the brand of modernity offered to them by the Soviets was far preferable than China's, since, in contrast to these contingents of rural Chinese, the Russians in the Mongolian capital were educated experts and managers.

The third image in the Mongols' Chinese triptych—that of the mysterious and cunning Oriental—tells a similarly complex and multilayered story. Dressed in silk robes and wearing a queue, this personage is firmly embedded in an Orientalist tradition. He is easily recognizable as a version of Fu Manchu but also reflects a uniquely Mongolian experience, refracted through a Russian imaginary of Asia. Like Fu Manchu, this evil Chinese is intent on political domination. Seemingly friendly, his ultimate aim is to take possession of Mongolia and to reintegrate it into the Chinese fold. Like Fu Manchu, he is also smart and seductive, as well as a consummate liar. He is customarily depicted as greedy, lusting after Mongolian women whom he is able to attract thanks to his financial resources.

If in Europe and the United States his potency has resided in his capacity to fuse Eastern and Western knowledge, in the Mongolian context he is feared for his physical similarities with Mongols. He is an expert at blending in, at "passing,"[22] and his liminal position—as both irrevocably alien and intimate doppelgänger—has been a regular fixture in anti-Chinese rumors. This tension between difference and sameness illuminates the fictive nature of the separateness in which Mongols are so deeply invested.[23] It also speaks to the ambiguous position of Mongols themselves, striving to align fully on a geopolitical formation that ultimately excludes them. Always potentially confused for Chinese, Mongols' physical similarities with the Chinese and other Asians always place this geopolitical alignment in jeopardy and require constant—and forceful—disengagement.

What is at the core of Mongolian Sinophobic discourse, then, is less a response to China's present economic rise than a cultural and racial hierarchy instilled in the Mongols in the course of the twentieth century. As the country was radically transformed into a socialist society, it had to embrace Eastern European socialist ideals and values, and jettison its prior cultural attachments to the Asian region. In the latter part of the socialist period, and especially from the 1960s onwards as the border between Mongolia and China was hermetically shut, all information about China came filtered through the Soviet Union. The image of China that formed during these decades was thus heavily mediated by Russia's views of Asia.

Russia's own place with respect to the West and to Asia is itself highly ambivalent and echoes in many respects the position of Mongolia on this continuum. Geographically straddling the two worlds, Russia is fully in neither, a liminality that has driven much of its soul-searching exercise. While some Russian historians and political scientists have seen this Eurasian identity as a source of pride and distinctiveness,[24] others have argued that this Asian component has been directly responsible for Russia's "backwardness." This has been made particularly explicit in discussions of the "Mongol-Tatar yoke" (*mongolo-tatarskoe igo*), which refers to the period of domination by the Golden Horde (1237–1480) (see Cherepnin 1977: 206).

If the dominant assessment of China—and to a large extent of Asia[25]—during the socialist period was one of a backward region requiring the guidance of a Soviet elder brother, these views were already well-established in Imperial Russia. *Kitaishchina*, the Russian counterpart of the *Chinoiseries* craze for all things Oriental, also encompassed a negative element indexed by the suffix "shchina" and became synonymous in Russian minds with inertia and conservatism. But unlike in Europe or the United States, for many Russians in the early nineteenth century this Chinese influence, in the form of *kitaishchina*, was also found in Russia itself (Lim 2013: 64). The brand of Orientalism deployed in Russia thus differed dramatically from versions found elsewhere. Not merely a fascination for an exotic Other, it was also reflective of negative traits found at home. The aphorism "Scratch a Russian, and you will find a Tatar" that is attributed to Napoleon speaks to the tenuousness and precariousness of Russia's membership in the West, with the attendant claims to coevality and modernity that this entails. Thus, as Nathaniel Knight (2000: 77) notes,

> Even after the reforms of Peter the Great, Russia's acceptance into the community of civilized western nations was conditional at best and applied only to the extent that Russian elites were able to shed their native traditions and assimilate into a pan-European culture of aristocracy.

Russia's colonial incursions into Central and East Asia were meant, in part, to rehabilitate the country and elevate its status in the eyes of Europeans. The use of Asia as a terrain onto which political and cultural aspirations could be actively projected was in fact made explicit by Fyodor Dostoyevsky (1993: 1374) in the late 1880s: "In Europe we were hangers-on and slaves, but in Asia we shall be the masters. In Europe we were Tatars, but in Asia we too are Europeans." But a significant difference with the British or the French colonial conquests was that, unlike the latter, which took place overseas, the Russian empire was territorially continuous. Its steady advance eastwards thus constituted an expansion of its own land frontiers. At the same time as Russia conquered new territories, to eventually become the largest state in the world, this very process transformed the meaning of Russia itself. The further east the borders moved, the more "Oriental" Russia became.

This problematic positioning of both Russia and Mongolia with respect to Asia means that perceptions of China differ in significant ways from Euro-American ones. A common genealogy undeniably exists—notably with the figure of the evil Fu Manchu or the common stereotype that Orientals are inscrutable and cunning[26]—but the discourse of the Yellow Peril that is deployed in both countries presents nonetheless its own cultural specificities. If, as noted in the introduction, Edward Said's thesis of Orientalism cannot be easily applied to East Asia, it is even more problematic in Russia or Mongolia given their own uncertain place with respect to that discourse.

Both Russia and China—and this is especially striking in the context of "Asian" Mongolia—have employed very vocal anti-Asian rhetoric in recent years. In Mongolia this has been seen in the discourse of right-wing xenophobic groups such as Dayaar Mongol who have drawn their inspiration from Nazi uniforms and paraphernalia, including the adoption of the swastika. As I have argued at length elsewhere (Billé 2015), these symbols purposely engage with a Western exclusionary discourse in order to express Mongolia's rupture from Asia as well as its alignment on the cultural West. If, as mentioned at the beginning of this chapter, these right-wing groups represent only the extremity of a much wider spectrum and are in fact considered hooligans (*tanhai*) by most Mongols, the same dynamics are at play in the anti-Chinese stories and rumors that circulate in Mongolia. This alignment even goes so far as to have appropriated the term "Yellow Peril," with all its stereotypes and connotations, to refer to China. Thus in 2005 an article titled "Yellow Peril" ("Shar ayuul" 2005) was published online that suggested a silent Chinese invasion (*chimeegüi ireh hyataduud*) was underway in the Russian Far East. This usage may be surprising given that Mongols are also classified as Asians, the name "Mongoloid" having been used in nineteenth-century racist ideology to refer to all East Asian groups. In Mongolia itself, however, "yellow" generally refers neither to Chinese nor to Mongols. Mongols have traditionally[27] described themselves as white (*tsagaan*) while the Chinese, with a darker hue, are brown (*bor*). When they refer to Caucasians, Mongols usually focus on features other than skin. To speak of their Russian neighbors, they may use the term *shonhor* (falcon) on account of their large noses, or even "yellow" (*shar*) in reference to their hair.

The term "yellow peril" (*shar ayuul*)—and to large extent "yellow" to refer to East Asians—is a neologism that has gained only limited traction in Mongolia.[28] However, the very possibility of its use in an East Asian setting, and its immediate comprehensibility as a racialized term excluding Mongolia, denote the close cultural alignment that exists between Mongolia and Russia. In fact, this 2005 article was the translation of an article published earlier in the Russian press. The decision to keep the same title speaks to the Mongols' cultural fluency with Russian discourse as well as to the high degree of translatability between the two cultures. Mongolian and Russian racial categories may not be identical, but they are sufficiently enmeshed to allow for commensurability. More importantly, their cultural stake in the excision of Asian elements within their own cultures tends to position them in similar ways respective to China.

Amorphousness

In 2012 China released a new passport featuring a watermark map of China that comprised Taiwan, disputed territories claimed by India, and a vast stretch of the South China Sea, including islands claimed by Vietnam, the Philippines, and other southeast Asian countries. In anger, Vietnamese border officials refused to stamp the new passports, while India decided to stamp its own version of the map onto visas issued to Chinese citizens. Chinese territorial extensions have been the focus of much media attention in recent years, particularly in the region of the South China Sea, where expansive activities have grated against other states. Terraforming—the creation of islands from reef just below, or flush with, sea levels—has been used to produce terrestrial toeholds to stretch the skin of the nation further out to sea. While China is not the sole nation involved in terraforming, and is in fact a latecomer to this practice, China's island-building exercise has far outpaced similar efforts in the area (Watkins 2015).

By contrast, the border between China and its northern neighbors is not subject to contestation. China recognized Mongolia's independence in 1949, and territorial disputes between the two countries were resolved in 1962. However, the fact that Mongolia was formally included within the Qing Empire until 1911, on a similar footing as Tibet or Xinjiang, is a constant source of anxiety for Mongols. The historical enmeshment of the two countries makes Mongolian political autonomy a very loaded issue, while the presence of 4.2 million Mongols in China's Inner Mongolian Autonomous Region (IMAR) underscores the ultimately unattainable fiction of the nation as an ethnically and culturally bound entity.

Until it was finally settled amicably in 2008,[29] the Sino–Russian border remained plagued for decades by unresolved territorial disputes, notably the question of "Outer Manchuria,"[30] the vast region to the northeast of Heilongjiang that was lost by China with the signature of the Treaty of Peking in 1860. The border clashes at Damanskii Island (Ch: *Zhenbao Island* 珍宝岛) in 1969, at the height of the Sino–Soviet split, nearly led to war and were followed by the hermetic closure of the border, which remained in place until 1989. Following the collapse of the Soviet Union, the Chinese and Russian governments resumed their dialog and finally came to an agreement in 2004 (finalized in 2008) without seeking the involvement of their respective citizens. This move elicited considerable public resentment in both countries. For Russians the decision to cede Tarabarov Island and part of Bolshoi Ussuriisk was seen as an admission of defeat. For Chinese nationalists, this agreement signaled the irrevocable sealing of the "unequal treaties" (*bu pingdeng tiaoyue*) imposed on China by colonial powers. For Russians and Chinese, both nationalists and ordinary citizens, the minuscule uninhabited river islands had been fetishized through history books and were felt to hold the very fate of the nation (see Billé 2014).

If today China enjoys excellent relations with both of her northern neighbors, and terms like "partners" and "friendship" dominate political narratives, both Russia and Mongolia continue to view China with much ambivalence. China's territorial hunger in the south, particularly in the South China Sea, has undeniably been a cause for concern for both. As Mongols watch China develop into a formidable economic powerhouse they worry, justifiably, that with increased power and self-assurance, China may decide to revisit its past territorial agreements with its northern neighbors. These anxieties express themselves in multiple ways. In Mongolia a body of rumors points to a poorly defined but impending threat about to strike. In Russia the ubiquitous trope of "Chinatown" sketches a geopolitical imagination of a weakened and disintegrating Russia gradually annexed through China's sheer demographic weight.

These anxieties have also proven economically inhibitive for both Russia and Mongolia. Since the reopening of the Sino–Russian border in 1989, the two sides have been eager to renew their commercial and social ties but development has been skewed in favor of China. The Russian border town of Blagoveshchensk thus saw the tiny settlement of Heihe, on the opposite bank of the Amur River, turn into a sizable town in a mere two decades, while its own development has been much slower. Unlike Heihe, which has given tax breaks to commercial establishments and offered visa-free visits for up to three days to Russian visitors, Blagoveshchensk offers no such incentives, and as a result has benefited far less from this international trade. Prioritizing security over economic opportunities, the Russian side has also continually delayed the erection of a bridge linking the two towns, despite China's offer to bear the full construction costs (Billé, 2016d). The same priorities have also been deployed in Mongolia, notably during the planned extension of a trans-border railway. Until 2014 most of the coal from Mongolian mines was transported to the Chinese border by trucks on paved roads, because a slight difference in rail gauge[31] made it impossible to ship it by rail. Fearing China's increasing hegemony in the region, Mongolia long resisted moving to the standard gauge, even considering building a railway track to China that would make a long detour through Russia.

These two examples illustrate the level of anxiety experienced by both Russia and Mongolia vis-à-vis their southern neighbor. Despite a lack of bellicose overtures toward them, and despite reiterations of official statements about "eternal friendship,"[32] China remains perceived as an imminent threat. In fact, the very absence of aggressive intentions tends to be interpreted as a sign that China is simply biding its time. If China's expansion in the South China Sea certainly plays a role in these anxieties, these readings are also informed by Orientalist views of China as an inscrutable and cunning nation, wearing a mask of friendliness but entertaining thoughts of world domination.

China's illegibility is also due, in part, to the misalignment between China's political borders and its cultural footprint. Traditionally China has seen itself as a set of nested cultural realms, from a cultural center located in the North China Plain extending outwards in an "ever-widening series of concentric borderlands" (Potter 2007: 240). The formation of the Chinese state has in fact often been described as a process of gradual expansion outwards, slowly incorporating lands on its margins in a process of Sinification or "cooking" of surrounding barbarian groups (Fiskesjö 1999). As a powerful cultural force that has shaped the cultures of its peripheries for millennia, China's influence continues to seep beyond its borders. Territories that were included within China's borders, such as Mongolia or parts of the Russian Far East, continue to be perceived as not wholly foreign, eliciting an affective force resembling "phantom pains."[33] This is especially true of territories lost to unequal treaties insofar as they are closely associated with traumatic events and with what is called the "Century of National Humiliation" (*bainian guochi* 百年国耻), i.e., the period of foreign intervention and imperialism by Western powers and Japan in China between 1839 and 1949. But cultural claims can also extend much further, to all land tied, however tenuously, to historical Chinese presence—a footprint that has occasionally claimed the entire northern Asia landmass, all the way to the Arctic.[34]

As William Callahan has perceptively noted (2010: 92–93), official Chinese maps are often imaginative and aspirational, and they inscribe territories not under state control but that could (or should) be part of China's sovereign territory. PRC maps thus include Taiwan as a province of China, along with the territory of Kashmir and numerous islands disputed by Japan, Korea, the Philippines, and other southern neighbors. In the same way, until very recently Republic of China (ROC) maps included Outer Mongolia as well as Tuva and other regions within the territory of the Qing Empire. These numerous, overlapping, and inconsistent cartographic footprints elicit both confusion and anxiety in China's neighbors, and perpetuate an image of China as imperialistic and land-hungry. Essentially, what China presents to the world is a contour in flux, a shape lacking firm anchor points and always liable to ooze out into its neighbors (Billé, 2016c).

Unlike in the South China Sea, where the objectives of its terraforming activities are to incorporate vast expanses of maritime territory, China's relation with its northern neighbors is neither contentious nor combative. Its borders with both Russia and Mongolia have been amicably settled, and its renewed ties of friendship are incessantly praised in the media. However, China's cultural and historical views of itself, combined with bitter resentment about its "lost territories," generate much anxiety for its neighbors. China's position via-à-vis Mongolia, and to some extent Russia as well, is not one of confrontation but one of cultural embrace, or "encompassment" in the phrasing of Baumann and Gingrich (2004),[35] where what we have is a *non-acknowledgment of difference*.

China's absence of firm cultural boundaries means that the line between self and Other lacks definitive clarity and that it is potentially subject to contestation and revision. China's cultural embrace may not be bellicose, but it is nonetheless just as threatening, especially for countries like Mongolia whose political existence is founded, and remains contingent, upon separation from China. When they travel to China, Mongols are not met with hostility but rather with the mildly curious "Oh, is Mongolia an independent country?" or, worse, the pitiful "Mongolia is quite poor. Why don't you come back?" Even when they are expressed in the most amicable way, what such condescending attitudes index is a non-recognition of difference, thereby undermining the very tenets upon which Mongolian political autonomy and cultural identity rests.

Conclusion

The anti-Chinese narratives prevalent in Russia and Mongolia tend to feel familiar to most Western European and North American readers in that they closely reverberate the Yellow Peril discourse to which they have grown accustomed through longstanding political and popular media representations. Both share the stereotype of the Chinese (and Asians overall) as cunning, calculating, inscrutable, and holding political and economic designs over the rest of the world. But the principal difference lies in Mongolia's and Russia's own positioning with respect to Asia.

Of course, Russia's and Mongolia's current brand of Sinophobia is partly related to China's increasingly assertive stance with regards to its borders, notably in the South China Sea, but it is more than simply a reaction to current events: encoded deep within Mongolian and Russian cultures, Sinophobia is in fact inextricably tied to both countries' self-identity. In both Russia and Mongolia, the figure of China stands for the extimate neighbor—both doppelgänger and alien, familiar and radically

Other (Žižek 2005).[36] Unlike the "West," these two nations are straddling the Euro-Asian continuum. Neither fully Western nor fully Asian, their discursive violence vis-à-vis China is radically and inherently different. For both, the path to modernity—and parity with the developed West— has required excision of this Asianness. Extending beyond xenophobia, this Sinophobic discourse thus constitutes a process of abjection (Kristeva 1980) insofar as anti-Chinese statements primarily seek to emphasize difference and create distance—a phenomenon also described by Carrico (this volume) in the context of Hong Kong. In the case of Mongolia, this desire for separation expresses itself more violently than appears historically justifiable. Mongolian resentment about prerevolutionary Chinese mercantilist practices does not seem to substantiate the discursive violence that has at times called for the murder of Chinese, especially when contrasted with overall positive assessments of Russia despite a very traumatic history.[37] Similarly, Russian violence against Asian groups, including populations that were constituent parts of the Soviet Union such as Central Asia or the Caucasus (Zarakhovich 2006), is also extraordinary in that it constitutes a complete reversal of the Soviet experience—and a reversal that has proven difficult to comprehend for the recipient groups.

To a large extent, this discursive and structural violence is in fact self-directed. In the case of Mongolia, it has been used primarily as a way to police the social body. While "China-themed," the chief recipients of anti-Chinese discourse have been Mongolian women, gay men, and other "bad subjects" (Billé 2015). In Russia, the fact that numerous attacks have taken place against migrants from the "Near Abroad"[38] and from ethnically Asian parts of the country such as Buryatia, Yakutia, and Kalmykia, substantiates David MacFadyen's argument (2006, xii) that, in these regions, Russia "went to war with the absent half of itself." The discursive, structural, and physical violence that in recent years has targeted migrants as well as visitors and tourists thus relates primarily to Russia's own Asianness with respect to the West.

In other words, the Mongolian and Russian forms of Sinophobia cannot be attributed solely to China's growing economic clout, nor even to its emerging geopolitical and territorial aspirations. In Mongolia, anti-Chinese discourse is less *reactive* than it is *productive*: Sinophobic statements primarily speak to a desire to create distance from an Asian continent that continues to rank lower than the West in the eyes of an elite educated in the Soviet Union and in Eastern Europe. While this "cultural hierarchy" has been challenged in recent years by a wider exposure to Asian forms of modernity, notably those deployed in Japan and South Korea, the mythical figure of China as archenemy remains a useful discursive device that retains much of its metaphoric force. In Russia, the established socialist imaginary in which China is embedded, namely that Asian societies are backward and stagnant, continues to endure. The recent sanctions imposed by the West on Russia have led to enthusiastic Russian declarations of a new "turn to the East" (*povorot na vostok*) and a renewed emphasis on closer ties with its Asian neighbors, and particularly with China. This new geopolitical orientation has not, however, unseated established cultural hierarchies. In the city of Blagoveshchensk in the Russian Far East, in a region that has badly suffered the brunt of the sanctions, the example of the rapidly growing Chinese city of Heihe, on the other side of the Amur River, has not destabilized Russian assumptions of cultural superiority (Billé 2016b).

If Russian and Mongolian Sinophobic narratives both reflect the historical specificities of the cultural contexts in which they are embedded, their particular genealogies and their survival also speak to their participation in wider global flows and imaginaries. In their mimetic reproduction of Euro-American representations—including Hollywood images of the bucktoothed obsequious Asian[39]—they concede their own subaltern position as not-quite-Western. In spite of their historical and cultural specificities, what Russian and Mongolian narratives ultimately do, then, is express a mimetic desire for an imagined and *idealized* West. Jettisoning their own Asianness proves that they, too, can achieve "modernity."

Notes

1 The term "hujaa" is a derogatory term somewhat equivalent to the English "Chink." It is likely to be a corruption of the Chinese term *huaqiao* (华侨), meaning "overseas Chinese."

2 See, for instance, China.com (2008).

3 The Chinese have been largely baffled by these nationalist excesses.

4 Sinophobia, as a state discourse, was already prevalent in Mongolia in the last two decades of the socialist era, notably when the relationship between China and the Soviet Union turned sour after the mid-1960s.

5 Till Mostowlansky reports similar anti-Chinese narratives along the Pamir Highway. Claims that the Chinese breed more aggressive and

poisonous mosquitos and horseflies to compel people to vacate the eastern Pamirs (Mostowlansky 2017: 126) resonate with many of the stories I heard in Mongolia (Billé 2015). In the context of 1860–1940s Japan, David Ambaras (Forthcoming) also notes similar anxieties of racial purity vis-à-vis China that echo contemporary Mongolian concerns.

6   See, for instance, the music videos by artists Dörvön Züg, Gee, and Tsetse (full references on page 196).

7   Recent work by Christopher Atwood has shown that the economic situation in Mongolia at the beginning of the twentieth century was much more complex, and that many British, German, Russian, and American firms competed with Chinese ones (2003: 66–67).

8   The Soviet rationale for suspending commercial relations between China and Mongolia was both geopolitical and ideological. As Mongolia was being transformed into a planned economy with state monopoly on foreign trade, China was a free market economy until 1949.

9   The Sino-Soviet split (*Zhong-Su jiaowu* 中苏交恶; *Sovetsko-kitaiskii raskol*), 1960–1989, was the lowest point of the political and ideological relations between the Soviet Union and the People's Republic of China during the Cold War. The deterioration of their relationship led them to the brink of war over the control of Damansky Island (*Ostrov Damanskii; Zhenbao Island* 珍宝岛) on the Ussuri River.

10 According to Mongolian writer Erdembileg (2007: 36), political depictions of China in Mongolia were in fact so simplistic and caricatural that China was symbolically equivalent to an ogre (*mangaa*) in fairy tales.

11 Urban influences can also be found in the very materiality of objects. In Ulaanbaatar, architecture and urban furniture, such as street lights, often have an undeniable Chinese "flavor." Because so much building material is imported directly from China rather than built locally, new urban developments often have a very Chinese character. Similarly, in Blagoveshchensk in the Russian Far East, trash cans are not only identical to the trash cans found all over China, they also bear the signs in Chinese that distinguish the recyclable from the non-recyclable goods, as well as stickers indicating the compartments where old batteries and cigarette butts should be deposited (Billé 2016a).

12 Mongols in South Korea form the world's largest population of Mongolian citizens abroad. In 2008 there were an estimated 33,000 individuals living in South Korea, i.e., 1.2 percent of the entire Mongolian population. Korean music, movies, and food have gained popularity in Mongolia through this extensive diaspora.

13 Rees (2015: 120) notes, however, some inroads of Cantonese pop in the 1990s through the popularity of Hong Kong movies.

14 A similar situation is seen with Chinese in the Inner Mongolia Autonomous Region. In the eyes of Mongols from the Republic of Mongolia, this lends a very Chinese flavor to the version of Mongolian spoken there. Conversely, Mongols from Inner Mongolia feel the Mongolian spoken in Mongolia has become heavily Russified.

15 Cyrillic acted as a linguistic prism, in that it forced spelling rules and phonemic constraints that were specific to Russian onto Mongolian. In Russian, foreign words starting with "h" are consistently transliterated as "g," i.e., "Gamlet" for "Hamlet" or "gamburger" for "hamburger," and since all these words were adopted into Mongolian via Russian, these phonetic constraints were needlessly brought along with them. In fact, as post-1990 direct borrowings tend to suggest, Mongolian would normally render these sounds with the voiceless velar fricative "kh" (Cyrillic "x").

16 See Billé (2015: 86–89) for a discussion of such images.

17 Karl Marx's theory of the Asiatic mode of production described Asian societies as stagnant societies dominated by a despotic ruler. While the theory was rejected in the Soviet Union in the Stalinist period, Asia has remained perceived in Russia, even to this day, as less "advanced" than its Western counterparts.

18 See Rees (2015).

19 In his ethnography of the Nivkh people of Sakhalin island, anthropologist Bruce Grant (1995: 40) noted a similar reluctance, with the Russian word "Azyat" used to refer to Asian groups beyond the Soviet border.

20 Witness, for example, the recent song by the band L.A. Face and titled "Fuck Them Chinese" (in English).

21 One of my interviewees, a Mongolian interpreter working for the UK border agency, related an incident that perfectly illustrates this. She was hired to interpret for a young Mongolian woman who had been arrested and was extremely agitated. "I expected that this young woman would be distraught about finding herself in jail given that her English was limited," she related. "However, the first thing she blurted out when I met her was that people kept referring to her as Chinese, and she wanted me to inform them that she wasn't."

22 However, even when they speak flawless Mongolian and appear indistinguishable from other Mongols, a Chinese, including an *erliiz* (someone of mixed Chinese-Mongolian heritage), cannot completely disguise their true identity, and their underlying foreign traits and accents will become progressively more apparent as they grow older (Bulag 1998: 159).

23 For an extended discussion of this issue, see Billé (2015: 90–94).

24 A prime example of this position is Alexander Dugin, an influential political scientist with close ties with the Kremlin and the Russian

military. His theory of Neo-Eurasianism (*neoevraziistvo*), which takes its inspiration from the Eurasianists of the 1920s and was also inspired by Lev Gumilev's work, argues that Russian civilization is distinct from the European one, which it should not strive to emulate.

25 A sole exception was Japan, which, after defeating Russia in the Russo-Japanese War (1904–1905), challenged this assumed European superiority.

26 While the figure of Fu Manchu is not dominant in Russian or Mongolian culture, variations on the personage (such as James Bond's Dr. No) are familiar and instantly recognizable. As discussed in the introduction, Hollywood representations are global images that intersect in unique ways with local cultures. In the context of Mongolia, the Fu Manchu character dovetails with the "prerevolutionary trader who exploited the Mongols."

27 Current Mongolian understandings of color and ethnicity are of course also informed by Western classifications, but "yellow" remains rarely used to refer to East Asians. Unlike in China, where the color yellow had positive cultural connotations through its associations with the Yellow Emperor and the Yellow River (see Dikötter 1997), which greatly facilitated the Chinese acceptance of Western racial categories, in Mongolia the culturally dominant color is blue, which refers to the sky. Often used as shorthand for "Mongol," blue has notably been appropriated by the nationalist group *Höh Mongol* (i.e., Blue Mongolia).

28 Except for this online article, usage of the term "shar ayuul" appears limited, with only a few hundred hits on Google. Although a few of my Mongolian interlocutors mentioned this 2005 article to me, it remains nonetheless difficult to evaluate its actual readership. The news site that published it, www.olloo.mn, is one of the main news aggregators in Mongolia with 9,500 Twitter followers, a reasonably high number if one considers Mongolia's very low population.

29 For an extended discussion, see Hyer (2015) and Urbansky (2015).

30 The term "Outer Manchuria" (外满洲), or "Outer Northeast" (外东北), is the unofficial term for the region formerly held by the Chinese Qing dynasty and now belonging to Russia. It includes the Russian regions of Primorsky Krai and parts of Khabarovsky Krai, Birobidzhan, and the Amur Oblast, as well as Sakhalin island.

31 Mongolia's 1,520-millimeter broad gauge dates back to the Soviet era. China uses the slightly smaller 1,435-millimeter standard gauge, 85 millimeters narrower than the rail gauge used in Mongolia.

32 The slogan "Rossia i Kitai—druzhba na vek" (Russia and China—Friendship Forever) has been ubiquitous in recent years, especially after the imposition of Western sanctions.

33 For a more detailed elaboration of this concept, see Billé (2014).

34 In his famous speech of July 1964 to a Japanese delegation, Mao Zedong spoke of 1 million square miles stolen by Tsarist Russia.

35 See also discussion in Fiskesjö, this volume.

36 The Lacanian notion of the extimate, developed from the Freudian "uncanny" (*das Unheimliche*), blurs this line between inside and outside, thereby provoking horror.

37 See Billé (2015) for an extended discussion.

38 The "Near Abroad" (*blizhnee zarubezh'e*) is the common Russian term for the recently independent former Soviet republics. While no longer within the nation, these newly independent republics have not become entirely foreign either.

39 See Billé (2015: 89–94) for a discussion of such images.

References

Ambaras, David. Forthcoming. *Japan's Imperial Underworlds: Intimate Encounters at the Borders of Empire*. Cambridge: Cambridge University Press.

Apple Daily. 2015 (April 5). "Zhongguo keyou menggu shouru xue di xia gui duanpian puguang" [中國客遊蒙古受辱 雪地下跪短片曝光], http://hk.apple.nextmedia.com/realtime/china/20150405/53603664.

Atwood, Chris P. 2003. "The Mutual-Aid Co-operatives and the Animal Products Trade in Mongolia, 1913–1928," *Inner Asia* 5, pp. 65–91.

Baumann, Gerd and Andre Gingrich. 2004. *Grammars of Identity/Alterity: A Structural Approach*. New York: Berghahn Books.

Billé, Franck. 2010. "Sounds and Scripts of Modernity: Language Ideologies and Practices in Contemporary Mongolia." *Inner Asia*, 12 (2): 231–252.

———. 2014. "Territorial Phantom Pains (and Other Cartographic Anxieties)." *Environment and Planning D: Society and Space* 32 (1): 163–178.

———. 2015. *Sinophobia: Anxiety, Violence, and the Making of Mongolian Identity*. Honolulu: University of Hawai'i Press.

———. 2016a. "模仿性竞争: 中俄边境城市的建筑演化" [Mimetic Rivalry: On the Evolution of Sino-Russian Border Architecture], 俄罗斯研究 [Russian Studies], Vol. 3 (June), pp. 122–138.

———. 2016b. "Futurs non linéaires: Modernité et imaginaires géopolitiques à la frontière sino-russe." *Études mongoles et sibériennes*, published online at http://emscat.revues.org/2809.

———. 2016c. "Cartographic Embrace: A View from China's Northern Rim," in Cartographic Anxieties, *Cross-Currents*, Vol. 21, pp. 88–110, published online at https://cross-currents.berkeley.edu/e-journal/issue-21/bille.

———. 2016d. "Bright Lights Across the River: Competing Modernities at China's Edge," in *The Art of Neighbouring*, edited by Martin Saxer and Zhang Juan. Amsterdam: Amsterdam University Press.

Bitsch, Jørgen. 1962. *Ukendt land: Rejse i Mongoliet*. Copenhagen: Gyldendal.

Branigan, Tania. 2010. "Mongolian Neo-Nazis: Anti-Chinese Sentiment Fuels Rise of Ultra-nationalism," *The Guardian*, August 2. http://www .theguardian.co.uk/world/2010/aug/02/mongolia-far-right

Bulag, Uradyn. 1998. *Nationalism and Hybridity in Mongolia*. New York: Clarendon Press.

Callahan, William A. 2010. *China: The Pessoptimist Nation*. Oxford: Oxford University Press.

Cherepnin, L. V. 1977. "Mongolo-tatary na Rusi (XIII v.)." In *Tataro-mongoly v Azii i Evrope*, pp. 186–209. Moscow: Nauka.

China.com. 2008 (June 20). "Zai Mengguguo de jianwen: Dangdi bushao ren bu xihuan zhongguoren" [在蒙古国的见闻: 当地不少人不喜欢中国人], http://club.china.com/data/thread/1011/2081/17/57/6_1.html

China Daily. 2015 (April 4). "Mongolia apologizes for attack on Chinese tourists by neo-Nazi group," http://www.chinadaily.com.cn/world/2015–04/04/content_20001155.htm

Dikötter, Frank. 1997. *The Construction of Racial Identities in China and Japan*. London: Hurst & Company.

Dostoyevsky, Fyodor. 1993. *A Writer's Diary*, tr. K. Lantz. Evanston: Northwestern University Press.

Erdembileg, H. 2007. "Hyatadyn mangaa." In *Tolbogüi mongol: Esse niitlelüüd*, pp. 36–47. Ulaanbaatar: Admon.

Fiskesjö, Magnus. 1999. "On the 'Raw' and the 'Cooked' Barbarians of Imperial China," *Inner Asia* 1/2: 139–168.

Genté, Régis. 2013. "Sentiments antichinois." Le Monde Diplomatique, March. http://www.monde-diplomatique.fr/2013/03/GENTE/48813

Ginsburg, Tom. 1999. "Nationalism, Elites, and Mongolia's Rapid Transformation." In *Mongolia in the Twentieth Century: Landlocked Cosmopolitan*, edited by S. Kotkin and B. Elleman. Armonk, NY: M. E. Sharpe, pp. 247–276.

Hamilton, Kitty. 2010. "Anti-Chinese Sentiment Sparks Alarm in Mongolia." Agence France Presse, August 31. http://www.mysinchew.com/node /44189.

Hyer, Eric. 2015. *The Pragmatic Dragon: China's Grand Strategy and Boundary Settlements*. Vancouver: University of British Columbia Press.

Hyer, P. 1978. "Mongolian Stereotypes and Images—Some Introductory Observations." In *Aspects of Altaic Civilization II, Proceedings of the*

XVIII PIAC, Bloomington, June 29–July 5, 1975, edited by L. V. Clark and P. A. Draghi, pp. 65–80. Uralic and Altaic Series, Vol. 134. Bloomington: Indiana University Press.

Kaplonski, Christopher. 2014. *The Lama Question: Violence, Sovereignty, and Exception in Early Socialist Mongolia*. Honolulu: University of Hawai'i Press.

Knight, Nathaniel. 2000. "Grigor'ev in Orenburg, 1851–1862: Russian Orientalism in the Service of Empire?," *Slavic Review* 59: 1 (Spring), 74–100.

Kristeva, Julia. 1980. *Pouvoirs de l'horreur: Essai sur l'abjection*. Paris: Éditions du Seuil.

Lattimore, Owen. 1962. *Nomads and Commissars*. New York: Oxford University Press.

Lim, Susanna Soojung. 2013. *China and Japan in the Russian Imagination, 1865–1922: To the Ends of the Orient*. London: Routledge.

MacFadyen, David. 2006. *Russian Culture in Uzbekistan: One Language in the Middle of Nowhere*. London: Routledge.

Mostowlansky, Till. 2017. *Azan on the Moon: Entangling Modernity Along Tajikistan's Pamir Highway*. Pittsburgh: University of Pittsburgh Press.

Moxley, Mitch. 2009. "The Neo-Nazis of Mongolia: Swastikas against China." *Time*, July 27.

Murphy, G. S. 1966. *Soviet Mongolia*. Berkeley: University of California Press.

Rees, Lucy M. 2015. *Mongolian Film Music: Tradition, Revolution and Propaganda*. London: Routledge.

Rupen, Robert A. 1964. *Mongols of the Twentieth Century*. Bloomington: Indiana University Press.

Sina.com. 2015. "Menggu shouru zhongguo youke zishu jingguo: Qiba ge xiaohuozi wei zhu wo" [蒙古受辱中国游客自述经过: 七八个小伙子围住我], April 4, http://news.sina.com.cn/c/2015-04-04/223531682627.shtml.

Tang, Peter S. H. 1959. *Russian and Soviet Policy in Manchuria and Outer Mongolia, 1911–1931*. Durham, NC: Duke University Press.

Urbansky, Sören. 2015. "Grenze im Fluss. China-Russland: Das historische Echo des chinesisch-russischen Territorialdisputs," *Osteuropa* 65: 5–6, pp. 125–136.

Watkins, Derek. 2015. "What China Has Been Building in the South China Sea," *New York Times* October 27, http://www.nytimes.com/interactive/2015/07/30/world/asia/what-china-has-been-building-in-the-south-china-sea.html.

Zarakhovich, Yuri. 2006. "Inside Russia's Racism Problem," *Time Magazine*, Aug. 23, accessed online on May 21, 2016, at http://content.time.com/time/nation/article/0,8599,1304096,00.html.

Žižek, Slavoj. 2005. "Neighbours and Other Monsters: A Plea for Ethical Violence." In *The Neighbour: Three Inquiries in Political Theology*, edited by Slavoj Žižek, Eric L. Santner, and Kenneth Reinhard, 134–190. Chicago: University of Chicago Press.

Songs

Dörvön Züg. "Büü davar hujaa naraa." http://www.youtube.com/watch ?v =zBOc9zalFm8
Gee. "Hujaa." https://www.youtube.com/watch?v=9P_z76bXCkM
L.A. Face. "Fuck them Chinese." https://www.youtube.com/watch?v =qoNJHcEWEJA
Tsetse. "Hujaa." http://www.youtube.com/watch?v=foBN3UpGVx4

CHAPTER 8

〜

Swarm of the Locusts

The Ethnicization of Hong Kong–China Relations

KEVIN CARRICO

"Fuck you chinks, go back to China."
"Chinese pigs, stay away!"
"No more Chinese locusts."

Such brazen declarations would be shocking anywhere in the world today. But, amazingly, these are anti-Chinese protest signs seen in 2012 and 2015 in China, specifically, in the Hong Kong Special Administrative Region of the People's Republic of China. In Hong Kong today, roughly 94 percent of residents are officially classified as ethnically "Chinese" (Home Affairs Department 2013), and the protestors holding these signs were in all cases members of this 94 percent. Can a "Yellow Peril"–type discourse, as a racialized expression of anxiety about China, exist within China itself? And if so, what are the implications of this internal anti-Chinese sentiment for thinking about identity and politics in the so-called Greater China region today?

In this chapter, I examine political and cultural tensions that have emerged in Hong Kong–China relations, particularly since 2011, and their evolution into perceived ethnic tensions, with attendant differentiating discourses. Seeking to account for the recent rapid escalation of ethnic tensions in China, academic studies and media commentaries have primarily analyzed ethnic tensions and nationalism through such familiar frontier regions of the People's Republic as Tibet and Xinjiang, where ethnic protest and conflict are clearly on the rise (Chinafile 2014;

Hillman and Tuttle 2016). By analyzing a new case, the recent emergence of ethno-nationalism in Hong Kong, I aim to develop a novel argument about the origins and implications of ethnic tensions in China today. Hong Kong may seem to be a highly unlikely candidate for the study of anti-Chinese ethno-nationalism, but in recent years there has in fact been a growing contingent of Hong Kong residents who have begun to view and actively construct the people of Hong Kong as an ethnicity distinct from the people of China, and who have begun to explore the idea of Hong Kong independence from the People's Republic of China (Sataline 2015).

Such ideas were largely unarticulated just a few short years ago, but have now begun to enter mainstream culture and political discourse: protests against Chinese visitors and traders occurred on a nearly weekly basis in the spring of 2015, and the Chief Executive of the territory took time in his annual 2015 report to call for vigilance against the "fallacies" of "self-reliance and self-determination" (Wong 2015). By 2016, localist political candidates had been nominated to, disqualified from, elected to, and expelled from the territory's Legislative Council, escalating tensions between Hong Kong and the People's Republic to unprecedented heights. Therefore, although Hong Kong seems an unlikely candidate for the study of ethno-nationalism and ethnic conflict, I argue here that in order to understand ethnic tensions in China today, one in fact needs to consider the case of Hong Kong, for the formative process of this new and unexpected form of nationalism can reveal new and unexpected facts about ethnicity and ethnic tensions in China today.

I begin this exploration of Hong Kong nationalism with an overview of two cases of Hong Kong ethnicization: the first being a racialized Yellow Peril discourse labeling the people of China as "locusts (*huangchong*)," and the second being a series of academic writings advocating for the idea of the people of Hong Kong as a distinct ethnicity with the right to self-determination (*minzu zijue*). These two cases, with their vastly different assumptions, highlight the complexities of the people of Hong Kong's relationship to China, as well as pointing toward vastly different directions for the future of the territory. After analyzing these two articulations of Hong Kong nationalism, I proceed to discuss the implications of these novel developments for our understanding of ethnic relations and ethnic tensions in China today, developing in particular a critique of sociologist Ma Rong's recent proposal for a new and "depoliticized" ethnic policy as a fundamental misrepresentation of the realities of ethnic identity formation. I then conclude with a brief reflection upon the relationship between real challenges and imaginary enmity in the formation of a Yellow Peril discourse in Hong Kong.

Two types of nationalism in Hong Kong: Swarm of the locusts

In February of 2012, a localized variation on the Yellow Peril discourse emerged in Hong Kong. Members of a popular local online forum, known as the Golden Forum (hkgolden.com, similar in many senses to Reddit), had pooled funds in the preceding weeks to place a provocative advertisement in the *Apple Daily*, one of the most widely distributed daily newspapers in Hong Kong,[1] expressing anger at an influx of immigrants from the north. Tensions had been rising for more than a decade in Hong Kong–China relations, as residents of the small but comparatively wealthy territory of Hong Kong found their massive and less developed neighbor to the north exerting growing pressure upon the territory's resources. A longstanding point of tension has been the availability of space in hospital maternity wards: Chinese mothers giving birth in Hong Kong not only enjoy considerably better medical care than that available to the north, but also have the added privilege of ensuring Hong Kong residency for their child (LaFraniere 2012; BBC News 2012). These children then have the right to access Hong Kong's attractive educational system, putting strains upon schools' capacity, in particular along the border where Chinese students can even live in the relatively less expensive city of Shenzhen and commute daily across the border to Hong Kong (Chong and Chan 2013; Pak 2013). In a city where real estate is already terrifyingly overpriced, many have also attributed further hikes in prices to hot money coming from the north, regardless of whether such beliefs are accurate or not. And there have been growing cultural clashes as ever more Chinese tourists descend upon Hong Kong for the nonstop growth industry of shopping tourism, with local residents bemoaning the overcrowding of central thoroughfares and a proliferation of litter and even in some cases, urine and feces (Demick 2014), all attributed to outsiders.

These emerging issues coalesced in the February 2012 *Apple Daily* advertisement into the image of a giant locust perched upon the iconic Lion Rock landmark and looking down menacingly upon the city of

Hong Kong, alongside a declaration that "the people of Hong Kong have had enough." Targeting in particular Chinese mothers crossing the border to give birth in Hong Kong to make use of the city's social welfare and educational system, the ad declared that the city spends 1 million Hong Kong dollars every eighteen minutes on supporting these new arrivals, represented therein as an ever-growing swarm of destructive locusts. The full text reads as follows:

> Are you willing to spend 1 million HKD every 18 minutes to raise children born to non-Hong Kong parents?
>
> The Hong Kong people have had enough!
>
> We sympathized with you after the poisoned milk powder crisis, so we let you come buy up milk powder.
>
> We had pity on your lack of freedom, so were willing to let you travel here freely.
>
> We understand that your educational system is backward, so we let you use our educational resources.
>
> We understand that you can't read traditional characters, so we used simplified characters.
>
> If you want to come to Hong Kong, please respect our local culture. If it wasn't for Hong Kong, you would all be screwed!
>
> We demand that the government revise Article 24 of the Basic Law![2]
>
> Stop undocumented Chinese mothers' refugee invasion of Hong Kong (taonanshi ruqin Xianggang)!
>
> This city is dying, you know? (Apple Daily 2012).

Thus began the rapid proliferation of the "locust" discourse in Hong Kong society, where it has since taken on a life of its own. Soon after this advertisement was placed in the *Apple Daily*, a number of anti-locust (meaning anti-Chinese) Facebook groups were formed, including "Hong Kong and China are not the same," "Oppose reddening, oppose colonization," "Hong Kong Independence Union," and "We are not locusts!" And soon after that, videos emerged of Hong Kongers forming spontaneous flash mobs to sing such locust-themed songs as "It's a Locust World (*Huangchong tianxia*)" and "The Advancing Locusts (*Jinji de huangchong*)" to perplexed Mainland tour groups in busy shopping areas in the spring and early summer of 2012.

By late 2012, the focus of this anger had shifted to a shortage of milk powder in Hong Kong, due to parallel traders buying imported milk in Hong Kong stores and selling it in China, making quick profits from the deep anxieties surrounding the milk industry and children's health in the aftermath of the distressing milk powder scandal of 2008 (Ko 2013). Similar to the portrayal in the original advertisement, Chinese were again represented as locusts swarming and gobbling up necessary resources from local families, mothers, and innocent children. And three years later, as clashes escalated between local residents and Chinese cross-border shoppers and traders in such commerce centers as Sheung Shui, Tuen Mun, and Yuen Long in the northern New Territories adjacent to Shenzhen in the spring of 2015, this inflammatory insect-animal metaphor was used again, its shrill implications all too familiar at this point to everyone's increasingly hardened ears.

Although "locust" is the most prominent and most inflammatory metaphor used to express anti-Chinese sentiment in Hong Kong in recent years, it is not the only example. Some Facebook users have uploaded images of Chinese visitors characteristically squatting in public while eating or talking in the streets, along with captions declaring that mysterious new "invertebrate creatures" had been spotted in various locations around Hong Kong. Other posters have compiled detailed lists comparing and contrasting the behaviors of Hong Kongers and the behaviors of Chinese visitors, portraying the two as essentially different species with objectively different characteristics: standing politely versus squatting while waiting; sitting properly in the metro versus sprawling out across the metro seats without concern for other customers; sitting properly on a Western-style toilet versus squatting on the toilet seat, leaving behind dirty footprints and fecal matter.[3] Following this theme, there is an eagerness to document Chinese visitors either urinating or defecating in public, a lasting visible and visceral material manifestation of divergent toilet cultures that, as it disperses material from inside the offender's body, is presumed to represent an essential dirtiness and difference at the deepest inner core of the Other's being. One particularly provocative form of satire has been to collect images of feces in public places such as MTR (public transit) cars, presumed to have been left behind by Chinese visitors, and juxtaposing these images with cartoons of locusts demanding "tolerance" and support from the Hong Kong people for locusts' "nonhuman rights" to defecate in public without repercussions.

Based in the slightly subtler yet still quite essentialist assumption that language forms produce moral character, a series of armchair analysts have pontificated on the relationship between language and personality in the People's Republic. Mandarin, the state-enforced national language, reflects the history of political power in early modern and modern China, insofar as its pronunciation is heavily influenced by northern and particularly Beijing-based pronunciation (DeFrancis 1984). Texts in classical Chinese (such as the standard example of the "Tang poem") lose some of their rhyme and indeed charm when read in this language as compared to Cantonese. This results in criticisms of Mandarin as a national language divorcing people from their self-declared rich cultural past. Similar criticisms with seemingly deeper moral implications have been lodged against the simplified characters used in the People's Republic, which provide easier-to-write forms of the traditional characters still used in Taiwan and Hong Kong. Yet critics of simplification, and by implication contemporary Mainland Chinese culture, argue that significant meaning has been lost in the process. Comparing, for example, the traditional and simplified characters for love, critics note that the simplified version 爱 lacks the heart radical 心 that can be seen directly at the center of the traditional character 愛. Similarly, the simplified version of the word for justice or righteousness 义 lacks the character 我 for "I" (or oneself) that can be seen at the base of the traditional character 義. Such linguistic discoveries have in turn been inflated into trite cultural caricatures claiming that, for example, people from the People's Republic do not fully put their hearts into love, or that they inherently lack a sense of justice or righteousness.

Here we see constructions of difference through animalistic and biological metaphors, alongside the cultural building blocks of language that are presumed to shape people's visions of the world. Such examples, ranging from the biological to the linguistic, are all presumed to reflect fundamental, innate differences in worldviews, beliefs, behavior, and indeed biology, a taxonomic portrayal fundamentally differentiating the people of Hong Kong from the people of China, with clear favoritism of course toward the former. In constructing an Other as invertebrate locusts who defecate freely and use a language that reflects not only a lack of connection to the past but indeed a fundamental inhumanity in the present, the people of Hong Kong are by contrast presumed to not be locusts, to have spines, to defecate in designated areas, and to use characters that express not only their humanity but indeed their supposed fundamental goodness. Animal metaphors are often essential, in both senses of the term, in the articulation of perceived racial differences, and have a long tradition in Chinese cultural views of "others" (Dikötter 1992). The animal and insect radicals long used to mark racialized groups along China's peripheries were replaced by the radical figure representing human beings only in the past century (Fiskesjö 2011). Yet there is more to these constructions than difference: underlying the obsession with and exaggeration of real cultural difference, such that the people of China have to be represented racially as another nonhuman species, is the acknowledgment, whether conscious or not, of the proximity of or overlap between these two groups, regardless of their many real sociocultural distinctions.

On the topic of discrimination against "peasants" in China, there is a well-known popular saying that if we look back only a few generations, everyone in China is descended from peasants. The widespread prejudice against "peasants" that one can easily observe among residents of China's cities is then a means of denying one's fundamental peasant origins, or, in other words, the common humanity of both city dweller and peasant. Similarly, the emerging obsession among some in Hong Kong with articulating and repeating this insect–human distinction through the language of the locust, a most extreme form of racialized difference, is a direct product of the unacknowledgeable, very marginal difference, in many senses, between the people of Chinese descent in Hong Kong and the people of China. Again, if one looks back a few generations, the overwhelming majority of current residents of Hong Kong and their ancestors were involved in precisely the type of journey from the north to Hong Kong that is now the target of protestors' anger. In his analysis of Sinophobic discourses in contemporary Mongolia, Franck Billé notes that it is precisely the eager and anxious denial of Mongolians' "Asianness" that drives the extensive Sinophobia in this country: "[T]he anxiety is not about becoming Chinese but about Chinese being *already present*" (Billé 2015, 56). In a similar sense, in Hong Kong today, it is precisely the common backgrounds between people, combined with real differences in behavior and culture along the Hong Kong–China divide, that lead to the anxious and indeed obsessive articulation of innate difference through the racialized metaphor of the locust. This is, I argue, how we might begin to make sense of an otherwise perplexing internal Yellow Peril discourse: the locust needs to be used in Hong Kong to refer to Chineseness as a form of absolute difference, because any less extreme metaphor would be at risk of revealing the historical production of this purportedly essential distinction. Yet while these racialized representations imagine radical differences so as to forget commonalities, we must still remember that there are very real and substantial distinctions between the two societies, which other Hong Kong–based critics of China have raised in more thoughtful ways in recent years, and it is to these that our discussion shall now turn.

Two types of nationalism in Hong Kong: Constructing a Hong Kong nation

Two years after the rise of the locust metaphor, in February of 2014, the University of Hong Kong's Undergraduate Student Union journal *Undergrad* published a special issue on the idea of a Hong Kong ethnicity and the corresponding right to self-determination, openly exploring a previously taboo topic within the politics of Hong Kong identity. *Undergrad* later followed this controversial special issue with subsequent issues on the territory's impending death under Chinese rule, the right to democratic self-determination, and the idea of a new nationalist movement in Hong Kong. The articles on ethnicity and self-determination in the original issue were later combined with articles by more established academics and commentators in an edited volume entitled *Xianggang minzu lun*, usually translated into English as *Hong Kong Nationalism*.[4] Needless to say, this new vision of Hong Kong nationalism is clearly not the type of politics that the Chinese leadership had hoped to cultivate in Hong Kong with their formula of "one country, two systems." Accordingly, in his 2015 policy address, Chief Executive Leung Chen-ying took time to criticize the *Hong Kong Nationalism* collection by name, stating that the authors had "misstated some facts" and that leaders of the student movement should avoid promoting fallacies (Leung 2015). Unsurprisingly, Leung's criticism immediately boosted the collection's sales (Wong 2015), suddenly doubling its print run. The sudden popularity of the volume after Leung's 2015 public criticism has led some to jokingly call the Chief Executive the spiritual leader of Hong Kong independence, an accidental imitator of former Taiwanese President and outspoken independence advocate Lee Teng-hui.

The English translation of the title as *Hong Kong Nationalism* can be misleading, insofar as this rendering evokes images of an extreme nationalist manifesto. The title could just as accurately be translated as *Theory of the Hong Kong People* or *On Hong Kong Ethnicity*, highlighting not only the emergence of nationalist thought or independence advocacy in the region, but also equally importantly registering the rise of a softer, more nuanced local ethnic thought and identity in Hong Kong. And upon close reading, the volume comes across as anything but hardcore nationalist, providing a deeply reflective discussion of ethnicity, nationalism, the cultural politics of Hong Kong–China relations, and Hong Kong's future political path. After all, how many nationalist manifestos begin with a quotation from Ernest Renan on the nation as a daily plebiscite, proceed to a discussion of Guibernau's notion of nations without states, reference Brubaker's analysis of civic nationalism versus ethnic nationalism, cite Anderson's analysis of imagined communities, and discuss Hobsbawm's work on nationalism and invented traditions? This employment of academic theories of nationalism, not necessarily legitimizing in and of itself, is significant as a manifestation of the critically self-reflective nature of the volume and the movement that it represents, which promote a particular brand of Hong Kong civic nationalism while nevertheless avoiding the many far more problematic implications of nationalist thought.

For example, in an article entitled "In search of moral courage for the Hong Kong nationality: Reflections on civic boundaries" in the August 2015 issue of *Undergrad*, the author Marcus Lau Yee-ching provides a vigorous denunciation of racial nationalism, promoting instead a vision of civic nationalism for Hong Kong. Deconstructing the notion of "blood and soil" that provided a foundation for German fascism, while at the same time implicitly referencing the blood-based nationalism (black hair and black eyes) and soil-based nationalism (expansive territorial integrity) that reigns uncontested in the People's Republic (Cheng 2015), the author highlights how such exclusionary and destructive ideologies have led to widespread disillusionment with the very idea of nationalism among those who have avoided its seductions. Civic nationalism, by contrast, is based not in the exclusion of others who are deemed to be unlike oneself and thus unworthy, but rather in culture and politics that embrace universal values. Civic nationalism is then an opportunity, in the author's argument, to recapture "nationalism" as a concept and a political movement (Lau 2014, 29–31). The author then proceeds to list three core aspects of Hong Kong's civic nationalist culture: southern culture based in the Cantonese language, civic values, and a common political life.

The idea of a unique Cantonese (or Hong Kong) culture is also elaborated in a *Hong Kong Nationalism* article entitled "There is a complete cultural system behind the idea of 'Hong Kong people'" (Tsou 2015). Both articles critique the uncompromisingly homogenizing and self-aggrandizing political culture based in Beijing, which has not just overlooked but rather actively suppressed Cantonese culture manifested in unique language, written characters, music, and film. The second concept, civic values, is based in such simultaneously universal and local Hong Kong values as an embrace of freedom, respect for the rule of law, and a determined opposition to corruption (Lau 2014, 29). The third concept of a common political life, according to the author, is based in a common experience of resistance to the Chinese empire, a process central to the rise of local Hong Kong identity. Arguing that this identity's foundation in the opposition to colonialism from the north makes it fundamentally defensive rather than offensive, the author calls for a civic nationalism based in local culture, values, and common experience that at the same time actively, openly, and importantly includes Hong Kong's half-million residents of non-Chinese descent (Lau 2014, 30). With this construction of a civic nationalism inclusive of all ethnic groups in Hong Kong, we have journeyed far away from the simplistic "locust" chorus described in the preceding section.

A second example from this collection entitled "Should Hong Kong have the right to national self-determination?" traces the history of Hong Kong, arguing that Hong Kong was not "an integral part of Chinese territory since the beginning of time" (Cheung 2014, 34). Rather, Hong Kong is portrayed herein as a land with a different history, culture, people, and language whose identity and indeed prosperity have evolved primarily as a result of its separation from China, and its residents' corresponding flight from war, chaos, and communist terror (Cheung 2014, 35–36). Tracing a different path to Hong Kong ethnicity, the author cites a newspaper article by Joseph Lian Yizheng applying the Stalinist definition of a nationality to the people of Hong Kong, noting (1) a common language, (2) a clearly defined geographic region, (3) a common economic life, and

(4) common "psychological characteristics" derived from a common culture.[5] Throughout this discussion of commonality, however, the author highlights how this is a diverse commonality characterized not by a forced internal homogeneity, but rather primarily by an obvious divergence from the obsessively enforced commonality to the north, noting that "there are probably many people in Hong Kong who dislike the *Apple Daily* or dislike TVB, but there are very few people in Hong Kong who will read the *People's Daily* or watch CCTV" (Cheung 2014, 35).[6] A molar unity in opposition to an external power opens onto a molecular embrace of internal contention, which maintains its difference precisely through this acceptance of contention.

Later in the article, the author addresses Tibet's troubling modern history within the People's Republic of China as a means of envisioning Hong Kong's future. Looking at the Seventeen-Point Agreement for the "Peaceful" Liberation of Tibet (quotation marks mine) drafted between the Chinese and Tibetan governments in 1951, the author notes the many similarities between this agreement and the city-state's Basic Law, raising the troubling question: Will their implementation, in the end, be the same? For example, guarantees of national regional autonomy and lack of interference in the political system of Tibet (points three and four in the Agreement) resemble guarantees of autonomy, executive, legislative, and independent judicial power (Article 2, Chapter 1, Basic Law). The subsequent history of Tibet, in which the promises of the Seventeen-Point Agreement remain empty and a mode of organization even vaguely resembling autonomy has never been truly realized, is far from reassuring for the people of Hong Kong, a region also witnessing promises of autonomy slipping away at an increasingly rapid pace. Considering the distinct experiences and ethnic characteristics of the people of Hong Kong alongside the disconcerting example of Tibet's "autonomy," the author argues that Hong Kong not only has the right to self-determination, but that indeed the struggle for self-determination is incumbent upon anyone who cares about Hong Kong's future (Cheung 2014, 37). Looking at the history of China's relationships with its nominal autonomous regions, as well as considering the convoluted path of Hong Kong's integration into China over the past two decades, such concern appears eminently reasonable.

A final example, entitled "The controversy surrounding CSSA residence requirements and the local political community" (Leung 2014,

24–26) discusses a 2013 case in which Hong Kong's Court of Final Appeal dismissed seven-year residence requirements put in place in 2004 for new Chinese immigrants to Hong Kong to receive social welfare, known in the region as Comprehensive Social Security Assistance (CSSA).[7] The court's dismissal of previously enforced requirements meant that new immigrants could receive social welfare after just one year of residence, a move likely to add an extra HK $750 million to annual social security expenses (Ngo and Chu 2013). Complaining about new immigrants living a lavish life on welfare certainly sounds like an all-too-familiar xenophobic nationalist argument. Yet moving beyond these assumptions, the article is anything but typical, instead basing the argument on the facts that (1) Hong Kong social services are vastly superior to those provided to the north in the People's Republic proper, (2) there are vastly more people to the north in the People's Republic than in Hong Kong, and (3) the porous border and increasingly porous residence requirements create the risk of severe overpopulation in an already overpopulated region, as well as continued overstretching of an already overstretched but vital social welfare safety net. The fundamental paradox of the welfare state is highlighted here, as it constantly expands to include the needs and interests of a constantly expanding population (Luhmann 1990, 34–39) without the capability of ever fully and finally attaining these goals, which then remain in perpetuity as goals (Luhmann 1997). In the end, the article's main argument is not about welfare or immigrants, but rather about the broader issue of the right of the people of Hong Kong to have a say in their own laws and policies, which are all too often left to the National People's Congress in Beijing to "interpret" and "explain," much to the detriment of the increasingly hollow official slogan of "Hong Kong-ers running Hong Kong (*Gang ren zhi Gang*)."

In each of these essays, as well as in other essays in these collections, one author after another self-critically dips his or her toes into the idea of a Hong Kong nationalism without, however, embracing the more extreme and xenophobic implications of traditional nationalist thought. Deconstructing the naturalized notion of the unified Chinese nation, the authors engage in their own self-conscious construction of a Hong Kong ethnicity and nation that avoids the presumptuous pitfalls so readily apparent within contemporary Chinese nationalism. Challenging the Han-centric racial nationalist narrative of Greater China, the authors promote an inclusive vision of Hong Kong identity that coalesces around a civic ideal rather than any fixed biological identity. And deconstructing the politicized misuse of the identificatory phrase "we are, after all, all Chinese (*dajia dou shi Zhongguoren*)" to silence the voices of the people of Hong Kong and all other internal critics of the status quo, the authors do not rush to declare in anyone's place that "we are, after all, all Hong Kong-ers," but rather attempt to lay the groundwork for a new and voluntary vision of identity. Although they promote the idea of a Hong Kong ethnicity and embrace the possibility of Hong Kong nationalism, there remains a self-critical attention to the dilemmas of such a discourse: authors highlight the need to promote civic nationalism over racial nationalism, point to the need for openness rather than exclusion, and, refreshingly, avoid reference to the term "locusts." Nationalism herein is rendered as a form of rationalism.

We thus have two contrasting articulations of the idea of a Hong Kong nation, with vastly different implications. Whereas the locust discourse troublingly racializes Chinese visitors as utterly different non-human insects devouring Hong Kong's resources and destroying its ecosystem, the authors of *Hong Kong Nationalism* promote a civic nationalism, advocating for the right to self-determination and the realization of democratic institutions that would protect the rights and freedoms of the people of Hong Kong. Although these two types of nationalism present their own clear prescriptions for the future of Hong Kong, their origins are not always understood. The emerging categories of ethnic nationalism in Hong Kong provide us with the opportunity to trace the formation and development of a new sense of ethnicity and national belonging that was not only not present even a decade ago, but was still largely unarticulated even just a few years ago. In the next section, I turn to an analysis of the formation of Hong Kong ethnicization or nationalism to develop a critique of recent theories of ethnic relations circulating in Chinese academia, reinterpreting the issue of rising ethno-national tensions currently at the forefront of political concerns in China today.

Rethinking ethnic politics through Hong Kong

Ethnic tensions in China are an increasingly pressing topic today, particularly in light of the recent rise of self-immolation in Tibet, riots and the emergence of terrorist attacks in Xinjiang and beyond, and growing tensions in Inner Mongolia and other frontier regions. Yet despite these rising tensions, no consensus has been found regarding how best to handle these tensions. James Leibold's recent review of ethnic policy debates in China introduces readers to the diverse array of opinions that have emerged over the past half-decade on the question of ethnic relations and ethnic policy in China: liberal and conservative voices, support for a return to "indigenous" traditions or an embrace of global norms, as well as calls for an enhanced sense of national belonging and a melting-pot view of identity (Leibold 2013). One of the more prominent voices within these debates has been Ma Rong, a sociologist currently based at Peking University, whose advocacy for the "depoliticization" of ethnicity in China, Leibold notes, was once a marginal view that has gradually made its way into mainstream discussions of ethnic policy (Leibold 2013, 14).

What is the "depoliticization" of ethnicity? According to Ma, the term "*minzu*" applied in Chinese ethnic categorization is the primary source of many of China's ethnic issues. *Minzu* is often translated as nationality or nation, and Ma Rong usefully points out the internal contradiction in terminology between the use of the term "*Zhonghua minzu*," meaning the "Chinese nation/nationality," and the 56 *minzu*, referring to the 56 nationalities presumed to be part of this nation. Accordingly, Ma proposes changing the designation of minority "*minzu*" or nationalities within the Chinese ethnic framework to the term "*zuqun*," one that he claims more closely resembles the term "ethnic groups" and thus provides a better orientation for "viewing, understanding, and managing ethnic relations" (Ma 2007, 202).

Ma's suggested change in terminology emerges from his belief that current Chinese ethnic policy is based in a "foreign" framework for ethnic identity, and that a return to authentic "indigenous" modes of handling ethnicity would begin to resolve or "harmonize" ethnic problems. According to Ma, the traditional ethnic framework in China viewed ethnicity through a cultural lens, expressed in the distinction between barbarism and civilization (*huayi zhi bian*). This cultural approach, he claims, promoted equality between peoples and provided space for individuals to cross this border toward the ideal of civilization: in Ma's words, "Following the principle of 'teaching without discrimination,' it was the Chinese cultural tradition to transform the 'uncivilized' minorities into 'civilized' members of society through acculturation" (Ma 2007, 204).

Setting aside the deeply problematic aspects of this portrayal of the past, such as the clearly racial aspects of this culturalism (Dikötter 1992) and most notably the irony of claiming equality between peoples in a self-declared Sinocentric distinction between civilization and barbarism, it is worth noting that Ma's construction of the romantic "culturalist" past is primarily a means of critiquing the ethnic framework in the present, which he views as having replaced the universally assimilating culturalization of ethnic groups with their politicization: the terminology of culturalization versus politicization in this narrative is then more important than the subtleties of historical reality. Following this distinction, Ma claims that the current ethnic framework in place since the early 1950s was copied directly from the Soviet Union,[8] and thus does not fit what he would call "Chinese tradition." The national identification project registered each and every Chinese citizen under a particular "nationality (*minzu*)," theoretically granted autonomy to ethnic minorities such that these groups could supposedly "play a leading role and manage their own affairs in autonomous areas," and put in place a "series of policies in favor of ethnic minorities in the administrative, educational, economic, and cultural areas" (Ma 2007, 214). The result of each of these aspects of the current ethnic framework, Ma claims, is tying minorities to a particular geographic area, granting these groups a political status as well as administrative power in their autonomous territory, thereby resulting in the politicization and institutionalization of these ethnic groups and the corresponding strengthening of their group consciousness. Furthermore, according to Ma's narrative, such consciousness, politicization, and institutionalization would otherwise supposedly never have happened.

Attempting to apply this theory in practice, Ma argues that the policy of recognizing, for example, Tibetans and Uighurs as minority nationalities in the 1950s has resulted in the politicization and institutionalization of these groups, thus leading to the ethnic tensions that we see today. Essentially, in unexpected curious variation on doing things with words, the act of acknowledging and labeling these groups as "nationalities," according to Ma, has produced a politicized and thus unstable situation for a singular nation. As a result, Ma proposes moving away from the Soviet-style politicization of ethnicity to the culturalization of ethnicity, prioritizing national identification as the source of political identity, and referring to minority groups as "*zuqun*" (ethnicities) rather than "*minzu*" (nationalities). Yet is this how identity and ethnic relations work in practice? A more careful reading of the history of interactions on the Chinese frontiers, looking at, for example, Uighurs' and Tibetans' unique histories relative to what we now call China, raises many questions about Ma's line of reasoning and in particular his founding assumption of eternal unity.[9] Yet the recent emergence of the notion of Hong Kong nationalism in particular challenges his analysis: rather than recognition resulting in the politicization of nationalities, I argue that it is precisely in the process of cross-cultural interaction, as well as in the experience of political stalling at best and suppression at worst, that nationalities can become politicized *even before they are recognized* by the state and even, in some cases, by their own constituents. The problem then is not outdated terms or labels misshaping reality that then need to be revised to more accurately reflect the underlying unity of the Chinese nation, but rather an outdated political system that is unable to deal with the full underlying complexity of an increasingly diverse society, which it tries to force into the constraints of an imaginary unified Chinese nation. The solution is not depoliticization, as Ma Rong recommends, but rather an understanding of how coarse authoritarian politics influences complex identities in practice.

How, then, did the notion of a Hong Kong nationality originate? As reprehensible as the locust discourse is, we should not lose sight of the fact that it emerged solely within rising cultural and political tensions between China and Hong Kong: we might also note that before the term "locust" had been used in Hong Kong, Chinese commentator and self-declared direct descendant of Confucius Kong Qingdong had nonchalantly called the people of Hong Kong "dogs" (*Oriental Daily* 2012). Such politicized name-calling occurred alongside growing sociocultural pressures in the form of decade-long tensions over the availability of hospital beds in Hong Kong on account of an influx of Chinese visitors giving birth in the territories, anger over parallel traders hoarding milk powder to the point that shelves were cleared in many areas of the territories, and tensions over dwindling spaces in local public schools. Such fear of outsiders, we must note, is not exclusive to Hong Kong: residents of many of China's first-tier cities such as Beijing and Shanghai fear being overwhelmed by the presumably unwashed masses, eagerly protecting the *hukou* that in reality provides them with few concrete benefits other than an urban identity apart from their rural compatriots. Yet the stakes are seen as higher in Hong Kong since the promotion of the "national security" amendment to the Basic Law in 2003, the National People's Congress decision on electoral reform in 2014, and the controversial disqualification of localist Legislative Council candidates in 2016, as these growing threats to Hong Kong's already fading autonomy have intensified these clashes. Examining these tensions, it becomes clear that in many cases, Hong Kong has served as an indispensable safety valve for the longstanding shortcomings in social services, food safety, and a general sense of security to the north, while its people have nevertheless been labeled as "dogs" by fervent Chinese nationalists. Insofar as imagined commonality ("we are all Chinese") is primarily employed as a pretext for rationalizing a losing situation to the people of Hong Kong, one can then begin to understand the origins of the emphasis upon difference via Hong Kong nationalism, while at the same time still disagreeing with the problematic expression of this difference through the dehumanizing label of the "locust," targeting the unknowing fellow victims of this same hegemonic political power.

Reviewing the alternative manifestation of Hong Kong nationalism described above, namely the civic nationalism employed in the collection *Hong Kong Nationalism*, this expression of Hong Kong nationalism through an embrace of democratic institutions and thinking runs counter to the Chinese state's attempts to racialize its current historically produced political framework as uniquely and naturally Chinese, or, in official parlance, "socialism with Chinese characteristics." In this culturalized authoritarianism that fills in ideological blank spaces in the present, state-sponsored political values are represented as "Chinese tradition" such that the former can not only derive value from the latter, but can indeed be viewed as the sole natural outcome of the latter: the "China model" (Bell 2015). The result of this constructed fusion is that the voicing of any doubts about such culturalized politics leads to doubts about one's proper "Chineseness," which in turn devalues one's opposition or criticisms as the muddled misunderstandings of an outsider: in a turn of *ressentiment*, a disillusioning state of political repression becomes a source of "uniqueness" that cannot be changed and that demands "understanding," in particular from Hong Kong residents with their perceived colonially polluted minds. In response to this framework, which attempts to ideologically graft Chineseness onto the current repressive political model, pushed onto Hong Kong through national education and growing restrictions on civil liberties, it is understandable that people disillusioned with this constraining vision of submission to authoritarian politics as the core of Chinese identity would respond with their own identity and politics, expressed in the Hong Kong nationalism volume's critique of Sino-centrism and embrace of democratic self-determination.

Thus, tracing the origins of the idea of a Hong Kong nationality and the emergence of Hong Kong nationalism, I find that this newest form of ethnicity and nationalism in the People's Republic is not the product of a state-sponsored nationality status, nor is it in any way related to state politicization of this label, thereby directly disproving Ma Rong's immensely political proposal for "depoliticizing" ethnic relations: such depoliticization, after all, could only be viewed as nonpolitical from Beijing's perspective. Rather than anachronistic labels that need to be abandoned for the sake of national unity, the emergence of Hong Kong nationalism shows that it is primarily an anachronistic political system, unable to cope with the complexity of contemporary Hong Kong and indeed Chinese society, that has resulted in the rise of such nationalism, generating an unexpected response to an essentially unsustainable political situation. Hong Kong ethnicization or nationalism has occurred not because of official recognition, but rather because of official dismissal of the Hong Kong people's concerns under the all-encompassing rubric of Chineseness, which can then in turn only be represented and addressed as a peril.

These findings on the rise of Hong Kong nationalism are thus also relevant to the study of national and ethnic identity in other frontier areas, such as Tibet and Xinjiang: rather than imagining with Ma Rong that a change in terminology and an increased emphasis upon a unified Chinese identity would somehow provide a solution to these ethnic tensions, we must note that the core issues herein remain similar to the issues in Hong Kong: mass migration, unflattering stereotypes and marginalization, ideological deployments of identity, and empty promises of autonomy. It is then not problematic ethnic labels, but rather problematic politics that generates and reinforces difference in China today. The core dilemma in ethnic relations and frontier areas in China today is not a prior ethnic identity itself, but rather a sociopolitical system unable to meet the needs of an increasingly complex society, creating new oppositional identities in the process. And wish though we may, there is no clear solution to this dilemma.

Conclusion: The promise and peril of the Yellow Peril discourse

This analysis of the rise of anti-Chinese and localist nationalist discourses in contemporary Hong Kong argues, in conclusion, two main points intended to add new layers of analytical complexity to our understanding of "Yellow Peril" discourses beyond simply pointing one's finger and denouncing them. First, not all expressions of concern or fear with regards to the "rise of China" are necessarily based in irrational or paranoid Sinophobic delusions, as can be seen in the discussion of the very real conflicts that have emerged in the course of the culturally "Chinese" territory of Hong Kong's integration into today's China. It would be easy and of course very politically correct, with our dog-eared copies of *Orientalism* in hand, to criticize the rise of anti-Chinese sentiment in Hong Kong as a product of the territory's presumably insidious British colonial legacy. But if we really want to take the issue of positioning seriously in academic work, we need to think beyond the East–West binary circuit that is continually reproduced in today's analyses to understand that oppressive powers exist across multiple binaries beyond East and West, including such binaries as China–Hong Kong or China–Tibet. Sometimes these hostile discourses emerge not as wild imaginings of an unfamiliar other but rather as the product of an all-too-great familiarity with an overpowering everyday other. Dismissive caricatures of anti-Chinese sentiment in places like Tibet, Xinjiang, and Hong Kong that attempt to attribute all such manifestations to "Western influence" then replace real political struggles with a new imaginary Orient, cleansed of internal conflict for the sake of a false analytical coherence and a feel-good narrative with reliably and comfortingly clear heroes and villains. Despite the substantial challenges involved, scholars of these processes should strive to move beyond such moralizing to reflect the full complexity of identity processes in the real world, focusing in particular upon the study of such fundamentally novel identity developments as those discussed above.

Second, however, not all criticisms of contemporary China and Chinese influence are created equal. The locust discourse discussed above claims to fundamentally racially differentiate the people of China from the people of Hong Kong, but in reality is nothing but a simplistic inversion of Chinese nationalism's essentialist assumptions about the people of Hong Kong: "dogs" are replaced by "locusts," colonial pollution is replaced by post-1949 communist moral pollution, and caricatures of crass materialism and lack of culture are replaced by mirrored caricatures of crass materialism and lack of culture. To simply replace one essentialist and exclusionary nationalism with another essentialist and exclusionary nationalism is to lose sight of the openness that fundamentally differentiates Hong Kong culture from contemporary PRC culture, producing a truly perilous situation in response to a perceived peril. The most powerful way to oppose the stifling political atmosphere and sociocultural issues currently bearing down upon Hong Kong from the north is then not to promote simplistic feel-good and click-friendly fantasies of the complete separation of Hong Kong and China but rather to, taking the lead from *Hong Kong Nationalism*, promote Hong Kong as a truly open society that rises above such tempting but in reality limiting views of the Other and the self. In this way, the fundamentally imaginary nature of Hong Kong nationalism, unlikely to ever be realized in practice as a result of insurmountable political realities, could nevertheless have very meaningful real-world effects in Hong Kong and, one might hope, beyond.

Notes

Research for this paper was generously funded by a New Staff Grant from Macquarie University. I would also like to express my thanks to Benjamin Garvey and Peter Gries for their thoughtful comments on this paper, and to Dan Garrett for his insights on the history of locust imagery.

1   Circulation figures for *Apple Daily* in the first six months of 2012 can be found at the Hong Kong Audit Bureau of Circulation Web site: http://www.hkabc.com.hk/admin/reports/1398.pdf

2   The Basic Law is the Hong Kong Special Administrative Region's constitution, ostensibly guaranteeing the territory a high degree of autonomy. A series of "interpretations" of the Basic Law in recent years by the Chinese state have raised serious doubts about the prospects for autonomy in Hong Kong. Article 24 of the Basic Law, which addresses the right of abode for immigrants from the People's Republic of China, has

been the subject of considerable controversy, discussed in a later section of this chapter.

3 See, for example, Local Studio, 2015, "Hong Kong is not China." Pamphlet.

4 These more established academics and commentators include former editor of the *Hong Kong Economic Journal* Joseph Lian Yizheng, Ho-fung Hung of Johns Hopkins University, independent scholar Eric S. Y. Tsui, and Wu Rwei-ren of Taiwan's Academia Sinica.

5 A similar argument about the distinctive nature of southern culture compared to the current Beijing-centered hegemony is made in Carrico 2012.

6 *People's Daily* and CCTV are Chinese state-run media.

7 The full decision can be read at "Kong Yunming (appellant) and the Director of Social Welfare (respondent), final appeal No. 2 of 2013." December 17, 2013. http://legalref.judiciary.gov.hk/lrs/common/ju/ju _frame.jsp?DIS=90670&currpage=T

8 The actual history of ethnic classification is considerably more complex. See Mullaney 2010.

9 An excellent summary of the history of Chinese–Tibetan interactions and the myths that have emerged around this relationship can be found in Elliot Sperling's *The Tibet–China Conflict: History and Polemics.* Honolulu: East–West Center, 2004. On the history of the Uyghur people and their current situation, readers can refer to James Millward's *Eurasian Crossroads: A History of Xinjiang.* New York: Columbia University Press, 2009, and Gardner Bovingdon's *The Uyghurs: Strangers in Their Own Land.* New York: Columbia University Press, 2010.

References

Apple Daily. 2012. "Locust" advertisement, placed by HK Golden Forum users. *Apple Daily.* February 1, 2012.

BBC News. 2012. "Hong Kong to limit Mainland China maternity services." *BBC News.* April 25. http://www.bbc.com/news/world-asia-china -17838280. Last accessed December 2016.

"Beida jiaoshou: Xianggang ren shi gou (Peking University Professor: Hong Kong people are dogs)." 2012. January 21. *Oriental Daily.* http:// orientaldaily.on.cc/cnt/news/20120121/00174_001.html. Last accessed December 2016.

Bell, Daniel. 2015. *The China Model: Political Meritocracy and the Limits of Democracy.* Princeton: Princeton University Press.

Billé, Franck. 2015. *Sinophobia: Anxiety, Violence, and the Making of Mongolian Identity*. Honolulu: University of Hawai'i Press.

Bovingdon, Gardner. 2010. *The Uyghurs: Strangers in Their Own Land*. New York: Columbia University Press.

Carrico, Kevin. 2012. "Recentering China: The Cantonese in and beyond the Han." In *Critical Han Studies: The History, Representation, and Identity of China's Majority*, edited by Thomas Mullaney, James Leibold, Stéphane Gros, and Eric Vanden Bussche. Berkeley: University of California Press.

Cheng, Yinghong. 2015. "Gangtai Patriotic Songs and Racialized Chinese Nationalism." In *Race and Racism in Modern East Asia*, edited by Rotem Kowner and Walter Demel. Leiden: Brill.

Cheung, Si-chai. 2014. "*Xianggang shifou yingyou minzu zijue quanli* [Should Hong Kong have the right to national self-determination?]" *Undergrad*, February 2014: 34–37.

Chinafile. 2013. "Are ethnic tensions on the rise in China?" February 13, 2014. http://www.chinafile.com/conversation/are-ethnic-tensions-rise-china. Last accessed December 2016.

Chong, Dennis, and Thomas Chan. 2013. "Fears of overcrowding in border school classes." *South China Morning Post*, March 23. http://www.scmp .com/news/hong-kong/article/1197448/fears-overcrowding-border-school -classes. Last accessed December 2016.

Cou Hiu-nok. 2014. "*Xianggang ren de beihou shi zhengge wenhua tixi* [An entire cultural system lies behind the idea of the Hong Kong people]." *Undergrad*, February 2014: 31–33.

DeFrancis, John. 1984. *The Chinese Language: Fact and Fantasy*. Honolulu: University of Hawai'i Press.

Demick, Barbara. 2014. "Toddler defecating riles residents of Mainland China and Hong Kong." *Los Angeles Times*. April 30. http://www.latimes.com /world/asia/la-fg-wn-china-hong-kong-defecating-dispute-20140430-story .html. Last accessed December 2016.

Dikötter, Frank. 1992. *The Discourse of Race in Modern China*. Stanford: Stanford University Press.

Fiskesjö, Magnus. 2011. "The Animal Other: Re-naming the Barbarians in 20th Century China." *Social Text* (Special issue, "China and the Human"), 29.4: 57–79.

Hillman, Ben, and Gray Tuttle, eds. 2016. *Ethnic Conflict and Protest in Tibet and Xinjiang*. New York: Columbia University Press.

Hong Kong Home Affairs Department, Race Relations Unit. 2013. "The Demographics: Ethnic Groups." July 30. http://www.had.gov.hk/rru /english/info/info_dem.html. Last accessed December 2016.

Hong Kong Undergraduate Student Union, eds. 2014. *Xianggang minzu lun* [Theory of a Hong Kong Ethnicity]. Hong Kong: Published by HKU Undergraduate Student Union.

Ko, Vanessa. 2013. "Mainland Chinese Traders Milking Hong Kong for All It's Worth." *Time Magazine*. February 4. http://world.time.com/2013/02/04 /mainland-chinese-traders-milking-hong-kong-for-all-its-worth/. Last accessed December 2016.

LaFraniere, Sharon. 2012. "Mainland Chinese flock to Hong Kong to give birth." *New York Times*. February 23. http://www.nytimes.com/2012 /02/23/world/asia/mainland-chinese-flock-to-hong-kong-to-have-babies .html?_r=0. Last accessed December 2016.

Lau, Marcus (Lau Yee-ching). 2015. "*Xunzhao Xianggang minzu de daode yongqi: guanyu gongmin jiexian de sikao* [In Search of Moral Courage for the Hong Kong Nationality: reflections upon civic boundaries]." *Undergrad*, August 2015: 28–31.

Leibold, James. 2013. *Ethnic Policy in China: Is Reform Inevitable?* Honolulu: East–West Center.

Leung, Brian. (Leung Gai-peng). 2014. "*Zongyuan sanxian zhengyi yu bentu zhengzhi gongtongti* [The Controversy Surrounding CSSA Residence Requirements and the Local Political Community]." *Undergrad*, February 2014: 24–26.

Leung, Chen-ying. 2015. "Uphold the rule of law, seize the opportunities, make the right choices: pursue democracy, boost the economy, improve people's livelihood." http://www.policyaddress.gov.hk/2015/eng/pdf/PA2015.pdf. Last accessed December 2016.

Local Studio. 2015. "Hong Kong is not China." Pamphlet.

Luhmann, Niklas. 1990. *Political Theory in the Welfare State*. Berlin: Walter de Gruyter.

———. 1997. "The Limits of Steering." *Theory, Culture, and Society* 14 (1): 41–57.

Ma Rong. 2007. "A New Perspective in Guiding Ethnic Relations in 21st Century China: 'Depoliticization' of Ethnicity in China." *Asian Ethnicity* 8 (3): 199–217.

Millward, James. 2009. *Eurasian Crossroads: A History of Xinjiang*. New York: Columbia University Press.

Mullaney, Thomas. 2010. *Coming to Terms with the Nation: Ethnic Classification in Modern China*. Berkeley: University of California Press, 2010.

Ngo, Jennifer, and Julie Chu. 2013. "Top court dismisses seven-year residency requirement for CSSA benefits." *South China Morning Post*. December 17. http://www.scmp.com/news/hong-kong/article/1383952/top-court

-dismisses-seven-year-residency-requirement-cssa-benefits?page=all. Last
accessed December 2016.

Pak, Jennifer. 2013. "School place shortage fuels Hong Kong tensions." *BBC News*. July 4. http://www.bbc.com/news/world-asia-china-23127940.

Sataline, Suzanne. 2015. "Meet the man who wants to make Hong Kong a city-state." *Foreign Policy*. May 18. http://foreignpolicy.com/2015/05/18/hong-kong-china-protests-democracy-nativism/. Last accessed December 2016.

Sperling, Elliot. 2004. *The Tibet-China Conflict: History and Polemics*. Honolulu: East–West Center.

Wong, Alan. 2015. "After criticism from Hong Kong's leader, publisher raises book's print run." *New York Times* Sinosphere blog. January 14. http://sinosphere.blogs.nytimes.com/2015/01/14/after-criticism-from-hong-kongs-leader-a-publication-raises-its-print-run/?_r=0. Last accessed December 2016.

CHAPTER 9

⌇

Who's Afraid of Confucius?

Fear, Encompassment, and the Global
Debates over the Confucius Institutes

MAGNUS FISKESJÖ

I T WAS PROBABLY INEVITABLE that the Chinese Party-State's global Confucius Institutes project would provoke a global round of accusations and counter-accusations, sometimes invoking the old idea of a "Yellow Peril."

The first Confucius Institutes (CIs) were opened in 2004, and there are now several hundred of them in institutions of higher learning on all major continents. If we also count the related "Confucius Classrooms" in high schools and the like, which are arrangements where the Chinese government pays foreign institutions to host Chinese teachers who use textbooks provided from China, the total number is about a thousand. They are all part of a strategic, global, and long-term Chinese Party-State campaign to increase its "soft power" around the world.[1] The CIs and the "Confucius Classrooms" are not independent, but lie under the direct control of the ruling Communist Party and its government, which funds them. The explicit agenda of the CI project is to use the considerable investments that have been made to help shape a positive image of China abroad, and this also includes the silencing or drowning out of critical views of China, or of its new global power.

Alarmingly, university administrators have often accepted CIs into their institutions without consulting their own faculty, not even those with knowledge about China. This accentuates the general erosion of faculty governance, which was at one time a key supporting ingredient in the once-popular idea of the university as an autonomous center of free inquiry. This is happening because in the current climate of stagnating or even declining public investment in education in their own countries, university administrators are eager to find new sources of financing and revenue—which often leads them to accept conflict-of-interest arrangements, and not just Chinese ones, against the opposition of faculty.[2]

Because of all this, the stage was set for a global debate over the interference and influence of the Confucius Institutes in the foreign universities or schools that accept to host them, and it is in this context that the CIs have been portrayed as a menace.[3] This, in turn, has provoked counter-accusations from the Chinese government, namely that intimations that the CIs pose a threat are unfounded, needless, or even tendentious and nefarious worries. These posturings and accusations and counter-accusations of fear and fearmongering sometimes draw on older "Yellow Peril" strains, which are sometimes visible immediately under the surface, and which sometimes surface. But the confrontations over today's Yellow Perils take new forms that turn on the new global situation, with a more powerful China under authoritarian Party rule today assuming a global position as a center of capital accumulation and consumption as well as military and political clout. This chapter is intended to discuss the multifaceted fears around China's Confucius Institutes—and the key role of Confucius himself in this saga, unfolding in the global arena.

From Portugal to Chicago

The debates over the CIs reached a new level of intensity in 2014. The programs had expanded exponentially and with few challenges until that time, but then, in 2014, there was a dramatic incident in which Confucius Institute officials moved to censor the program of the biannual meeting of the European Association of Chinese Studies, which took place in Portugal in July 2014, causing an outrage. The background was that the CI central office (the Hanban) had partially sponsored the event financially, and the CI officials therefore assumed they could dictate to the organizers. What appears to have transpired was that the Hanban director, Madame Xu Lin, first noticed that the conference program included advertisements from other sponsors, one of them being the Chiang Ching-kuo Foundation, located in Taiwan (a long-standing sponsor of these meetings, which advertised its fellowships for Chinese studies). Seeing an advertisement from an entity on autonomous Taiwan provoked the ire of Mme. Xu, even though there was no adversarial content. She then appears to have ordered the collection of all meetings brochures that could be found, and then had her staff rip out all the pages containing these advertisements. The altered brochures were then redistributed. The event's organizers and participants were utterly confounded: the excised pages had included vital program information, which was laboriously restored. A formal protest was lodged, unprecedented in recent history.[4]

This kind of behavior may seem outrageous outside China, but inside China, Party officials not infrequently cancel scheduled academic meetings, festivals, and the like at the last minute, often without explanation, and see this as their natural prerogative. Chinese organizers are often embarrassed, but powerless; foreign participants are generally bewildered by these shows of authoritarianism. But for Chinese officials to take such drastic action outside China, to bring this domestic capriciousness abroad and impose it on an international host was a violation of the normal international rules of engagement. Therefore, this incident caused widespread concern, and to many must have looked like a harbinger of future ominous Chinese interference and the setting aside of accepted norms—of exactly the kind that many had feared was inherent in the CIs, either openly, as in this incident, or through more subtle censorship behind the scenes. The Portuguese example looked like an attempt on the part of the Chinese to suddenly, willfully, and unilaterally rewrite the rules of engagement. If Chinese representatives were behaving like this in the open, some thought, should we not worry about what they may be doing behind the scenes? (For example, are officials instructing China-dispatched teachers in what topics to suppress, and how to suppress them? Are they wielding their influence when representatives are wining and dining docile foreign university administrators, for the sake of "friendship"?)

In the same year, 2014, several other Confucius Institutes were suspended or cancelled, including notably the one at Stockholm University, in Sweden, which had been among the very first CIs to open back in 2004 (*South China Morning Post* 2015). There, the university ultimately decided—exactly as many critics had long argued—that hosting the CI within itself created untenable suspicions of undue influence.

Also in 2014, another incident strongly suggested the same aggressive Chinese attitude as that exhibited in Portugal the same summer—but with a twist that provided further insight into the Chinese regime's conception of hard power and soft power. This was the rather sudden termination of the CI at the University of Chicago. This was in itself a significant loss of prestige for the Chinese project as a whole, even though several other prestigious American universities have continued to host the CIs. Although considerable debate had taken place at the university over the merits and dangers of hosting the CI there,[5] the announcement of the termination came as a surprise. The actual trigger seems to have been offensive remarks made by the same Mme. Xu, Director-General of the Hanban, belittling the university's president as a meekly obedient figure. The comments were made to a domestic Chinese newspaper interview, published only in Chinese for domestic consumption, and neither Mme. Xu nor the paper thought to anticipate that Americans might read her remarks, and how they may then react, if insulted in this way. The interviewer, having first discussed with the Director-General her motherly concerns for the welfare of CI teachers dispatched to work in faraway Africa, turned to note how

> Xu Lin's toughness has been felt by many. In late April this year, more than 100 retired professors at the University of Chicago in the U.S. petitioned for the closing of its Confucius Institute. Xu Lin directly sent a letter to the University of Chicago President and made a call to its Beijing representative and pronounced just one sentence: "I'm fine, if your University decides to drop out." Her attitude made the other side anxious, and they soon replied that the university leadership had decided to continue to do a good job of running [ban hao] the Confucius Institute.[6]

This patronizing treatment of a remorseful American university president, portrayed as duly promising that he and his staff wouldn't be naughty again, would have left a bitter aftertaste for the decision-makers at the University of Chicago regardless of the fact that they apparently never received such a letter, which may have been made up anyway, for the sake of projecting toughness in the interview. In China, such an image of Chinese Communist toughness would have played very well to Communist leaders at home, letting them feel good in their all-powerful domestic position in which they can always show who's the boss, and where the press exists to enhance this state of affairs, not disrupt it.

Yet to anyone else, and especially to those of us who know Chinese history, this propaganda image of the pliable barbarian also uncomfortably evokes the all-too-common Chinese "imperial" inability to deal with others as equals. It suggests that all the previous talk about equal footing and equal benefit for the parties involved (here, the Chinese Party-State versus the University of Chicago) was but empty platitudes. I will return to this key problem further on.

The curious recruitment of Confucius

The developments leading up to the current situation, with a vast network of Chinese state–sponsored institutions implanted in foreign schools and universities around the world, are quite bewildering. They are emblematic of China's rapid transformation into a global power that is both new and old at the same time.

First of all, we must note the re-appropriation of the ancient philosopher Confucius as a representative of China under the rule of the Chinese Communist Party. This in itself is, hands down, the most curious, striking, and interesting aspect of the whole affair. In the past, the very same Party vehemently condemned Confucius as a reactionary thinker who served the ruling classes.

The Party's paramount figure, Mao Zedong, was himself decisively, explicitly, and virulently anti-Confucius. We get a very interesting glimpse of Mao's own thinking about Confucius in relation to the mission of his revolutionary Party, in a fragment of his conversations with his nephew Mao Yuanxin, himself a zealous revolutionary who was very close to Mao in his last years. Mao argued the following, in about 1975:

> We Communists arose from criticism of Confucius. And we will never follow the route of those who came before, criticizing and then once again revering [Confucius]. After we have established our position [of power], if we once more pick up Confucius' thought and hand it to the people, then we [too] will fall into [that] cycle of history. And we cannot do that. Whenever the Communist Party can no longer govern, or runs into trouble, and then asks for Confucius to come back, then that means you too are soon finished.[7]

Confucius can, of course, be many things to different people; there continue to exist various disparate interpretations of Confucius.[8] But Mao here is addressing the particular brand of "imperial" Confucianism that in his view, as a self-declared revolutionary, was revived time and again by incoming Chinese emperors who wished to perpetuate an unequal class society. There is a particular usefulness to this Confucius, the emphasis on obedience to authority, which is what each of those emperors cherished, and which was why they bothered to revere him, mark his birthdays, and so on. It was this use, and this "cycle," that Mao had wanted his own Communist revolution to finally put a stop to.

We can disregard the fact that Mao and his Party, just like in the Soviet Union that served as the model for China's own socialist economy and society, themselves soon formed a new class hierarchy of their own. Regardless, Mao still held on to his analysis of Confucius—born out of a Marxist notion of class contradictions driving history—as an arch-conservative figure, with a special place in the specifically Chinese "cycle of history" that he sought to break with. His fear was that if the Confucius of the emperors was rolled out again, this would mean that his Communist-revolutionary dream had been set aside by a new ruling class seeking to build a Confucian-style, fundamentally conservative reverence for an unequal social status quo dressed up as "harmony."

And the central surprise about China now is, of course, that Mao's fear is exactly what is coming true in China today. It is almost as if Mao-the-purported-revolutionary gave us a forecast that has now come true, Confucius included. Only three decades after economic reforms started, stagnating state socialism has been transformed into a state capitalism in which the Communist Party presides over a sharply divided society, with a class of new rich who are loyal to the Party because they rely on it for their wealth. The Party's members are themselves firmly integrated with this transformed class hierarchy, commanding tremendous wealth as part of an elite social stratum that includes and merges with a new class of the privately wealthy. Even as the "anti-corruption" campaigns roll on, many Party officials exploit state power to enrich themselves, often simultaneously serving as the chieftains of networks of wealth ownership in key industries and resources.

At the same time, the state apparatus crushes dissent from everyone—writers, lawyers, environmental activists, and others—including exploited workers who try to form labor unions (Friedman et al. 2016; see also Fiskesjö 2017)—all in the name of social order. It is no wonder that even inside the Party, few believe the still-listed but increasingly anachronistic Party dogmas about class struggle for a worker's and peasant's Socialist state and a Communist future.

Against this background it is also no wonder, but no less paradoxical, that the Party itself is reaching for Confucius. The Party leader himself has personally attended birthday celebrations for the sage, and personally spoken there about the relevance of Confucius for contemporary social morals, harmony, and order.[9]

This very public and symbolic embrace is taking place along with celebrations of ancient and mythical emperors for whom enormous new monumental memorials and solemn sacrificial rituals have also been recreated; they are the stuff of an emergent, comprehensive neo-nationalist narrative that also would be useful to eventually displace and replace Communism and Marxism as a national ideology or religion. However, in contrast to Confucius, the revived cult of the ancient emperors has so far not yet been fully and officially embraced by top-level officials of the still-wavering, still-officially-Communist ruling Party.

But Confucius, for his part, has been invited back in, and is being mobilized in earnest—despite protests by a minority of die-hard "Leftists" who remember and approve of Mao's stance.[10] In January 2016, news came (*People's Daily* 2016) that the Party Politburo had invited and heard a special lecture itself by a Confucius scholar, a leading representative of the conservative-styled *guoxue*, or "national learning." In past years, Central Party School officials have assembled in the hundreds for similar lectures (Pu Rui 2015), and the school has sent delegations on tour around China to preach the same message to local officials, about the merits of traditional values and how they can be deployed today to promote "harmony" (that is, social order defined as a positive value).

Mao the revolutionary must be turning his torso in his glass box in the mausoleum on Tiananmen Square, but there is no mistaking that Party leaders are reviving the Confucius of the emperors—in the face of a near-total loss of faith in official Communism and Chinese State Marxism as a national religion, in a new social landscape that is heavily marked by the new class divides. I think it is possible that the leaders are even preparing, when the time comes, to formally abandon Communism, change the name of the Party, revive the Empire with its mythic ancestry, and introduce a new Neo-Confucianism as the accompanying new state religion—something neo-conservatives have already been clamoring for.[11]

In this flurry of a political revival of Confucius, one very interesting move, which helps explain the curious choice of the sage's name for the Confucius Institute project, is the identification of (selective) Confucian tenets with Chinese national culture. Even though Confucius (ca. 551–479 BCE) lived long before the empires, and in a world two and a half millennia before the organization of the present nation-state of China, the current recruitment of Confucius is as an ambassador of modern yet enduring Chinese national values, as defined by the current government. The choice of name for the "Confucius Institutes" must have been made in 2003 or so, a decade earlier than the Party's official embrace of Confucianism took off; but the CI baptizers must have had a certain sense of premonition in this fusion with current national identity[12] that made "Confucius" the ideal choice for the "Confucius Institutes"—which teach only the mainland version of the modern Chinese language, and which promote only images of China that are promoted under Communist Party rule. As the Australian China historian Michael Churchman writes (2011, n.p.),

> The control through Confucius Institutes of what can and cannot be taught as Chinese is as equally rooted in the politics of the People's Republic as the control of what can and cannot be discussed about China. It is by nature detrimental to a wider understanding of China as is the exclusion of certain censored topics.

That is to say, foreigners hoping to learn about China through Confucius Institutes will be fed a "Chinese culture" approved by the ruling Party and defined as directly continuous with the time in which the sage himself actually lived, however different that was.

Confucius as cultural ambassador

This also seems to shed more light on just why Confucius, rather than any other figure, has been recruited: he was chosen not because he is the only other Chinese figure aside from Mao who has any name recognition outside China, but because of the hope that, notwithstanding his centuries-old authoritarian reputation, his name will help assuage foreigners' fear of a China so powerful that it can dictate its own terms and rewrite the rules of international engagement and diplomacy.

At the same time, if a more benign Confucius is revived, recast, and re-appointed as the front man for contemporary China-the-nation, itself merged together with the Communist Party that has appointed itself as ruler of that nation and is channeling Confucius (cf. *New York Times* 2014a), then those foreigners who point out the danger of censorship at universities hosting Confucius Institutes can be conveniently framed as criticizing "China" itself, not just its current Party-State regime.

The Confucius Institutes teach the Chinese language as defined in the mainland (on this see Churchman's discussion of the limitations that this places on the foreign student), using pre-vetted teachers who have been instructed in what topics to avoid (and how to avoid them—for hilarious examples of these awkward silences, see Hubbert 2014). This includes sponsored and hosted events and programs, in which the CI custodians will steer away from anything criticizing the harsh Chinese rule over Tibet, etc.[13] For the teachers dispatched to undertake this work—who may of course themselves often be nice people—there can be no question that as designated soldiers in the soft-power army, they must toe the Party line on just what is national language, culture, and politics, and on what must be omitted, avoided, or suppressed.[14] As with the press at home and in the Chinese-controlled media abroad, this will be reinforced by updated instructions transmitted from home, reinforced in gatherings on the home front, and in selective teaching materials, and so on.[15]

This works together with the most peculiar and ingenious aspect of the arrangement with Confucius Institutes: the Chinese government strategy to pay (from their huge trade surpluses) to have their institutes (and "classrooms") embedded *inside* host country institutions, creating a situation of indebtedness and dependence that is couched in the concept of "friendship" familiar from Chinese official relations—a very heavily instrumentalized, and politicized, kind of friendship that is often used to muzzle and silence inferior and dependent "friends"[16] in the name of "harmony," very much in tune with the emphasis on hierarchy in the "imperial" style of Confucianism.

The awkwardness of the Confucius Institute arrangement is unlike other comparable ventures like the Alliance Française or the Goethe Institutes, which have their own addresses in the host cities or towns and which are easily identified as promoting their respective nations. In the case of China's Confucius Institutes, however, because they are housed inside universities and schools, their host institutions in effect endorse them—in exchange for Chinese funds. This arrangement of implantation and "indebted endorsement" evidently works well in many places, but it is also exactly what prompted several cancellations of CIs hosted at universities in Canada, the US, and Sweden, after the initial ten-year period of unbridled CI expansion into ever more countries around the world.

Yet the Confucius expansion still continues—above all because of the money, but certainly also because of increased curiosity about China in a multipolar world, and perhaps because of their mascot's appeal. However, as the world's curiosity about China comes up against the authoritarianism and unequal relations that so profoundly define and characterize China today, the debates about the arrangement and its potential consequences for the independence of the host institutions, and for the possibility of a bias-free picture of China and Chinese affairs, are bound to continue. Unavoidably, fears and worries will continue to arise, especially when curious students discover the desire of the CI authorities to censor the way China is discussed and taught.

In response, the administrators of host universities, who are above all interested in Chinese money, can be expected to defend the arrangements as innocuous—and as "not unusual." They are of course either ignorant about contemporary China, or they have become personally indebted to the CI bureaucracy because they have been entertained and pointedly named "China's friends." Their observation that external funding is not unusual is of course valid, because with shrinking public support, universities are nowadays increasingly losing their standing as independent institutions as part of the drift toward "corporatization." But this too will be up for debate when people follow the money.[17]

Many academics, for their part—especially those who know something about China—can see that Chinese state funds come with dangerous strings attached. Some have argued to the contrary, that the strings are still limited, not very dangerous, and manageable (cf. McCord 2014, Redden 2014; ChinaFile 2014). Sometimes these arguments also seem to echo one line of argument launched from Chinese authorities and state media: that the worries about the CIs imply a "loss of self-confidence" in "weak" Americans and other aliens (*Global Times* 2014).

But we should note that these defenses of the CI implantations largely came *before* the Portugal incident in July 2014; before the appearance of

Sahlins' [2015] compilation of documented incidents of censorship; and, perhaps most consequentially, before the currently ongoing (2015–2018) very harsh campaigns of political arrests and show-trial treatment of all sorts of freethinkers, lawyers, writers, and others in China. With these developments, the Confucius Institutes' welcome abroad may have faded, even with the otherwise irresistible money they bring with them.

Fearing Confucius Institutes

In Western debates, the issue of "fear" has mostly come up in relation to worries over the threat to academic freedoms, and specifically as regards how we talk about China in an arena paid for by an arm of the Chinese Party-State—at least at weaker academic institutions where this money talks even louder, but also in the most prestigious places in academia.

These fears have not come up in the shape of a revived, racialized "Yellow Peril," or the current debates elsewhere about China as an economically "rising," authoritarian, and militarily powerful superpower—although outside academia these fears have indeed sometimes related to such concerns,[18] such as about the Chinese punitive measures against foreign news media attempting to investigate Chinese affairs.[19]

On the contrary, because they naturally anticipate such accusations, academic critics have often tried to preempt them altogether by insisting they are not against China itself, but rather against the lodging of a Chinese state–sponsored institution inside their own.

Interestingly, in the official Chinese responses to these foreign concerns regarding academic freedoms, a different "fear" has been invoked. This move in itself suggests that the underlying conception for the mission of the CIs is in fact by now profoundly nationalistic and essentialist in nature (that is to say, not very Communist, in the original sense of that term). For example, in 2012 the Chinese ambassador to Britain tried to deflect the criticism by instead denouncing the offending British academics as clinging to an "outdated 'Cold War' mentality" (Branigan 2012; Hughes 2014, 73–74), harking back to the competitive ideological divide of the Cold War era, during which, ostensibly, the capitalist/socialist divide covered up any openly racist motivations.

Most Chinese official responses to the foreign criticisms, intended to counter Western concerns about interference and censorship, have similarly tended to portray critical Westerners as fearful of a cultural China, supposedly embodied by the Confucius Institutes and their promotion of a spirit of "harmony." This is intended to deflect the political character of the criticism, and justified fear, that academics and others have. Early on, the Party newspaper the *People's Daily* (2006) prominently cited a university administrator involved with the CI initiative as arguing that "culture is a soft power that effectively penetrates to quench misunderstanding and hostility between people of different races" and therefore, he argued, with aid of the CIs, "once [the world's people] come to know the Chinese people better, they will find out that harmony is an essential part of Chinese tradition, and a country that values harmony poses absolutely no threat to the rest of the world."

Some foreigners may swallow this harmony shtick (cf. Metz 2015), but to many outsiders, it is a discourse that will appear hollow in the light of the recent trends toward harsh censorship inside China itself, including the newly reasserted Communist Party control of all universities and the anxious prohibitions against using Western-origin textbooks and teaching "Western values" there[20] (which casts a big cloud of irony over all the official Chinese attempts to portray Confucius Institute critics as fearful and weak), not to mention China's increasingly aggressive foreign policy, including the ongoing military expansion in the South China Sea.

It also will appear hollow to many Chinese, in light of how "harmony" has become a central domestic political term in China continuously deployed by officialdom as the justification for its widespread censorship of various forms of expression. The term has been widely ridiculed on Chinese domestic social media, for example through the invention of the new passive verb "to be harmonized," meaning censored and silenced, and through the mocking use of homonymous Chinese characters for an imaginary "river crab," which they substitute for the "harmony" of Chinese government Newspeak. They know that whether or not it is labeled "Confucian," the official Chinese term "harmony" obviously involves the enforcement of limitations on speech, writing, and expression.[21]

Official counterarguments with foreign critics since that time have continued on this tack, with what I would argue is a new type of essentialist-nationalist Chinese discourse that leaves behind past Communist causes (but not the power of the "Communist" Party), and centers on identifying traits like harmony as essential attributes of the Chinese nation, represented by the revived and remodeled Confucius—and actively associated with the CIs. In another such putdown of foreign critics (who are often left unnamed, a classic power tactic), it was argued that "what Confucius Institutes are doing is simply opening a window through which foreigners can catch a glimpse of traditional Chinese culture if they so desire" (*People's Daily* 2010); and disharmonious foreigners who worry about censorship are dismissed as "biased" against China as a country.[22]

When the American Association of University Professors (AAUP 2014) advised against hosting CIs because of concerns over academic freedom, a more substantive official Chinese response was broadcast (*Xinhua* 2014a; see also reports in the *New York Times* 2014b). This response was striking, on the one hand, for its plain statement of the AAUP concerns, but much more so for its plain insistence that the Confucius Institutes, supervised and controlled by the Chinese Communist Party and its government organs, are not at all about Communism, but about traditional China, which has very little to do with Communism! According to the broadcast, the AAUP

> claimed that Confucius Institutes function as an arm of the Chinese state and are pushing political agendas, since they are sponsored by Hanban, a state office dealing with Chinese culture run by the Chinese government and the Communist Party of China (CPC). Such claims expose not so much Communist propaganda as their own intolerance of exotic cultures and biased preconceived notions to smear and isolate the CPC.
>
> The shaping of traditional Chinese culture in the past thousands of years hardly has any direct relations with Communism or its ideology, and those seeking to stem Confucius Institutes as disseminators of world culture are trying to hold back a pure form of human communication.[23]

Here we have almost a disavowal of any Communist agenda (in great contrast with the Party's continuing strident claim, at least domestically, to actually be Communist). This forms part of a claim that even though the government-approved CIs teach contemporary Chinese language and hold events and classes on contemporary culture, they really represent, and teach, a traditional, eternal Chinese culture, as part of a world culture, that no reasonable person could fear.

Again, this is a rhetorical move that attempts to cast the critics as critics of China the eternal nation (here even of world culture and human communication as such!), and thus deflect criticism of the soft-power initiative of a formidably authoritarian state. Just as striking here is the claim to what I identified earlier as a shift in Chinese politics itself, away from the erstwhile Communist agenda. The rhetorical mobilization here by the state's central media of "The great Chinese sage Confucius" might be an attempt to put Confucius out front, to deflect or overcome the fears of foreigners. But here even Communism itself is minimized as a parenthetical or peripheral concern compared to the weight of traditional China ("The shaping of traditional Chinese culture in the past thousands of years hardly has any direct relations with communism or its ideology . . ."). This is, I think, a revealing indication that—as could well be expected from my account of the changing place of Confucianism in Chinese society and politics, in the beginning of this chapter—there are changes afoot in Chinese state ideology itself. Even with the glaring contradictions on display here, it may be that the state ideological agenda is itself shifting toward the embrace of an imperial Confucius—much as Mao once feared. This would mean that the empire is back—which indeed would be something to be even more afraid of!

And yet, while the Chinese authoritarian state discourse may seem hegemonic, due to its formidable capabilities for monopolizing the public voice in China and successfully influencing foreign audiences, imperial Confucianism in support of a neo-imperial state formation may not be the only conceivable outcome of China's trajectory. The persistent state propaganda, including the dismissal of foreign critics of the Confucius Institutes program as being fearful of China itself (but not necessarily of Communism, any more), also hides conflicting views that exist not far under the monolithic state media surface. Some Chinese citizens outside the government are laughing, either incredulously or cynically, at the Confucius Institutes program, and/or at the foreigners who are being drawn into it. On the home front, it is unclear where this may lead, but it is closely related to mistrust in the government's management of China's assets—now including the full-frontal deployment of Confucius, the disarmer.

Chinese-styled encompassment, and other forms of alterity

One might well ask what kind of influence the ongoing CI project will have on the possible futures of Chinese foreign relations. One tool that may be useful for thinking about this is the intriguing anthropological theory of the *Grammars of Identity/Alterity* (Gingrich and Baumann 2004), which addresses the distinct ways in which identity and alterity are always linked.

On a basic level, this is relevant here since fear centrally involves concerns regarding one's own integrity and identity, faced with invading others. In the case of the Confucius Institutes, I believe the central concern is the relation with a powerful country that seems incapable of adopting the concept of respect for equal relations, including freedom of expression, and instead insists on erasing the voices and views of others unless they are "friendly" and "harmonious."[24]

This concern is not alleviated when we see how the Chinese government is using the CI project to promote an ostensibly peaceful and open China, but at the same time, inside China, it is cultivating a newly intensified discourse of fear and suspicion directed against foreigners as potentially hostile, and as agents of disruptive change.

Venturing beyond the basic point that identity requires alterity as a prerequisite for itself and for its own defensive integrity, Gingrich and Baumann also argue, daringly, that humans entertain just three fundamental "grammars," or patterns, of relations with others. These govern both discourse and interaction. Among these "three grammars" of identity and otherness, the most egalitarian is the "segmentary" grammar, under which people are able to regard and respect each other as different, yet equally legitimate.

The two other grammars are more unequal: "orientalism," which involves a simultaneous fascination and contempt for an other, one seen as inferior because it is backward, yet also admired for preserving qualities that civilization has lost; and, finally, the more extreme grammar of "encompassment," in which the self does not acknowledge the other as different, except as a lesser, dependent version of the self.[25] A hallmark example of this would be, for example, the creation of Eve from Adam's rib bone—a cardinal example of how, for some men, women are merely incomplete and inadequate subsets of the standard self, which is male.

Similarly, in caste society, high castes regard the lower castes as substandard versions of themselves, who by definition, as incomplete beings, cannot have, propose, or maintain a legitimately different view of anything, not even their own true identity.

Obviously, in both its domestic policies and in its foreign relations, official China's mindset is singularly dominated by such an "encompassment" grammar—for example, in refusing to allow dissident voices, and in its inability to acknowledge Tibet or Taiwan as legitimate interlocutors (something many Taiwanese and Tibetans would surely wish to see, under a "segmentary" grammar). Official China insists on "encompassing" the other in a "correct" and unassailable view of their relation, leaving no room for the other to dispute the nature of the relation. It dismisses any attempts by the other to reread or redefine the relation as untutored and showing a need of correction from above: In Chinese parlance, they are "not listening," which simply means they are not hearing what the Master wants them to hear.

This sort of unidirectional "encompassment" also shines through in Chinese officialdom's frequent belittling of fearful-because-ignorant (and therefore un-"friendly") foreigners who make trouble over the motivations of China's Confucius Institutes, as well as in some recent, rather ominous, neo-conservative Chinese discourses of the Chinese people as a (new-old) world "master race" imposing its will on the world.

And yet, even though official China is so deeply mired in ideas of hierarchy and superiority as ideals conforming to the encompassment model or grammar, and seems incapable of relating to others other than by encompassing them as a lesser version of itself, the "orientalist" and potentially even the "segmentary" model do remain in play in Chinese peoples' relations to others.

In the classic fashion of the "orientalist" stance, there is widespread fascination in China with the alluring qualities of uncivilized or barbarian others. The somewhat confusingly named but (in the Gingrich–Baumann theory) precisely defined "orientalist" stance allows the foreigner to approach and engage in conversation, even as the two parties may often be speaking past each other and become confused by the titillating mix of fears and attractions.

I believe the phenomenon of the "Yellow Peril" discourse of the past is exemplary of what Baumann and Gingrich meant by "orientalist," on both sides: in the Western "orientalist" stance the imaginary China is both alluring and menacing; likewise, mixed up with the predominant Chinese tendency toward all-knowing encompassment, there is indeed also an on-again, off-again Chinese "orientalist" stance toward the imaginary West that involves a tense combination of admiration and contempt. This is a relation in which either aspect is present and can therefore be mobilized—such as in the dormant "Yellow Peril" stereotype that can be mobilized and hurled along at any time, generating another round of repulsion and attraction.

However—and here I intentionally try to strike an optimistic note—even though China certainly is predominantly "encompassing" towards others and occasionally "orientalist," the potential is also present for a "segmentary" grammar that would emphasize a fearless equality, a relationship on the same plane. This would not seem possible in light of the "encompassing" attitude so often displayed by China's official representatives, which is to insist on one's own view as the only one permitted, and to refuse to accept the legitimacy of alternate voices or different views, and only occasionally play with "orientalism."

Yet if Confucius the philosopher is presented not as a world-encompassing super-sage in the service of the empire, but as a figure of humility, on an equal footing and open to dialogue with figures such as the Goethe of Germany's Goethe Institutes or the Cervantes of Spain's Cervantes Institutes, this would be a different story. Such a stance may also very well be closer to that of the historical Confucius himself.

Notes

I wish to thank the editors for their interest, encouragement, and great patience.

1 Whether it is actually succeeding at this is dubious (Yuan et al. 2016; Zhou and Luk 2016). Note: I could write "government," but I start out here writing "Party-State" to better indicate how in China there is no government independent of the Communist Party, which installs members in every government office, who make all major decisions.
2 There is a large literature on these effects of the "corporatization" of the university. For a snapshot view, see Mihalyfy 2014.
3 For more context on these debates, see Sahlins 2013, 2015; Hughes 2014; AAUP 2014; ChinaFile 2014; Mulhere 2014; Hubbert 2014; also Barr 2011,

etc.; see also Jennifer Hubbert's forthcoming ethnography-based book on the CIs.

4 EACS 2014a and 2014b. The director-general further compounded the incident in the BBC interview (BBC News 2014) where she first appeared to condone her actions, but then asked the BBC to censor the interview. She did not apologize.

5 See Schmidt (2010) on how both a Milton Friedman Institute and a Confucius Institute had been accepted by the administration without the knowledge, much less the approval, of the Faculty Senate, supposedly charged with the university's educational affairs. (Full disclosure: As an alumnus of the University of Chicago, I too participated in the debates over hosting a CI there, including in the alumni magazine.)

6 Xu Lin et al. 2014; see also Schmidt 2014.

7 From Conversations about the Criticism of Confucius with Chairman Mao and Comrade Mao Yuanxin, ca. 1975. This book is unavailable but is widely quoted on the Chinese sector of the internet (see the listed secondary sources), and is widely regarded as authentic, since it fits eminently with Mao's other pronouncements.

8 On alternative views of Confucius and his potential as a critical or even pro-democracy thinker, for our times, see for example Yu Ying-shih 2015. For a broader account of the current revival of Confucius, see Billioud 2015; on the Confucius revival in the preceding decades of the post-Mao era, also see Makeham 2008. The best edition of Confucius' teachings, the Analects (Confucius et al., 2014), carries a collection of very useful essays commenting on the revival and on the different interpretations of Confucius. Another very useful essay in this vein is El Amine 2015.

9 Xinhua 2014b, etc., on the famous occasion of the Party leader's speech at the 2565th birthday celebrations. For a brief discussion, and links to Xi's speech, see Gardner 2014.

10 It is only on the barely tolerated Leftist Web sites that fragments of Mao Yuanxin's conversations still circulate. Another tragicomic expression of leftist influence, as well as the irresolvable contradiction between Communism and Confucianism, came when a new, very large Confucius statue erected outside the National History Museum on Tiananmen Square in Beijing suddenly vanished from its spot in front of the museum one night in April 2011—only to reappear, compromised and devalued, in the museum's back yard.

11 The emperor cult might be embraced, soon, if the Peoples' Republic generation of Chinese can just fade away some more—see Fiskesjö 2015.

12 This is in some ways akin to the identification of Goethe in Germany's Goethe Institutes or Spain's Cervantes, even though of course Cervantes

and Goethe were primarily writers and never Confucius-styled philosophers integrated with imperial rule.

13 See, again, the compilation of incidents in Sahlins 2015.

14 See John Fitzgerald's recent incisive remarks (2016) on the workings of the Chinese propaganda apparatus.

15 CI staff are evaluated for political reliability before they are dispatched, as evident in the case of the Toronto CI for which the original ad in China listed "political ideology" as the first aspect to be certified by the applicant's current employer (Hunan City University 2014). With the current trends in China, the supervision of CI employees dispatched from China must have become even stricter than before.

16 The best discussion available of this particular notion of "friendship," and its close relative, "collaboration," is probably Bulag 2010.

17 Interestingly, at home in China, nongovernmental public discussion about the CIs has largely focused on this expenditure choice and on suspicion of funds embezzlement (for example, curious netizens noted that the CI's central Web site was one of the most expensive ever designed in China!), as well as asking why the large sums of state funds spent on promoting the CIs should not instead go to poor rural areas, where education is deteriorating—and this not least because Westerners seem so ungrateful for the Chinese government's largesse (see Ruan 2014, etc.; also Yuan Zhenjie et al. 2016).

18 On the separate but inevitably conflated phenomena of the "rise of China" and the situation of Chinese abroad, such as Chinese-Americans, who do not necessarily identify or affiliate with the People's Republic of China, see for example Wu 2013.

19 For example, when Bloomberg's news service was seen as curtailing its Chinese news reporting for fear of having its financial reporting rights terminated—in the context of the prohibition in China of the *New York Times*, after that paper published investigative reporting on top Communist leaders' wealth networks (*New York Times* 2012), as Bloomberg's had also done.

20 See China Digital Times 2015; Phillips 2016. These trends could themselves be construed as evidence of fearfulness and anxiety.

21 As mentioned, in the teaching activities by China-dispatched staff, the soft-power tactic for dealing with unwelcome topics (Tiananmen, Tibet, Taiwan, etc.) seems to be not to aggressively attempt to shut students and others down, but to ignore them and to try to steer them away from disapproved topics.

22 Or even somehow deranged: see for example China Daily (2014): "Those who dislike Confucius Institutes are more often than not people who have

a deep bias against China. They seem unable to avoid putting a political label on what is nothing but a language and cultural program . . ."

23 This astonishing text was broadcast by Xinhua (2014a), the official state news agency; see also reporting in the *New York Times* (2014b).

24 Loewen's hilarious yet profoundly sad story (2010) about censorship, disrespect, and the impossibility of Chinese reciprocity is an outstanding example of this.

25 Baumann and Gingrich underline that different grammars may well be deployed by different sides in the same relation, and alternately in different contexts. They may also be deployed by different social strata. We can see this in, for example, how Chinese Party bosses only believe in "encompassment," and will not publicly admit to "orientalism"—even as they send their children to be educated in Western countries.

References

AAUP [American Association of University Professors]. 2014. "On Partnerships with Foreign Governments: The Case of Confucius Institutes." Report prepared by the American Association of University Professors Committee on Academic Freedom and Tenure in June 2014. http://www.aaup.org/report/partnerships-foreign-governments-case -confucius-institutes

Barr, Michael. 2011. *Who's Afraid of China?: The Challenge of Chinese Soft Power.* London: Zed Books.

Baumann, Gerd, and Andre Gingrich, eds. 2004. *Grammars of Identity/ Alterity: A Structural Approach.* New York: Berghahn Books.

BBC News. 2014. "Confucius institute: The hard side of China's soft power." [Interview with director-general Mme. Xu Lin] By John Sudworth, December 22, 2014. http://www.bbc.com/news/ world-asia-china-30567743.

Billioud, Sébastien. 2015. *The Sage and the People: The Confucian Revival in China.* Oxford; New York: Oxford University Press.

Branigan, Tania. 2012. "Chinese ambassador attacks 'cold war' fears over Confucius Institutes." *The Guardian*, June 15. http://www .theguardian.com/world/2012/jun/15/confucius-institutes-universities -chinese-ambassador

Bulag, Uradyn E. 2010. *Collaborative Nationalism: The Politics of Friendship on China's Mongolian Frontier.* Lanham, MD: Rowman & Littlefield.

China Digital Times. 2015. "Unraveling China's campaign against western values." March 5. http://chinadigitaltimes.net/2015/03/unraveling -chinas-campaign-western-values/

ChinaFile, with Perry Link, and others. 2014. "The debate over Confucius Institutes," *ChinaFile*, June 23. Parts I-II. http://www.chinafile.com /conversation/debate-over-confucius-institutes

Churchman, Michael. 2011. "Confucius Institutes and controlling Chinese languages." *China Heritage Quarterly* 26 (June 2011), n.p. http://www .chinaheritagequarterly.org/articles.php?searchterm=026_confucius .inc&issue=026

Confucius et al. 2014. *The Analects: The Simon Leys Translation, Interpretations.* Edited by Michael Nylan. New York, NY: W. W. Norton & Company.

Conversations about the Criticism of Confucius with Chairman Mao and Comrade Mao Yuanxin, text as cited on several Web sites, for example as "Mao Zedong's farsighted view," n.d., http://www.sunomoon.com/me/7 -shizheng/maozedongdeshenkeyuanjian.htm; and cited in "The Confucian Return in an Age of Extremes," by David Brophy, October 1, 2014, http://www.thechinastory.org/2014/10/the-confucian-return-in-an -age-of-extremes/ (citing http://www.wyzxwk.com/Article/lishi/2011 /02/205279.html).

El Amine, Loubna. 2015. *Classical Confucian Political Thought: A New Interpretation.* Princeton: Princeton University Press.

European Association for Chinese Studies (EACS). 2014a. "Report: The deletion of pages from EACS Conference materials in Braga." July 30, http://chinesestudies.eu/?p=584.

European Association for Chinese Studies (EACS). 2014b. "Letter of protest at interference in EACS Conference in Portugal." July 30, http:// chinesestudies.eu/?p=585.

Fiskesjö, Magnus. 2015. "Heritage and Ancestors: The politics of Chinese Museums and historical memory." Elvera Kwang Siam Lim Memorial Lecture at the Center for Chinese Studies, University of California-Berkeley, November 6. Web cast: http://ieas.berkeley.edu/ccs /webcasts.html.

Fiskesjö, Magnus. 2017. "The Return of the show trial: China's televised 'confessions.'" *Asia-Pacific Journal: Japan Focus*, Vol. 15, Issue 13, Number 1 (2017). http://apjjf.org/2017/13/Fiskesjo.html

Fitzgerald, John. 2016. "Beijing's *guoqing* versus Australia's way of life." *Inside Story*, September 27. http://insidestory.org.au/ beijings-guoqing-versus-australias-way-of-life

Friedman, Eli, Aaron Halegua, and Jerome A. Cohen. 2016. "Cruel irony: China's Communists are stamping out labor activism." *Washington Post*, January 3. https://www.washingtonpost.com/opinions/cruel-irony -chinas-communists-are-stamping-out-labor-activism/2016/01/03

/99e986f2-b0bb-11e5-b820-eea4d64be2a1_story.html?hpid=hp_no
-name_opinion-card-b%3Ahomepage%2Fstory

Gardels, Nathan. 2014. "Xi launches cultural counter-revolution to restore
Confucianism as China's ideology," *Huffington Post*, September 29. http://
www.huffingtonpost.com/nathan-gardels/xi-jinping
-confucianism_b_5897680.html?utm_hp_ref=world (+ link to http://
news.xinhuanet.com/politics/2014–09/24/c_1112612018.htm)

Global Times [Huanqiu]. 2014. "Wang Dehua: US universities killing off CI
indicates lack of confidence." October 6. http://opinion.huanqiu
.com/opinion_world/2014–10/5158339.html

Hubbert, Jennifer. 2014. "Ambiguous States: Confucius Institutes and
Chinese soft power in the U.S. classroom." *PoLAR: Political and Legal
Anthropology Review* 37.2, 329–349.

Hughes, Christopher R. 2014. "Confucius Institutes and the university:
Distinguishing the political mission from the cultural." *Issues & Studies*
50, no. 4, 45–83. eprints.lse.ac.uk/60790/

Hunan City University [Hunan chengshi xueyuan]. 2014. "Guanyu tuijian
2014 nian fu Jianada Duolunduo Kongzi Xueyuan jiaoshi de tongzhi
[Circular on recommending teaching staff for the CI in Toronto, Canada,
for 2014]." http://www.hncu.net/content.jsp?urltype=news.NewsContent
Url&wbtreeid=1017&wbnewsid=2012 (June 2014).

Jian Junbo. 2011. "Blind hatred lurks in Western views." *Asia Times*, October
21. http://www.atimes.com/atimes/China/MJ21Ad02.html

Loewen, James W. 2010. "Not Aesopian enough: A Chinese publishing fable."
The China Beat, June 8. http://www.thechinabeat.org/?p=2158

Makeham, John. 2008. *Lost Soul: "Confucianism" in Contemporary Chinese
Academic Discourse*. Cambridge, MA: Harvard University Asia Center.

Mattis, Peter. 2012. "Reexamining the Confucian Institutes." *The Diplomat*,
August 2. http://thediplomat.com/2012/08/reexamining-the
-confucian-institutes/

McCord, Edward. 2014. "Confucius Institutes: Hardly a threat to academic
freedoms." *The Diplomat*, March 27. http://thediplomat.com/2014/03/
confucius-institutes-hardly-a-threat-to-academic-freedoms/

Metz, Thaddeus. 2015. "Values in China as compared to Africa." In *The Rise
and Decline and Rise of China: Searching for an Organising Philosophy*.
Edited by Hester Du Plessis. Johannesburg: Real African Publishers, on
behalf of the Mapungubwe Institute for Strategic Reflection (MISTRA),
75–116.

Mihalyfy, David Francis. 2014. "Higher ed's for-profit future." *Jacobin Magazine*,
6.7.14. www.jacobinmag.com/2014/06/higher-eds-for-profit-future/

Mulhere, Kaitlin. 2014. "China and Academic Freedom." *Inside Higher Ed*, December 5. https://www.insidehighered.com/news/2014/12/05/lawmakers-look-chinese-influence-american-universities

New York Times. 2012. "China blocks Web access to *Times* after article." By Keith Bradsher. *New York Times*, October 26. http://www.nytimes.com/2012/10/26/world/asia/china-blocks-web-access-to-new-york-times.html

New York Times. 2014a. "Xi touts Communist Party as defender of Confucius's virtues." By Chris Buckley. *New York Times*, February 13, 2014. http://sinosphere.blogs.nytimes.com/2014/02/13/xi-touts-communist-party-as-defender-of-confuciuss-virtues/

New York Times. 2014b. "'Fear or ignorance drives Confucius Institutes' critics, Xinhua says." *New York Times*, Sinosphere. By Bree Feng. June 24, 2014. http://sinosphere.blogs.nytimes.com/2014/06/24/fear-or-ignorance-drives-confucius-institutes-critics-xinhua-says/

People's Daily [Beijing]. 2006. "'China threat' fear countered by culture." May 29, 2006. http://english.peopledaily.com.cn/200605/29/eng20060529_269387.html

People's Daily / Xinhua. 2010. "No need to fuss over Confucius Institutes." August 12, 2010. http://en.people.cn/90001/90782/90873/7103027.html

People's Daily / Xinhua. 2016. "Scholar of Confucianism lectures Politburo members." January 15, 2016. http://news.xinhuanet.com/politics/2016-01/15/c_128631705.htm

Phillips, Tom. 2016. "China universities must become Communist Party 'Strongholds,' says Xi Jinping." *The Guardian*, December 9, 2016. https://www.theguardian.com/world/2016/dec/09/china-universities-must-become-communist-party-strongholds-says-xi-jinping

Pu Rui. 2015. "When National Learning entered the Central Party School." *Pengpai* [The Paper], September 25, 2015. http://www.thepaper.cn/newsDetail_forward_1378746

Redden, Elizabeth. 2014. "Confucius controversies." *Inside Higher Ed*, July 24, 2014. http://www.insidehighered.com/news/2014/07/24/debate-renews-over-confucius-institutes

Ruan, Lotus. 2014. "Chinese doubt their own soft power venture." *Foreign Policy*, October 17, 2014. http://www.foreignpolicy.com/articles/2014/10/17/chinese_people_also_dont_like_confucius_institutes

Sahlins, Marshall. 2013. "China U." *The Nation*, October 29, 2013. http://www.thenation.com/article/176888/china-u

Sahlins, Marshall. 2015. *Confucius Institutes: Academic Malware*. University of

Chicago Press; distributed for Prickly Paradigm Press. http://prickly -paradigm.com/titles/Confucius-Institutes-Academic-Malware.html

Schmidt, Christine. 2014. "University to end partnership with Confucius Institute: Move comes in response to article implying that Hanban director strong-armed University into renewing partnership." *Chicago Maroon*, September 30, 2014. http://chicagomaroon.com/2014/09/30 /university-to-end-partnership-with-confucius-institute/

Schmidt, Peter. 2010. "U. of Chicago's plans for Milton Friedman Institute stir outrage on the faculty." *The Chronicle of Higher Education*, June 1, 2010. http://chronicle.com/article/U-of-Chicagos-Plans-for-M/65737/

South China Morning Post. 2015. "Swedish University severs ties with Confucius Institute." January 9, 2015. By Laura Zhou. http://www.scmp .com/news/china/article/1677976/swedish-university-severs-ties-confucius -institute

Wu, Ellen D. 2013. "Is the 'Yellow Peril' dead?" *History News Network*, November 18, 2013. http://historynewsnetwork.org/article/153958

Xinhua 2014a. "China Voice: Fear, ignorance behind calls to stem Confucius Institutes." Xinhua, June 23, 2014. http://news.xinhuanet.com/english /china/2014–06/24/c_133431220.htm

Xinhua 2014b. Speech by Xi Jinping at the International Symposium on the Occasion of the 2565th Birthday of Confucius. Xinhua, September 24, 2014. (In Chinese) http://news.xinhuanet.com/politics/2014–09/24/c _1112612018.htm

Xu Lin with Wang Yi. 2014. "Xu Lin, Wang Yi: Duihua Kongzi xueyuan zhangmenren: Wenhua de kunjing zaiyu buzhi bujue [Conversation with Xu Lin, director of the Confucius Institutes: The dilemma of culture lies in awareness]." *Jiefang ribao* (Shanghai), September 20, 2014. http:// newspaper .jfdaily.com/jfrb/html/2014–09/19/content_17605.htm; http://blog.sina .com.cn/s/blog_9da15c960102v36w.html

Yu Ying-shih. 2012. "Kongzixue yuan jiqi yingxiang—zhuan fang Yu Yingshi [The Confucius Institutes and their influence—Special interview with Yu Ying-shih]." *Zonglan Zhongguo* [China in Perspective], March 2012. Part I http://www.chinainperspective.com/ArtShow.aspx?AID=15064; Part II http://www.chinainperspective.com/ArtShow.aspx?AID=15071. (In Chinese).

Yu Ying-shih. 2015. "The Chinese Communists are not Confucianists." Interview in *China Change*, July 1, 2015. http://chinachange.org/2015 /07/01/the-chinese-communists-are-not-confucianists/

Yuan Zhenjie, Junwang Guo, and Hong Zhu. 2016. "Confucius Institutes and the limitations of China's global cultural network." *China Information* 30.3, 334–356.

Zhang, Taisu. 2015. "Why are China's leftists embracing Confucius?" *Huffington Post*, April 27, 2015. http://www.huffingtonpost.com/taisu -zhang/china-leftists-confucius_b_7147498.html

Zhou, Ying and Sabrina Luk. 2016. "Establishing Confucius Institutes: A tool for promoting China's soft power?" *Journal of Contemporary China* 25.100: 628–642.

CHAPTER 10

~

Fears Abroad, Propaganda at Home

*Reflections on the Yellow Peril
Discourse in China*

SÖREN URBANSKY

I N THE PAST TWENTY YEARS OR SO, anti-Asian discourses related to the
Yellow Peril theme have received considerable attention from scholars
of various disciplines, yet their focus has been mainly on European and
North American forms and specifications of this phobia. The reverberations of the discourse in Asia have so far received little attention. While
two chapters in this volume (Billé and Carrico) seek to overcome this gap
in Asia, debates in the People's Republic of China, the biggest and most
populous country in Asia and a major target of the Yellow Peril ideology, have been almost completely neglected (Fiskesjö).[1] But what happened when the Yellow Peril moved to China? What role did the Yellow
Peril discourse play inside China during its tumultuous transition from
a once-mighty empire that by the turn of the nineteenth century had
become weak and vulnerable to a new world power of the twenty-first
century? This essay shifts the focus and explores the reflections on the
Yellow Peril discourse among Chinese intellectuals during the last one
hundred years. It also examines the political function and usage of this
term in China by analyzing the main themes and major shifts in the
Chinese debate.

Europeans began to perceive Asians as "yellow" when racial theories were developed from the mid-nineteenth century onwards (Demel
1992, Keevak 2011). Among receptive audiences, the fear of Asians arose
within the cultural context of psychologically volatile societies shaped

by "yellow" journalism hungry for clichés, and prevailing cultural pessimism. The economic and demographic anxieties were further reinforced by military events. The slogan "Yellow Peril" itself was coined in Germany in 1895 following Japan's victory over China (Sösemann 1976) and spread rapidly across the globe, particularly after the Boxer Uprising (1900), when it referred to a Chinese threat and, after the Russo-Japanese War (1904/1905), to a Japanese threat. While the fear of the Yellow Peril in Europe and America has remained a part of cultural consciousness up to the present day, the enemies it identifies, along with its manifestations, have nevertheless changed over time. It has been a fractured discourse with a moving target. For some authors it was about "Asia," for others it was about China specifically (Frayling 2014), and for yet others it was about Japan (Kowner 2000). For some the term denoted racial threats, for others political or economic threats, and for still others it was an amalgam of both of these.

In the United States, as discussed in the introduction, the Yellow Peril was first associated with the effects of Chinese immigration in the nineteenth century (Lee 2003, Wu 1982). After Tokyo's attack on Pearl Harbor in 1941, Japan became the ultimate target in the United States (Dower 1986), and discussions of the Yellow Peril extended their focus to Japanese immigrants and their American-born offspring (Robinson 2003). Then, throughout the Cold War, it resurfaced as a fear of China (Hensman 1968, Huang 2010), North Korea, and Vietnam, and in the 1980s briefly referred once again to a temporarily prosperous Japan (Morris 2013). Since the advent of the "Asian century," which has been largely shaped by China's rapidly growing economy and increasing military power, the fear has re-emerged as a subject of political and economic discourse under the catchphrase "China Threat" (Huang 2010, Pan 2012). So, while the term "Yellow Peril" has remained the same, it has referred to different anxieties at different places and times.

The Yellow Peril discourse (*huanghuo lun*) also left its trace on Chinese intellectuals, politicians, and scholars after the term was coined and popularized in the West and beyond. With notable authors such as Lu Xun and Sun Yatsen referring to it during the early 1900s, it became a hotly debated topic among the wider public in Republican China. Early reflections found in late Qing- and Republican-period journals and newspapers often simply added anti-colonial comments to translated Western writings on the Yellow Peril. After 1949, politicians and journalists increasingly utilized the Yellow Peril trope in articles published in *Renmin Ribao* (*People's Daily*) and other official media outlets for propaganda purposes. In recent years the discourse has shifted once again, with the term Yellow Peril—just as in the West—going largely out of fashion, due to a marginalization of racial discourses in evaluation of social relations. It has been replaced by the so-called "China Threat Theory" (*zhongguo weixie lun*)—a new phrase used in the West that has been included in a discourse of patriotism and economic confidence in debates in China today (Yee and Zhu 2002, Lu and Guo 2004, Song et al. 1996, Song et al. 2009). Unlike a century ago, when many of the China-related Yellow Peril writings were targeted against Chinese immigrants in the United States, evoking fears of a threat to the health and the moral values of their predominantly white environments (Lui 2007, Shah 2001, Urbansky 2016), the new concept depicts China as a hygienic and morally unobjectionable incarnation of hyper-modernity, despite accusations of a supposed lack of creativity of its citizens (see introduction). This new China is seen as a threat to the existing geopolitical and global economic world order (Huang 2010).

In what follows I will argue that over the past century the shifting Western Sinophobic discourses have been reflected on by Chinese intellectuals and politicians and used in China for a variety of reasons, first to throw off the shackles of colonialism, then for propaganda purposes, and then, under the term "China Threat," as a discourse of patriotism and economic confidence. My examination of changes of perceptions from a *longue durée* perspective is thus not about how China has been perceived in the West and other parts of Asia, but about Chinese perceptions of themselves and the role of their nation on the world stage. More generally speaking, it will reflect upon the question of how to situate racial and post-racial Sinophobic discourses in a shifting setting of competing empires over time. Often enough, as the following pages will demonstrate, it was not in the context of a struggle between Asia and the West but of rivalries within Asia that the Yellow Peril trope was used.

Yellow Peril narratives in late Qing and Republican China

Chinese intellectuals were aware of the Yellow Peril discourse in the West from quite early on, with the Chinese public first learning about the anti-Asian catchphrase in the last years of the nineteenth century. The first article on this subject most likely appeared in 1898 in the Shanghai journal *Changyan Bao* (*Justified News*). During the next decade, about fifty texts appeared in *Xinmin Congbao* (*New Citizen Journal*), *Waijiao Bao* (*Diplomatic Review*), *Zhongwai Ribao* (*Chinese and Foreign Daily*), *Jingzhong Ribao* (*Alarm Daily News*), *Dongfang Zazhi* (*The Eastern Miscellany*), and other Chinese periodicals. Given the still-nascent Chinese press, this number illustrates a serious interest among Chinese intellectuals and journalists. Despite their interest, however, Chinese authors wrote only about a third of these articles; the majority were translations of English, American, and Japanese texts, some written by illustrious figures like Japan's Prime Minister Ōkuma Shigenobu (Luo 2001: 35–36, Luo 2007: 290–308).

Japanese translations were by no means written in defense of the "yellow people" in general. Instead, they often painted a negative picture of China. In order to avoid being seen as a part of the Yellow Peril themselves, many Japanese authors, but far from all of them, listed a variety of differences in order to draw a clear line of distinction between Japan and China.[2] Their texts mainly argued that the contemporary conflict was not simply a struggle between races, but a struggle between the civilized and the uncivilized world. Some Japanese articles went so far as to advise Western countries not to open their doors to Chinese immigrants, as their citizens would lack the means to resist a Chinese invasion. Others, written during the height of the Russo-Japanese rivalry over influence in Northeast Asia, blamed Russia for having fabricated the Yellow Peril theory with the purpose of isolating Japan, and went on to blame the Russians for being "barbarians" themselves (Luo 2001: 36–38). Yet others stressed that Russia's defeat by Japan demonstrated that it was not the race but the national system that was crucial to the success or failure of a country (*Zhongwai Ribao*, February 13, 1904).[3] These Chinese translations of Japanese writings, however, failed to convey a comprehensive picture of the various faces of the Yellow Peril discourse of that time, which varied greatly from country to country. In the United States, the discourse was shaped by a reflexive reaction to the massive influx of Chinese immigrants, while in Germany it was a geopolitical doctrine, based on civilizational and racial categories, and in Russia it was determined by a distinct fear of losing the Russian Far East as a result of Chinese immigration or Japanese aggression (Gollwitzer 1962). Despite their differences, they each gave readers a broad idea of some of the hidden strategies behind the Yellow Peril myth. Turn-of-the-century Japanese publications on the Yellow Peril exemplify that the trope was never solely a Western one targeting Asia but from early on was also based on concerns about conflict and distinction within Asia itself.

During the last years of the Qing dynasty, Chinese intellectuals no longer simply digested translations of foreign texts on the Yellow Peril, but increasingly published their own opinions on that topic. A wide spectrum of Chinese authors painted quite a different picture than their Japanese peers in the nation's burgeoning press. They drew clear distinctions between the moral, racial, political, and economic aspects of the Yellow Peril discourse. Most writers had two main arguments as to why China did not constitute a peril. First, they portrayed the Boxer Rebellion as an act of self-defense against the spread of Western influence in religion, trade, and politics. Second, they countered the Yellow Peril argument by reminding readers of China's great contribution to human civilization, and condemned the Yellow Peril ideology as a creation of white racism. These accounts stress the harm done to China by the theory, as well as the lack of understanding of this damage among the Chinese, and urge a resolute reaction. Some articles are written in a sanguine, often bold tone, pointing to the many advantages of Chinese civilization and referring to the numerous examples from the past when the "yellow people triumphed over the white" (*Dongfang Zazhi* 1906). While Japanese authors were careful to show that the Chinese were different from them, some Chinese intellectuals instead defended all Asian peoples, not just the Chinese, despite China's defeat in the Sino-Japanese War and despite the Sinocentric tendency to regard their own culture as superior to other cultures.

Some authors were confident about China's future. In their eyes, the conditions needed to rule the world of business and industry were favorable since they perceived that the nation's environment offered the advantages of strength and autonomy, its people were blessed with abundant knowledge and were good at doing business, and their wages were low. Such projections were usually highly selective, however, and avoided any actual advice as to how to change China's miserable status quo or how to respond to the Yellow Peril idea (Luo 2001: 38–39). As some authors' writings failed to unmask the primary causes of Yellow Peril accusations in the West, such as the xenophobic sentiments in regions with a significant

Chinese diaspora population, they repeated the ethnocentric argumentation patterns of their opponents in Europe and North America.

Lu Xun (Zhou Shuren), one of China's greatest writers and a leading figure of modern Chinese literature during his seven years in Japan, criticized the Chinese for precisely these shortcomings. "Breaking the Sound of Evil" ("Po e sheng lun"), published in the Magazine *Hunan* in 1908, was the last article he published during his time there. In many ways, it also became the epitome of reflection on the then-contemporary Chinese culture. Lu Xun criticized the Chinese response to the Yellow Peril, calling it a long-term self-submission to violence. He saw the Chinese as gradually becoming the slaves of the imperial powers, forgetting about the original causes, and repeating word for word what others said:

> Considering those people who are gifted to win a war, they are actually people who have long been oppressed; therefore their features are like those of slaves. Among them those who forget their origin and on the contrary applaud the invaders are the worst. Those who have no own ideas but always agree with others are somewhat better. Sometimes there are people who belong to neither of those two groups. Sometimes they reverse their nature that they had before they became human beings, which I saw in one or two poems, whose authors agreed with the Yellow Peril theory of the German Kaiser Wilhelm II, and, full of pride, were exclaiming that London will be destroyed, Rome will be reversed, Paris, the place of sexual pleasure, will be taken, etc. Although persons advocating the danger of yellow people often compare them with beasts, in fact yellow people were not so extreme at all. Today I dare to tell the Chinese soldiers: be brave and strong, be determined and have no fear of war; that is what life should be like. We are stressing this in order to succeed ourselves, not to destroy innocent countries. When our country is safe and firm, and when we still have some bravery, then we should [. . .] put an end to oppressions. Taking the middle, when there are countries in danger, we should help them. First we should support those countries that have amicable relations with us, then others. If we help others then we succeed in creating a just and peaceful world, and in making the white people lose their slaves. Then indeed

the Yellow Peril would be realized. But today we should put off the heart of admiring violence. On the contrary, we should talk about the importance of self-defense. Sigh, our China is also a country which is under aggression, should we not be thinking about that first? (Lu 1908)

Lu Xun was not the only famous Chinese intellectual of the early twentieth century to reflect on negative racial stereotypes. Sun Yatsen (Sun Zhongshan) embarked on the path of revolution to overthrow the Qing Dynasty precisely at the time when the Yellow Peril ideology was most virulent in the world. In a series of articles directed at an educated Chinese readership, the founding father of the Republic of China criticized and profoundly exposed the Yellow Peril myth of the West. In Sun's view, China was an important force in maintaining world peace, and only with Chinese independence, unity, and prosperity could the world become a more secure and peaceful place. In 1904, in "The True Solution of the Chinese Question—An Appeal to the American people" ("Zhongguo wenti de zhen jiejue—xiang Meiguo renmin huyu"), the revolutionary condemned these Western anxieties:

It is often argued that China has a large population and abundant resources, and if it awakes and adopts Western methods and ideas, it will be a threat to the entire world. The most sensible policy that other countries should therefore follow is to suppress the Chinese, as much as possible [. . .]. This argument seems very interesting but [. . .] it is untenable. In addition to the rational side of the question, whether a country should wish for the decline of another country, this issue has its political side. The nature of the Chinese people is hard-working, peaceful, law-abiding, and peace-loving. If they had ever waged war, it was just for self-defense. [. . .] If the Chinese were to be autonomous, they would prove to be the most peace-loving people in the world. From an economic point of view, the awakening of China and the establishment of an enlightened government would not only be good for the Chinese, but also for the entire world. [. . .] Interstate relationships are just as the relationships between individuals. From an economic point of view, it is more beneficial to have a wealthy and smart neighbor instead of a poor and ignorant one. Therefore the Yellow Peril theory in fact can be turned into a yellow blessing [*huangfu*]. (Sun 1956: 61–62)

Sun Yatsen and other Chinese writers did not collapse the racial, moral, economic, and political narratives into one. They carefully distinguished between the different elements of the Yellow Peril. For Sun, racially the discourse was clearly negative, but politically and economically it suggested that China had in fact the potential to be a powerful nation in Asia and to become a blessing for the world. Yet the detailed analyses of Lu Xun and Sun Yatsen remained individual responses to widespread biases against China that were read only within narrow circles of educated and politically motivated citizens.

Chinese writings on Yellow Peril narratives shifted during the Republican period. With Japan emerging as the most belligerent opponent, Chinese intellectuals projected the Yellow Peril complex increasingly onto Japan. Perhaps no publication epitomizes this trend better than Zhou Zhiming's book *The Yellow Peril is in fact a Japanese danger* (*Huanghuo ji Ri huolun*). Published in 1944, this political essay is a long list of arguments presenting Japan as a global threat. Chapter by chapter, the author lays out why Japan is the only Asian threat to the world, and claims that the German Kaiser's speeches and other anti-Asian texts in Germany are supposedly all about a Japanese, not a Chinese, menace. In a similar vein, he rightly argues that it was the Russo-Japanese War that gave rise to the Yellow Peril discourse in Russia, and that it was the Japanese immigrants who were seen as an instrument for infiltrating the United States during World War II. In the last chapters, Zhou elaborates on the contemporary war situation in Asia and argues that the Greater East Asia Co-Prosperity Sphere was a masquerade conducted by Tokyo to present its imperial mastery over Asia as an egalitarian structure of independent nations. Only by virtue of Sun Yatsen's Three Principles could China end Tokyo's oppression and escape the Japanese peril (Zhou 1944).

Zhou Zhiming's book is thus another telling example of how Chinese reflections on the Yellow Peril trope were in fact often discourses of competing powers in Asia, and to a much lesser degree of a struggle between the West and Asia. His book again underlines that, unlike Japanese authors, who often were careful to show that the Chinese were different from themselves, Chinese authors frequently defended all Asian peoples against the Occidental threat—and increasingly against Japan. Several key factors contributed to such divergent reverberations of anti-Asian narratives in Japan and China: first, Japanese authors' frustration with Western Yellow Peril writings stemmed from their desire to become a nation of equals with the West. For China the imperialism of Western powers was the major cause of disagreement with Russia, the West, and Japan. Another key factor was the pressing issue of immigration and the poor image of the Chinese communities in Russia and the United States. Compared to authors in Japan, Chinese writers argued much more strongly for the historically unique situation of their nation. In their Sinocentric world, China was the unchallenged and pristine representative of Asia, protecting all its neighboring nations from Western imperial threats. Also, in their eyes the color yellow had no negative connotation. As the emperor's color in imperial China, it was considered the most beautiful and prestigious (Dikötter 1992). Furthermore, the color symbolized racial loyalties within Asia, in contrast to Japan, where people did not see themselves as belonging to the same single racial category as other Asians (Keevak 2011).

In their own reflections on the Yellow Peril writings, Japanese and Chinese authors increasingly broadened and deepened those distinctions between their nations. This shift in meaning and interpretation becomes apparent when we compare the first articles in the Chinese press of the late nineteenth century with Zhou Zhiming's book. Whereas early publications were either translations or vague explanations of the various anti-Asian myths of the time, Zhou's book is in fact a Chinese manifesto against Japanese aggression, which not only exemplifies the internalization of a Western concept in China, but also provides an insight into the purposeful utilization of this discourse in the Sino-Japanese rivalry prior to communist rule.

The Yellow Peril discourse in communist China

Since the mid-twentieth century, the Yellow Peril discourse has undergone significant changes in China and the West. Although the notion of yellowness as a racial marker had by then gradually faded away in Europe and North America as societies became more postcolonial and multicultural, the discourse nonetheless enjoyed another renaissance as an ideological fear of communist China in the West in the postwar decades.

After the founding of the People's Republic of China in 1949, the Yellow Peril trope took on a new role in China as well. Due to higher literacy rates, newspapers began to gain wider readership throughout the country. In combination with a centrally controlled media system, the catchphrase was now being used as a weapon of propaganda by the Chinese government. The changing audience and purpose affected the media rhetoric on the Yellow Peril. Reading the *Renmin Ribao*, the official mouthpiece of the Chinese Communist Party, one gets an idea of how the circulating myth was either neutrally portrayed or, as was more often the case, abused for the party's own political agenda.

Between 1946 and 2014, the term "Yellow Peril" (*huanghuo*) appeared in 79 articles in *Renmin Ribao* and was relatively equally distributed among the decades, with the highest frequency (16 articles) occurring during the 1960s.[4] With statistically only slightly more than one article per year, one might assume that this topic had become irrelevant. When one considers, however, that the Yellow Peril myth in the West had begun to vanish as a racial discourse many years earlier, those figures begin to appear much more significant.

So why, and under what circumstances, did the Chinese media reintroduce the term to their readers? Chinese newspapers reinstated the term from days long gone by for propaganda reasons, even after it had lost its racial and moral significance as a catchphrase in the West. Beijing's propaganda now mainly accused non-Western opponents of instrumentalizing Sinophobic motifs to stir up public animosity toward the People's Republic. Similar to the first decades of the twentieth century, the Yellow Peril trope was once again utilized by China in an internal Asian discourse, this time targeting not mainly Japan but other opposing powers. Whether or not India, Indonesia, the Soviet Union, and other rivals were airing anti-Chinese propaganda using old Yellow Peril motifs did not matter. For the Chinese state media, the Yellow Peril trope was a perfect means of discrediting its international opponents at home. Therefore, it is hardly surprising that this discursive and performative motif was used mainly in connection with foreign politics. *Renmin Ribao* informed its readers regularly that, in the words of Cheng Qian, a Chinese military general who was then Governor of Hunan Province, the "'Yellow Peril' catchphrase is an imperialistic rumor to injure others' reputation" (April 24, 1959: 3). But in the post-1949 context, it was often used in the Chinese press to condemn other powers, particularly those at odds with Beijing in the communist or decolonized world, and to present the People's Republic of China as an advocate of the anti-imperialist nationalist movement in the postcolonial world and a proponent of equal relations among the races. Yellow, in this sense, was no longer the color of imperial China or the skin of Asian people. The term "Yellow Peril" was now entirely detached from its original meaning.

At first, the motif appeared in relation to border disputes and ethnic conflicts on China's southern periphery. Without supporting evidence as to whether Indian nationalists really used the term, the official newspaper of the government of China accused India of attempting to establish a widespread new Yellow Peril phobia to smear China as an aggressor during a series of violent border incidents after the Tibetan uprising of 1959, which eventually led to the 1962 Sino-Indian War (ibid., November 21, 1959: 5). During the Tibetan uprising, local Tibetan feudalists and imperialist powers allegedly conspiring behind the scenes against China were accused of oppressing the Tibetan people (ibid., April 24, 1959: 3). In contrast to the past, the Yellow Peril trope presented here bore a closer resemblance to Western allegations against Japan's aggressive imperial expansion in the first half of the twentieth century.

The trope was also used to stress strong ties between China and other countries of the Global South. According to *Renmin Ribao*, imperialists and reactionaries retained the cliché to slander China. With regard to Beijing's influence on revolutionary movements in Southeast Asia, *Renmin Ribao* quoted a vice-chairman of the Central Committee of the Communist Party of Indonesia as saying, "[T]he claims of a so-called 'aggression from the North,' 'Yellow Peril,' and 'an attack by the People's Republic of China' that some people even in a yellow country [Indonesia] spread are ridiculous and stupid nonsense" (ibid., October 7, 1964: 5).[5] The opinions of African political leaders, such as a high-level politician from Mali, were presented in a similar way: "The people of all countries no longer believe in the 'Yellow Peril,' because there is no 'Yellow Peril.' They can't believe the 'Yellow Peril,' because it is the imperialists who confuse right and wrong and attack the views of others" (ibid., April 27, 1965: 3). But who were those imperialists? The United States, as the main enemy in the 1950s and 1960s, was painted as an imperialist force that continued to stir up the "Yellow Peril" phobia throughout the world (ibid., October 5, 1964: 6).

As the amicable relations between Moscow and Beijing turned sour, however, the main target of accusations of Yellow Peril hysteria became the USSR. According to the Chinese press, however, the Sinophobic hysteria had generally abated. There were many places in the world—such as Bulgaria and other socialist sister countries—in which the people cared about the struggle of the Chinese people for national liberation, because they all shared a common destiny and wished to become masters in their own countries (ibid., September 7, 1959: 6). In the context of its relations with Moscow, however, Beijing used the Yellow Peril motif as a propaganda weapon in all state media channels. In the press, for instance, the Soviet Communist Party leadership was accused of resorting to the most reactionary racial theories and of inheriting German Kaiser Wilhelm II's legacy of belief in the Yellow Peril. Moscow was charged with falsifying history and creating a big commotion over communist China as the new Yellow Peril or the reincarnation of Genghis Khan. In relation to China's role in the Third World, *Renmin Ribao*, in an open letter to the Central Committee of the Soviet Communist Party, quoted an unnamed Soviet party official describing how Moscow was trying "to replace class theory with race theory [. . .] to stir Asian and African people's nationalism and racial prejudice [. . .] in order to erect racial and geographical barriers" (ibid., October 22, 1963: 1).[6] The objective of this anti-Chinese hysteria was to organize a hostile campaign against the revolutionary spirit and socialist construction of the People's Republic of China and to spread suspicion and hostility against China among people of Third World countries in order to gain support for new aggressive plots against China. Last but by no means least, its objective was to alter public opinion within the Soviet Union in support of Moscow's imperialist policy (ibid., June 10, 1969: 6).[7]

An article entitled "The specters of Wilhelm II" ("Weilian ershi de youling") concludes with a heated reminder to Moscow's agitators:

Aren't you not often talking about such fine words like "nationalism" [*guojia zhuyi*] and "anti-racism" [*fandui minzu zhuyi*]? Aren't you repeatedly saying that you are opposing the division of power in world politics "according to skin color"? But now, as you actually follow in the footsteps of Wilhelm II, blurting out the "Yellow Peril," is this really going to your nation's glory? Aren't you aware that not only the vast majority of the Asian nations are yellow skinned peoples, but that there are also thousands of thousands of yellow skinned people in your country? In what position do you really want to put yourself as you vigorously promote the "Yellow Peril" in the world? Gentlemen, while you are promoting Wilhelm II's "yellow peril" theory, don't forget the fate in which the Emperor ended up! (ibid., April 19, 1979: 6)

The article was published one month after the end of the Sino-Vietnamese War. Though Moscow was not directly involved in the conflict, it provided intelligence and equipment support for its ally, Vietnam, and a war between Beijing and Moscow appeared more likely after the bloody clashes on the Ussuri River in March 1969. To the Soviet Union, the self-perceptions of Asiatic people within the USSR were not irrelevant, although most ethnic minority populations in the Asian territories of the Soviet Union would not have thought of themselves as "yellow people." And to maintain an "ethnic harmony" within its own borders, Yellow Peril motifs were not part of Moscow's propaganda campaign against the People's Republic during the Sino-Soviet split. For the regime in Beijing, in turn, using Yellow Peril accusations from days long gone by against the Soviet Union at home and abroad (Urbansky 2012) was one way in which Moscow could be discredited as the legitimate leader of the communist bloc. By doing so, China cast itself as an anti-imperial alternative to an alleged xenophobic Soviet Union for the leadership of the communist and developing world. After the 1950s, the Chinese Communist Party elite thus used Yellow Peril accusations against ideological and geopolitical opponents in Asia and the world.

Though the discourse was in many ways a thing of the past and "Yellow Peril" was mainly employed by Beijing as a treacherous argument detached from its actual historical context, *Renmin Ribao* ran a few reports about the history of the Yellow Peril, such as a text on discrimination and exclusion of Chinese in the United States during the second half of the nineteenth century (ibid., June 3,1960: 7). Only on a few occasions were articles published at times of actual discrimination against the Chinese, in particular against the Chinese diaspora in Southeast Asia. Sinophobic rallies found an obvious echo in the Chinese press, particularly as a reaction to anti-Chinese ethnic cleansings in Indonesia during the mid-1960s. Addressing the Indonesian government, the official newspaper of the Chinese Communist Party said,

For ten months now we have observed anti-Chinese sentiments and exclusion of Chinese on a daily basis. Overseas Chinese are being persecuted and massacred, the Chinese Embassy is attacked openly, and the Chinese Consulate General is occupied and destroyed. You encourage thugs to draw graffiti and shout "Crush the People's Republic of China," "Hang the Chinamen," "Kill the Chinamen" and other Sinophobic slogans on the streets of Jakarta, in order to stir up fascist and racist sentiments. You are also making use of your mastery over the newspapers, news agencies, and the radio to attack China, insult China as "Chinese colonialists," "Communist imperialists," "Yellow Peril" [. . .] every day. (ibid., April 27, 1966, p. 4)[8]

Nevertheless, such accounts remained the exception. The majority of reports were detached from the typical Yellow Peril themes but followed a political agenda of their own. On the whole the term was primarily used in China for propaganda purposes, by no means reflecting any authentic utilization of Yellow Peril motifs in other countries. Only during a few episodes, such as the Indonesian killings of 1965–1966 targeting communists, ethnic Chinese, and alleged leftists, were the Chinese responding to actual anti-Chinese violence or sentiments. By the late 1970s, however, the term itself practically disappeared from the official Chinese newspapers. Whenever it came up it was no longer used as a rhetorical weapon against foreign powers, but was rather mentioned in its historical context on rare anniversaries such as the centennial of the Boxer Uprising in 2000 (ibid., October 6, 2000: 2).

From Yellow Peril to China Threat: Debates since 1978

The death of Mao Zedong and the beginning of Deng Xiaoping's reform and opening-up policies in the late 1970s marked a period surprisingly free from the reporting of foreign anti-Chinese sentiments in the Chinese media. This lull in reporting was brief, however, and soon the old motif was taken up again. It resurfaced because China took on a new role on the world stage as East Asia's economic powerhouse and a rising military power in the region and beyond. For several reasons, its form and content had changed. As we have seen earlier, the prefix "yellow" had gone out of fashion in the West, and had been replaced by other less ethnically discriminatory terms and concepts by the end of the Cold War, most prominently the so-called China Threat Theory. This new form of anti-Chinese speech is not simply a latter-day version of the Yellow Peril, but refers to claims that China's rise may result in economic and military threats to other countries, in particular its neighbors and the United States (Goldstein 2005, Huang 2010, Jiang 2012). To date, the government in Beijing perceives the China Threat Theory as a toxic ideology invented by foreign powers to harm Beijing's peaceful intentions abroad (Tiezzi 2014). Unlike the old Yellow Peril, the new motif does not arise from racial critiques, although it still represents all Chinese as a group. Yet, its focus is much narrower (directed solely against the People's Republic of China, but not any other Asian nations or parts of Greater China) and as a concept it is far less fluid. However, the transformation of the dominant Sinophobic discourse did not signal the disappearance of racial fears as such. While linguistic changes have also been reflected in the Chinese press, its usage as a propaganda tool against foreign powers has remained surprisingly stable.

Renmin Ribao mentioned the term "China Threat Theory" for the first time in 1983 when accusing Vietnam of seeking an excuse for its own invasion of Cambodia by bullying China, which it painted as aggressive (March 1, 1983: 6). This was the only time the term was used in the 1980s in the paper. From the 1990s, however, worldwide public debates, scholarly discourses, and media reports on China's rise to the position of global player were echoed in the Chinese press. It was, however, not just the growing global interest in China that was reflected in its re-emergence. After the Tiananmen massacre in 1989, the Chinese government launched a "patriotic education campaign" in which they deployed emotive memories of the "hundred years of humiliation" and portrayed the Communists as the party of national salvation (Callahan 2010, Gries 2004). This policy shift partly explains the sharply increased coverage *within* China of the idea of China as a threat to the world. According to state media, foreign experts, journalists, and politicians who were calling China a threat thus epitomized a new form of national humiliation.

Beginning in the 1990s, the issue was most commonly brought up in Chinese media as a reflection of the concerns of other powers over the steady increase in China's military spending and China's economic boom, in which a Cold War–style hysteria was displayed (ibid., April 17, 1993: 6). Often it was a combination of both, being particularly virulent in the Western press, where it presented the alarming subtext of "economic development going hand in hand with military expansion," which sooner or later "will pose a threat for regional or world security." The Chinese leader Jiang Zemin and other high officials issued reassurances in the Chinese press that such prognoses lacked any factual basis and demonstrated only the narrowmindedness of their originators: "China is not a superpower, and will not seek to become a superpower" (ibid., June 1, 1993: 7).

Just as the party propaganda had accused foreign powers of being Sinophobic back in the day, it would now employ the motif of a conspiratorial China Threat Theory to suspect and brand rivaling nations in Asia. In fact, most articles of the 1990s deal with Japan (ibid., July 9, 1996: 6), the Philippines (ibid., November 1, 1995: 1), India (ibid., October 23, 1996: 6), or other Asian neighbor states and the contexts within which the theory is brought up in these countries. This shows that China was at that time much more concerned with its position in Asia than with its relations with the United States. The articles emphasize that it was usually not the government or common people but certain elements within those societies that created rumors about a Chinese threat from ulterior motives. These were aimed at inciting public opinion to put pressure on China, to interfere in China's internal affairs, and to damage China's reputation among its neighbor states—often in order to maintain a hegemonic position themselves: "In a nutshell, they attempt to start a new Cold War in Asia Pacific" (ibid., October 23, 1996: 6).

The China Threat trope slowly shifted when China's rise became increasingly tangible on a global scale and China was more and more recognized as the second superpower of the twenty-first century. In July 2002, for instance, the then Chinese Ambassador to the United States, Yang Jiechi, stressed during a meeting with American Chinese and Chinese students held in Washington, D.C., that the People's Republic was to be seen not as a threat, but as an opportunity. More interesting than the contents of his speech itself was the fact that it was targeted at Chinese living overseas and that it was widely covered by the Chinese media. According to Yang, the influence of "Cold War thinking" and the "China Threat Theory" needed to be eliminated in order to achieve the healthy and stable development of bilateral relations between Washington and Beijing (ibid., July 18, 2002: 3). A peaceful China and a stable development were thus common tropes used by intellectuals, politicians, and writers as different as Lu Xun, Sun Yatsen, and Yang Jiechi.[9] At different points in time they rejected the Yellow Peril notions and speculations about China as a threat to the peace and security of other countries. On the contrary, China in their eyes was an important player in maintaining world peace. Their metaphorical reassurances were used to gain support for the claim that it was China that was the victim of defamation (see *Fiskesjö* in this volume) and that the real peril was a "white" one. Unlike early twentieth-century Chinese intellectuals and politicians, who had been merely reactive to a Western discourse, Chinese leaders of today try to shape the discourse not only at home but also abroad.

Conclusion

Over the course of the last century, anti-Asian discourses and theories on China underwent a shift from the Yellow Peril discourse to the China Threat Theory, representing different periods of Western and non-Western views of the Chinese. While their content varies and they do not form an integral system, what they did have in common was that at times they had a far-reaching impact by forming a negative image of China in the United States, India, Russia, Germany, and various other countries of the world. Chinese intellectuals were and are aware of these discourses. At first, when Kaiser Wilhelm II was popularizing the fear of the Yellow Peril in his Sinophobic rhetoric during his notorious "Hunnenrede" (Hun Speech), Chinese reflections of the Yellow Peril myth largely echoed discourses in Japan and in the West. Chinese newspapers reported extensively on anti-Asian sentiments during the Boxer Uprising and the Russo-Japanese War. Just a few years later, Lu Xun criticized his fellow countrymen for falling into the trap of inflated self-esteem, while Sun Yatsen called China a "yellow blessing."

All these responses, as varied as they are, were directly related to the different nuances of the Yellow Peril myth that was virulent in Europe, North America, and beyond. The situation changed after 1949, when direct contacts between Mainland China and the West shrank significantly, while contacts between Western-aligned parts of China (Taiwan, Hong Kong, Macau) and the world increased. In addition to disrupted communication with the outside world, the Chinese discourse on the Yellow Peril had entered much wider parts of the population under the communist regime, compared to the narrow circle of readers of the writings of early twentieth-century Chinese intellectuals. The larger audience and the lack of communication with the West affected the rhetoric in the media outlets. The bygone Yellow Peril discourse, which had been a propaganda tool to some degree during the Republican era, now became a motif completely gutted of its historical racial and moral context, and was used in relation to political and ideological adversaries in world politics, such as the Soviet Union or India, that in most cases did not belong to the West. The two exceptions were of course the Korean and was Vietnam Wars—both of which were, somewhat surprisingly, not portrayed in the Chinese press within this old scheme.

During the 1990s, when China's ties with the world were deepening again, Sinophobic tropes had their day in the Chinese press. But just like the situation in the West, the Yellow Peril was gradually replaced by new phrases, new ways of self-perception, and others' changing perceptions. It was now the term "China Threat" that began to replace the old catchphrase in the press. Yet, unlike "Yellow Peril," the term "China Threat" has a much narrower range, as it refers specifically to China (not to Japan or Asia in general) and denotes solely political and economic threats, but does not portray the Chinese as inferior in any form. While the sentiments attached to the "China Threat" are very different from the wide and fractured range of alleged threats contained in the traditional Yellow Peril trope, both terms likewise remain important elements in Chinese debates about China's place on the world stage. Both notions reflect China's position in the global rivalry with other nations and empires and within Asia in particular. They echo China's continuous search for its place in the world in a turbulent century, its journey from an empire under siege to a nation-state to a new rising empire. Looking at Chinese responses to these motifs also reminds us that anti-Asian and Sinophobic ideologies, such as the Yellow Peril and the China Threat Theory, were not monopolized by the West but adapted in diverse contexts in China and other parts of Asia as well.

Notes

1 The two most notable exceptions are perhaps the publications by Luo Fuhui of Wuhan's Central China Normal University. The historian of modern China has published two books on the Yellow Peril, one monograph and one collection of sources. Yet even those two works

deal with Chinese perceptions of the Yellow Peril discourse during late Qing and Republican China only at the end of each publication and do not discuss post-1949 China (Lü 1979, Luo 2007). Cf. also Tsu's (2005) study on the making of modern Chinese identity, which includes some reflections about Chinese perceptions of the Yellow Peril.

2   In his famous book *Bushido*, Inazō Nitobe (2002) studied the ethos of his nation during a time of deep transformations while becoming a modern nation. Other Japanese scholars, in turn, stressed the similarities of Japan and other Asian nations. The most prominent example is, perhaps, Okakura's (1920) *The Ideals of the East*, a cultural history of Asian civilizations in which he stresses a spiritual unity throughout Asia.

3   Cit. in Lü (1979: 373–374).

4   During the same time period the term "Yellow Peril discourse" (*huanghuo lun*) is mentioned only nine times. Beginning in the 2000s, the Yellow Peril acquires an additional meaning related to cellphone addiction, which I excluded in my calculations.

5   In a similar vein, directed against the United States and the Soviet Union, Norodom Sihanouk, the King and effective ruler of Cambodia and loyal ally of the People's Republic of China and North Vietnam, was quoted in *Renmin Ribao* (October 19, 1965: 1).

6   In almost identical wording, *Renmin Ribao* (February 18, 1968: 6).

7   *Renmin Ribao* frequently reported on Moscow's Sinophobic Yellow Peril motif during the Sino-Soviet split, for example in *Renmin Ribao* (June 16, 1977: 1). The Chinese paper also reproduced suitable extracts from foreign media whenever the subject was taken up there. See, for example, passages of an article in the German paper *Die Welt* that appeared in the *Renmin Ribao* (February 24, 1974: 6).

8   Cf. also *Renmin Ribao* (June 11, 1966: 1).

9   A comparison of Sun Yatsen's arguments against Yellow Peril discourses and Deng Xiaoping's arguments against the China Threat Theory has been made by Liu (2001).

References

Callahan, William A. 2010. *China: The pessoptimist nation*. Oxford: Oxford University Press.

Demel, Walter. 1992. "Wie die Chinesen gelb wurden: Ein Beitrag zur Frühgeschichte der Rassentheorien." *Historische Zeitschrift* 3, Vol. 255, pp. 625–666.

Dikötter, Frank. 1992. *The discourse of race in modern China*. London: Hurst & Company.

Dongfang Zazhi. 1906. "Lishi shang huang bai liang zhong zhi jingzheng." *Dongfang Zazhi*, no. 13.

Dower, John W. 1986. *War without mercy: Race and power in the Pacific War*. New York: Pantheon Books.

Frayling, Christopher. 2014. *The Yellow Peril: Dr. Fu Manchu and the rise of Chinaphobia*. New York: Thames and Hudson.

Goldstein, Avery. 2005. *Rising to the challenge: China's grand strategy and international security*. Stanford: Stanford University Press.

Gollwitzer, Heinz. 1962. *Die Gelbe Gefahr: Geschichte eines Schlagworts. Studien zum imperialistischen Denken*. Göttingen: Vandenhoeck & Ruprecht.

Gries, Peter Hays. 2004. *China's new nationalism: Pride, politics, and diplomacy*. Berkeley: University of California Press.

Hensman, Charles Richard. 1968. *China: Yellow peril? Red hope?* London: SCM Press.

Huang Xinghua. 2010. *"Zhongguo wei xie lun" de you lai yu fa zhan*. Nanchang: Jiangxi gaoxiao chubanshe.

Jiang Jialin. 2012. *Zhongguo weixie haishi weixie Zhongguo? "Zhongguo weixie lun" yanjiu*. Beijing: Waisen chubanshe.

Keevak, Michael. 2011. *Becoming Yellow: A Short History of Racial Thinking*. Princeton, NJ: Princeton University Press.

Kowner, Rotem. 2000. "'Lighter than yellow, but not enough': Western discourse on the Japanese 'race', 1854–1904." *The Historical Journal* 1, Vol. 43, pp. 103–131.

Lee, Erika. 2003. *At America's gates: Chinese immigration during the Exclusion Era, 1882–1943*. Chapel Hill: University of North Carolina Press.

Liu Yaling. 2001. "Sun Zhongshan bochi 'huanghuo lun' yu Deng Xiaoping pibo 'Zhongguo weixie lun'." *Huanggang shifan xueyuan (zhexue shehui kexue ban)* 2, Vol. 14, pp. 18–22.

Lu Xun. 1908. "Po e sheng lun." *Henan*, no. 8 (December).

Lui, Mary Ting Yi. 2007. *The Chinatown trunk mystery: Murder, miscegenation, and other dangerous encounters in turn-of-the-century New York City*. Princeton, NJ: Princeton University Press.

Luo Fuhui. 2001. "Qingmo Zhongguo baokan dui 'huanghuo' lun de fanying." *Xiaogan Xueyuan Xuebao*, no. 4: 35–41.

———. 2007. *Huanghuo Lun—Dongxi Wenming de Duili Yu Duihua*. Taibei: Tuxu wenhua shiye *Renmin Ribao*.

Lü Pu, ed. 1979. *"Huanghuo lun" Lishi Ziliao Xuanbian*. Beijing: Zhongguo shehui kexue chubanshe.

Morris, Narrelle. 2013. *Japan-bashing: Anti-Japanism since the 1980s*. London: Routledge.

Nitobe, Inazō. 2002 [1900]. *Bushido: The Soul of Japan*. Tokyo: Kodansha International.

Okakura, Kakuzō. 1920 [1903]. *The ideals of the East: With special reference to the art of Japan*. New York: E. P. Dutton and Company.

Pan Chengxin. 2012. *Knowledge, desire and power in global politics: Western representations of China's rise*. Cheltenham: Edward Elgar.

Robinson, Greg. 2003. *By Order of the President: FDR and the internment of Japanese Americans*. Cambridge, MA: Harvard University Press.

Shah, Nayan. 2001. *Contagious divides: Epidemics and race in San Francisco's Chinatown*. Berkeley: University of California Press.

Song Qiang et al. 1996. *Zhongguo keyi shuo bu: Lengzhan hou shidai de zhengzhi yu qinggan jueze*. Beijing: Zhonghua Gongshang Lianhe Chubanshe.

Song Xiaojun et al. 2009. *Zhongguo bu gaoxing: Da shidai, da mubiao, ji women de neiyou waihuan*. Nanjing: Jiangsu renmin chubanshe.

Sösemann, Bernd. 1976. "Die sog. Hunnenrede Wilhelms II: Textkritische und interpretatorische Bemerkungen zur Ansprache des Kaisers vom 27. Juli 1900 in Bremerhaven." *Historische Zeitschrift* 2, Vol. 222, pp. 342–358.

Sun Zhongshan. 1956 [1904]. "Zhongguo wenti de zhen jiejue—xiang Meiguo renmin huyu." *Sun Zhongshan xuan ji*. Beijing: Renmin chubanshe, Vol. 1: 56–64.

Tiezzi, Shannon. 2014. "Beijing's 'China Threat' theory," *The Diplomat*, June 3, accessed online on December 23, 2016, at http://thediplomat.com/2014/06/beijings-china-threat-theory/.

Tsu Jing. 2005. *Failure, nationalism, and literature: The making of modern Chinese identity, 1895–1937*. Stanford: Stanford University Press.

Urbansky, Sören. 2016. "Für Clan und Vaterland? Loyalitätsstrukturen in Chinatown San Francisco während der ersten Hälfte des 20. Jahrhunderts." *Geschichte und Gesellschaft* 4, Vol. 42, pp. 612–650.

———. 2012. "The unfathomable foe: Constructing the enemy in the Sino-Soviet borderlands, ca. 1969–1982." *Journal of Modern European History* 2, Vol. 10, pp. 255–278.

Wu, William F. 1982. *The Yellow Peril: Chinese Americans in American fiction, 1850–1940*. Hamden, CT: Archon Books.

Yee, Herbert, and Zhu Feng. 2002. "Chinese Perspectives of the China Threat: Myth or Reality?" In *The China Threat: Perceptions, Myths, and Reality*, edited by Herbert Yee and Ian Storey. London: RoutledgeCurzon, pp. 21–42.

Zhou Zhiming. 1944. *Huanghuo jiri huolun*. Shanghai: Duli chubanshe.

Contributors

Ross Anthony is the director of the Center for Chinese Studies at Stellenbosch University. His work focuses on China's relationship to its peripheries, particularly Xinjiang, as well as its engagements with Africa. His most recent work examines the China–Africa link through the concept of the Anthropocene and the consequences this has in terms of territorial imaginaries. Anthony is also involved in developing teaching curriculum on East Asia from an African perspective.

Franck Billé is a cultural anthropologist based at the University of California, Berkeley, where he is program director for the Tang Center for Silk Road Studies. His work has been published in *Environment and Planning D, Cultural Anthropology, Cross-Currents, Cambridge Anthropology,* and *Asian Anthropology,* among others. His first book, *Sinophobia: Anxiety, Violence, and the Making of Mongolian Identity,* was published by University of Hawai'i Press in 2015. His latest book, *On the Russia-China Border* (coauthored with Caroline Humphrey), is under contract with Harvard University Press.

Kevin Carrico is a lecturer in Chinese Studies in the Department of International Studies (Modern Languages and Cultures) at Macquarie University. He is the author of *The Great Han: Race, Nationalism, and Tradition in China Today* and the translator of Tsering Woeser's *Tibet on Fire.* He is currently researching the origins and implications of the Hong Kong independence movement.

Romain Dittgen is a human geographer and holds a PhD from the University of Paris (Panthéon-Sorbonne). In his research, often comparative, he has mostly been interested in studying the impacts of various forms of capital on economies and societies in Africa. Prior to joining the South African Research Chair in Spatial Analysis and City Planning at the University of the Witwatersrand, he held positions at the South African Institute of International Affairs, the African Studies Centre, and the International Institute for Asian Studies (both at Leiden University), as well as within the Geography Department at the Sorbonne. Having conducted research in several countries in Africa (Chad, Ethiopia, Gabon, Senegal, and South Africa) as well as in China, his areas of focus range from exploring transnational and adaptive capital, migrant spaces, and related imaginaries, to the governance of future cities in Africa and in China.

Magnus Fiskesjö was educated in his native Sweden and at the University of Chicago, where he received a joint PhD in anthropology and East Asian languages and civilizations in 2000. Earlier, he served in the Swedish embassies in Beijing and in Tokyo, and in 2000–2005 was director of the Museum of Far Eastern Antiquities in Stockholm, Sweden. Since 2005, he has taught anthropology and Asian studies at Cornell University. His research interests include ethnic relations and ethnopolitics, history, and archaeology, as well as heritage and critical museum studies, mainly focused on East and Southeast Asia.

Christos Lynteris is senior lecturer in social anthropology at the University of St Andrews and principal investigator of the European Research Council–funded project "Visual Representations of the Third Plague Pandemic." He is the author of *The Spirit of Selflessness in Maoist China: Socialist Medicine and the New Man* (Palgrave Macmillan 2012) and *Ethnographic Plague: Configuring Disease on the Chinese-Russian Frontier* (Palgrave Macmillan 2016).

Yu Qiu was trained at University of Cambridge where she received her PhD in social anthropology in 2017. Yu has research interests in a range of theoretical areas: the emotional, affective, and intimate dimension of China–Africa interactions; Sino–African friendship politics; gender relations; and racial and national identities in China. In her recent research, Yu takes an interdisciplinary approach to unpacking the private and intimate life of Nigerian migrant traders in Guangzhou (China), and pays particular attention to the sociocultural logic behind the gendered establishment of both intimate and business partnerships between these traders and Chinese women. She explores the rich and diverse practices of what she terms "complicit intimacy" in the people's way of navigating a better and promising future. In the past years, she has conducted ethnographic fieldwork in China and Nigeria.

Sören Urbansky is research fellow at the German Historical Institute in Washington, D.C. His research has been published in *Geschichte und Gesellschaft*, *Journal of Modern European History*, *Kritika*, and other journals. He is author of *Kolonialer Wettstreit: Russland, China, Japan und die Ostchinesische Eisenbahn* (Frankfurt: Campus, 2008). Currently he is completing a book manuscript on the history of the Sino–Russian border (under contract with Princeton University Press) and embarking on a new project that examines anti-Chinese sentiments in a global perspective.

David Walker has written extensively on Australian representations of Asia. His prize-winning book, *Anxious Nation: Australia and the Rise of Asia, 1850 to 1939* (UQP, 1999), has been translated into Chinese and Hindi. He is the co-editor of *Australia's Asia: From Yellow Peril to Asian Century* (UWA Publishing, 2012). A collection of his Asia-related essays has been published under the title *Encountering Turbulence: Asia in the Australian Imaginary* (Readworthy, 2013). His recently published personal history, *Not Dark Yet* (which explores family, memory, and the experience of becoming "legally blind"), has been translated into Chinese (光明行) and published by The People's Literature Publishing House, Beijing (2014). From 2013 to 2016, Walker was the inaugural BHP Billiton Chair of Australian Studies at Peking University, Beijing. He is an Honorary Professorial Fellow in the Asia Institute, University of Melbourne, and Emeritus Professor at Deakin University. He holds visiting professorships at Beijing Foreign Studies University and Renmin University, Beijing. David Walker is a Fellow of the Academy of the Social Sciences in Australia and the Australian Academy of the Humanities.

Xiaojian Zhao is professor of Asian American studies and history at the University of California, Santa Barbara. She received her PhD in history from the University of California, Berkeley, in 1993. She is the author of *Remaking Chinese America: Immigration, Family, and Community, 1940–1965* (Rutgers University Press, 2002; winner of the History Book Award from the Association of Asian American Studies), *The New Chinese America: Class, Economy, and Social Hierarchy* (Rutgers University Press, 2010), and *Asian American Chronology* (Greenwood Press, 2009). She is also co-editor of *Asian Americans: An Encyclopedia of Social, Cultural, Economic, and Political History* (ABC-Clio, 2013).

Index

Page numbers in **boldface** type refer to illustrations.

academic freedom, 231, 233
Amerasia Journal. See newspaper
anti-Chinese: discourse, 8, 178, 188,
    215; hostility, 24, 84, 94, 100–101;
    narratives, 5, 13, 98, 101–102,
    177–178, 180, 182, 187–188, 260;
    sentiments, 5, 23–25, 41, 75, 85,
    98–101, 170–171, 197, 201, 215, 255,
    257–259
Apple Daily. See newspaper
Asia(n): century, 8, 247; diseased
    Asian world, 7, 46, 66–68;
    future, 17, 62; immigration, 20,
    66–67, 73; intellectual power, 66;
    invasion, 4, 22, 61–62, 65–66, 69,
    76; markets, 78; Northeast, 4,
    249; women, 16
Australia(n): continent, 6, 66, 74;
    indigenous, 60–61; women, 62,
    65, 71; resources, 74; separation
    from Asia, 61
autonomy: economic, 38; individual,
    153, 161; political, 143, 172, 176,
    184, 187, 250; regional, 207, 211,
    213–214

barbarian(s), 22, 186, 225, 236, 249
Berkeley, University of California,
    15, 47
Black Death. *See* disease(s)

Blagoveshchensk, city of, 171, 185,
    189
Boxer Uprising, 247, 259, 262
BRICS, 117, 124, 128
Britain, 6, 47, 61–64, 67, 71, 73, 75,
    231; British Empire, 2, 22–23,
    60, 63, 113; British imperialism,
    7, 13, 25, 60, 67, 69–70, 157–158,
    164, 182, 215. *See also* United
    Kingdom

California, 4, 6, 15, 35–36, 47, 92,
    100–101
Canada. *See* North America
China: development of, 24, 37, 78,
    110, 124–125, 161, 163, 177, 225,
    261; economic rise of, 8, 171–172,
    180; fear of, 39, 98, 247; learning
    from, 161–164; opening to the
    West, 76, 128; People's Republic
    of, 46, 74, 115, 197–198, 207, 246,
    255–257, 260; role in Africa,
    143–144, 257; trading partner,
    76–77, 117, 142; Threat Theory
    (*Zhongguo weixie lun*), 27, 248,
    260–263
China Central Television (CCTV),
    121, 207
Chinatown, 7, 23, 36, 41–42, 47–49,
    90, 121–123, 185

271

Different types and styles of chin implants. The white implant on the left is made of Teflon, the next one is a silicone gel implant. The other implants are various types of silicone rubber implants. The implant on the far right is used to determine the proper size during the procedure.

When the Chin Is Very Small, It May Be Better to Have the Actual Bone Changed with a "Sliding Genioplasty"

As with all foreign materials, the larger the implant, the more frequent the problems. When a large augmentation is needed, a horizontal cut in the chin bone can be made. The bottom portion is advanced and held in place with tiny titanium plates and screws. Not every plastic surgeon performs this procedure, but those who do claim it is no more risky than an implant and has numerous advantages. No foreign implant is present to move or get infected, although the plates themselves are foreign. And the chin can be vertically shortened or lengthened and advanced forward or backward. The downside, however, is that most genioplasties require general anesthesia.

Once successfully placed, a chin implant should be permanent. After a few weeks, the brain incorporates the implant into its body image. As with a dental filling, the implant no longer feels foreign.

The Procedure

Digital imaging is useful in determining the size of the proposed chin implant.

A chin implant can be performed under local or general anesthesia. A three-centimeter-long incision is made in the crease under the chin and is deepened to the bone. A pocket is made directly over the bone, fitted precisely to the size of the implant. The implant is washed with antibiotic solution and placed in the

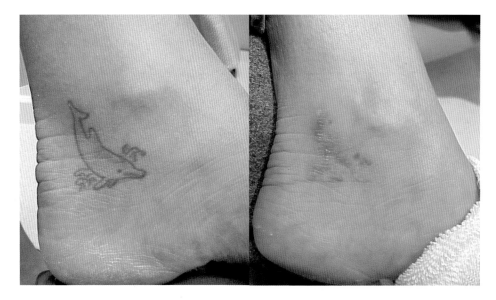

This woman underwent seven laser treatments to get rid of the pesky dolphin. Even so, some pigment remains. Left, before treatment; right, postop.

This tattoo had the most common color, blue-black. The photo on the right is after just three laser treatments. Notice the scarring left behind by the laser, or perhaps by the tattoo itself.

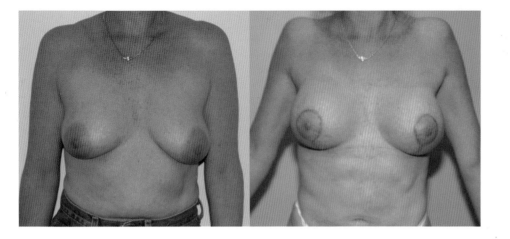

Bad scars occur in 3–5 percent of patients. Assuming your plastic surgeon has closed the wound properly, this hypertrophic scarring is genetically predetermined and largely unavoidable. This woman had small, droopy breasts. On the right, her appearance after a combined lift/augmentation procedure. She developed red, raised scars, although she had soft-feeling breasts.

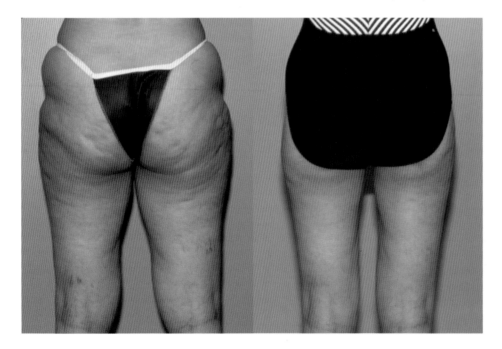

This woman underwent two rounds of sclerotherapy after having liposuction of the hips, thighs, and knees. Postop on the right.

18

Chin and Cheek Implants

Chin Augmentations

The first cosmetic procedures on the chin were actually performed during World War II. Cuts were made in the bone, and the bone was pushed outward and held in place with steel wires. The first chin implants were used in the 1960s and presented a much simpler method of making the chin larger.

A small chin is commonly called a weak chin—and that says it all. The impression is of a weak personality. A strong chin, particularly in a man, is associated with strength and leadership. Chin implants can be placed onto the bone, changing a weak chin into a more powerful, domineering chin. In men, the change increases the image of masculinity. In women, chin implants balance the face. In both sexes, however, a weak chin makes a large nose seem even larger.

Chin implants can be placed on the front of the chin, improving the profile by as much as a centimeter. Extended versions of implants are available that allow the width of the chin to be increased. Depressions in the jaw line can even be corrected with the creative use of these implants. Clefts can be created or removed. Most implants today are made of silicone rubber, although some surgeons use other materials, such as Gore-Tex (polytetrafluoroethylene), Medpor (polyethylene), and a bone-like hydroxyapatite.

Chin augmentations with silicone rubber implants are examples of a low risk, high-benefit procedure. Thirty-two thousand procedures were performed in 2005, making it the eleventh most common cosmetic surgery operation.

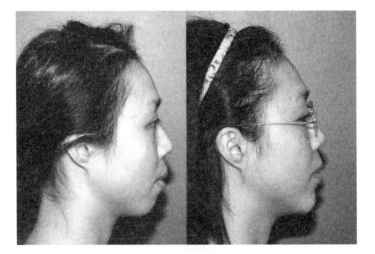

This 28-year-old woman had a very small chin (left). On the right, after chin augmentation with a silicone implant. The operation elevated the lower lip muscles and allowed better closure of her lips. See color plates.

pocket. The muscle and skin are then closed over the implant. Some surgeons prefer to make the incision inside the mouth, below the lower teeth. Although an incision made in this location is invisible, the chance of infection or slippage of the implant is higher.

The Risks

A chin implant can extrude through the skin. If it becomes exposed, it must be removed. Some surgeons recommend using antibiotics before dental procedures if the patient has a chin implant; others disagree. If the implant becomes infected, it must be removed.

An implant can shift in position, requiring a second procedure for repositioning. It needs to be placed carefully, so that the nerve that supplies sensation to the lower lip is not injured. All implants gradually erode the very bone that they were intended to augment. Sometimes the result is a loss of the improved projection of the chin. In extreme cases, the implant can erode into the roots of the teeth. Pain and sensitivity of the teeth result and sometimes a root canal is required.

Cheek Implants

The cheekbones are seen most easily with the head turned 45 degrees, the oblique angle. High cheekbones are considered beautiful by many cultures.

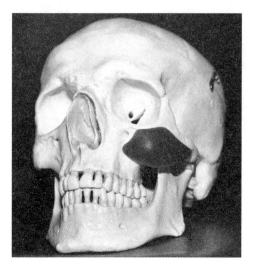

This silicone rubber implant sits on the cheekbone in this skull model.

Cheek implants are one method of restoring the cheek height that is lost with advancing age. Also called malar implants, the implants are usually made of silicone rubber. Midface or thread-lifts are other methods.

Cheek implants receive more mentions in the press than in the operating room. In fact, only 12,000 procedures were performed in 2005, making it the eighteenth most common surgical procedure.

Some have proposed making cuts in the cheekbones and advancing them to increase their prominence. Bone grafts and plates with screws are then necessary to hold the bone in place. This technique can also be used to decrease the size of cheekbones that are too big. Unless there is a major deformity, I would be reluctant to have my facial bones cut and moved if I were a patient. Implants are simple and straightforward.

Current face-lift techniques and minimally invasive suture lifting techniques raise the sagging cheek pads to a more youthful position, eliminating the need for foreign material in the face.

The Procedure

Cheek implants can be inserted either through the mouth, with incisions made above the upper molars, or through a lower-eyelid incision. They can also be placed through the skin incision during a face-lift. Usually general anesthesia is used, although local anesthesia is adequate for a motivated patient. A pocket is made directly on the cheekbone, and an appropriately sized silicone rubber implant is washed in antibiotics and positioned. The skin is then closed.

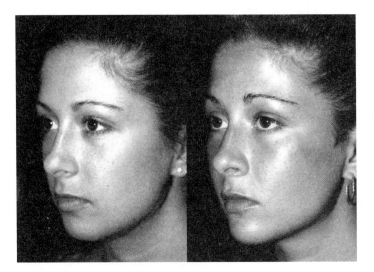

Preop on the left; postop rhinoplasty, chin and cheek
augmentation on the right. Facial balance is achieved.
See color plates.

The Risks

Like other implants, cheek implants can become infected. If this happens, they
will need to be removed. Cheek implants are harder to position than chin implants and are more likely to be placed too high, too low, or off to the side. Since
these implants are paired, they must be perfectly symmetrical in order to look
good. The cheek implant is placed very close to the nerve that supplies sensation
to the cheek, upper lip, and nose. If this nerve is injured, an annoying sensation
is experienced until it grows back. Worse, the nerves that supply the muscles of
the upper lip and cheek may be injured during the operation, resulting in either
weakness or paralysis. Needless to say, this is a potentially devastating compli-
cation. Fortunately, when it does occur, it is usually temporary.

The Cost

Cheek implants cost $2,700 on average and chin implants cost $2,100. This does
not include the cost of the implants themselves, which averages about $150
apiece.

19

Lip Augmentations

In the mid-1980s, lip augmentations were virtually never performed. Then, sometime around the early 1990s, large lips became desirable. Goldie Hawn's hilarious lip augmentation in the 1996 movie *The First Wives Club* actually increased my lip enlargement business. It is hard to know just how many of these operations are performed annually, since organized plastic surgery counted only the 50,000 *surgical* lip augmentations in 2005, exclusive of augmentations from the injection of fillers. The popularity of lip augmentation certainly has increased over the last decade.

Foreign materials do not belong in the lip. Silicone or Gore-Tex do not do well there. The newer filling materials Artecoll and Radiesse can cause hard nodules in the lips.

Surgical procedures to alter the shape of the lips are not popular. They leave scars and are really not totally successful.

Dermal-Fat Grafts

This type of graft is more durable than other techniques. It has been around for over half a century, and the lip augmentation is simply a new use for an old technique. With dermal-fat grafts, an area of skin somewhere on the body is excised in the shape of an ellipse. The upper skin (epidermis) is removed, leaving the lower level (dermis). The skin is then cut out, keeping a layer of fat attached. The location where the skin was removed is closed as a straight line. Often I remove the skin in a scarred area, in hopes of improving the existing scar, giving a secondary benefit.

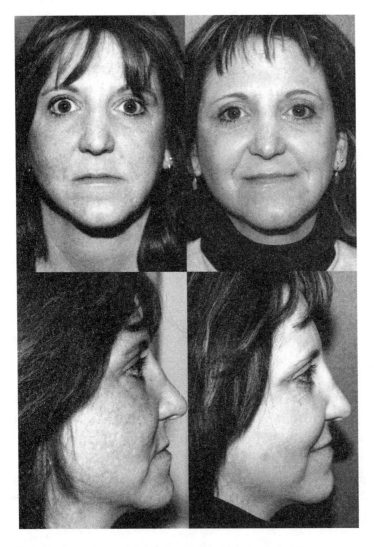

This woman underwent a dermal-fat graft to the upper lip, balancing the lower lip. A TCA peel also improved her skin tone and reduced the number of freckles. See color plates.

The dermal-fat graft is then shaped. For the lips, it is made into a narrow strip. The lips are numbed and tiny incisions are made in the corners on the inside of the lip. A space is made in the lip, under the red lip skin. With a long clamp, the dermal-fat graft is threaded through the lip and the incisions are closed.

This type of graft behaves just like any other skin graft. It gets its own blood supply within three days, and becomes part of the lip by three weeks. The percentage of graft that survives should be very high.

Not everyone wants this operation, however. It is most popular in people who already have a scar somewhere. Usually abdominal, back, or buttock scars work well. If your body is scarless, it is unlikely that you will choose to have a five-to-seven-centimeter scar created just for this purpose.

Fat Grafting Is a Much More Common Method of Lip Augmentation

Through tiny incisions inside the belly button or on the hip, the fat is numbed and liposuction is performed. Only a few teaspoons of fat are required. This fat is drained of blood and reinjected through tiny incisions in the lip. In actuality, the fat is not injected, but layered into the lip by lifting the lip skin with the injecting needle. Fat is extremely pressure sensitive and will not survive a true injection. To live, it must contact tissue but must not be placed under pressure. I use the instrument to create multiple tunnels not only through the tissue just under the lip skin, but also in the lip muscle.

After the procedure, the lips swell comically. Pleco fish come to mind. The profound swelling goes down rapidly, however, and within five days is almost gone. I graft extra fat, because much of it will not survive. Less survives in the lips than in the nasolabial folds. No one knows why, but I believe it is because the lips cannot remain at rest. Eating and talking probably disrupt some of the fat in the early days following the graft. My feeling is that about one-third of the fat survives long term. I tell my patients that in three to six months they will require a second augmentation. It seems that a higher percentage of fat survives during the second procedure. This makes sense biologically: for a time, the blood supply of the lips is increased after surgery, and grafts survive longer with a better blood supply.

If a Surgical Procedure Is Not Desired, Then "Lips from a Bottle" Can Be Created

I prefer Restylane for temporary lip augmentation. After the lips are numbed with lidocaine, Restylane is injected slowly and carefully. It will last between six and twelve months. One of the advantages of Restylane is that we can add another syringe the following week if even larger lips are desired.

Often a patient is not sure just how big her lips should be. In this case, I inject her lips with saline and have her look into the mirror. We record the amount of saline injected, and this is the amount of fat or Restylane that I use.